VNR COLOR DICTIONARY OF

MUSHROOMS

VNR COLOR DICTIONARY OF

MUSHROOMS

Edited by
COLIN DICKINSON & JOHN LUCAS

 VAN NOSTRAND REINHOLD COMPANY

NEW YORK   CINCINNATI   TORONTO   LONDON   MELBOURNE

ACKNOWLEDGMENTS

Acknowledgments are due to the following sources for photographs used in this book: Heather Angel, S.C. Bisserot/Bruce Coleman, R.B. Bock/Bruce Coleman, Alberto Cappelli, Claude Carre/Jacana, Centro Fotografia Scientifica, A. Colombi, C. Del Prete, Rene Dulhoste/Jacana, E.D.E.N.A., E. Ferrari, Harry Fox, Roberto Galli, Brian Hawkes/Jacana, P.J. Jamoni, R. König/Jacana, Yves Tanceau/Jacana, Ruffier Lanche/Jacana, R. Longo, Angelo Lucini, J.C. Maes/Jacana, Marka, A. Margiocci, Riccardo Mazza, Pierre Pilloud/Jacana, S. Prato, D.A. Reid, J. Roberts/Jacana, S.E.F., G. Tomisch, H. Veiller/Jacana, M. Viard/Jacana, Fred Waldvogel.

CONTENTS

INTRODUCTION:
THE NAMING OF FUNGI

One of the most impressive features of the natural world is the enormous diversity of living organisms. Describing and naming all the different types of plants, animals and microbes is a formidable task facing the biologist. The fungi are no exception to this rule; it has been estimated that there are at least 50,000 different species of fungi, and some authorities put the number at nearer 100,000. Obviously, if we are to make some sense of this enormous group we need to devise a workable system for identifying and classifying the many different types.

The perfect natural classification system remains for most groups of organisms, including the fungi, an ideal rather than a present-day reality. This is largely because to establish beyond doubt the evolutionary history of a group we need to have a comprehensive fossil record in which all the ancestral types are preserved. For the vast majority of biological groups the fossil record is sketchy, and for some such as the fungi, it is almost non-existent. This is no doubt due to the fact that fungi are too fragile and ephemeral to stand up to fossilization. In the absence of any preserved evidence our attempts to devise evolutionary trees for the fungi are at best speculative, but biologists believe that similarities in the fundamental structure and life cycles of present-day species often reflect a common evolutionary origin, and use this as a basis for achieving, as far as possible, a natural classification. This approach relies on recognizing the importance, or non-importance, of certain features. For instance, the agaric genera *Russula* and *Lactarius* are believed to be closely related as both have a characteristic tissue anatomy in which rounded cells are found as well as the more usual filamentous ones. This feature is not found in any of the other agarics, and as it is unlikely to have arisen twice in two entirely unrelated groups it seems reasonable to suppose that *Russula* and *Lactarius* share some common ancestry. Biologists describe this as a good natural group. In contrast, all the different genera of fungi classified as Gasteromycetes are grouped together

The large bracket fungus, Ganoderma applanatum, *which commonly attacks beech trees*

on the basis of a single negative feature, namely non-violent discharge of basidiospores. This character may well have arisen on several occasions in evolutionary history, simply by the loss of the ability to discharge the spores. For this reason the Gasteromycetes are almost certainly an unnatural or artificial group, and the species within this group are placed together more for reasons of convenience than because they share a close evolutionary relationship. In fact, recent evidence from comparative anatomical and developmental studies suggests that many of the Gasteromycetes are more closely related to various agarics than to each other.

Having dealt briefly with some of the theoretical aspects of classification, we should now consider how the fungi are divided into groups sharing certain characteristics. The major divisions are based upon reproductive structures and similarities in life cycles. Vegetative characters, that is, morphological details of the mycelium, are of limited use because in most cases the differences are subtle or can be detected only by using sophisticated microscopic or biochemical techniques. With the exception of the slime moulds, a group of uncertain affinity possessing a creeping vegetative phase rather like a giant amoeba, nearly all the fungi have a filamentous mycelium which is superficially similar in a wide variety of species. For this reason fungi cannot be readily identified on the basis of the mycelium, and it is usually necessary to have a fruiting structure to find out what a fungus is.

Biologists attach special significance to the details of sexual reproduction because it is a fundamental event in the life cycle of an organism and is also a stable character. The mechanism of sexual reproduction is therefore used as the initial criterion in defining the major subdivisions of the fungi (Table 1). One of the subdivisions, the Deuteromycotina, is undoubtedly an artificial group as the common feature is the absence of a sexual stage, and in many cases this merely reflects the fact that the sexual stage has eluded discovery. The fungi of most interest to the mushroom collector are grouped either in the Basidiomycotina (the mushrooms, bracket fungi, fairy clubs,

Outline Classification of Major Groups of Fungi

Division	*Myxomycota*
	The slime moulds and allies. Vegetative phase is an amoeboid plasmodium.
Division	*Eumycota*
	The true fungi. Vegetative phase is typically a filamentous mycelium.
Subdivision	*Mastigomycotina*
	These are microscopic mould fungi in which sexual reproduction leads to the formation of a thick-walled oospore. Many of the more primitive types are aquatic and also form mobile zoospores.
Subdivision	*Zygomycotina*
	These fungi form a characteristic sexual spore known as a zygospore. Many are well known as moulds on bread and rotten fruit.
Subdivision	*Ascomycotina*
	Sexual reproduction leads to the formation of ascospores inside a specialized cell, the ascus. This group includes mainly microscopic types, such as the yeasts and *Penicillium*, but some larger fungi, such as the truffles, morels and cup fungi are also placed here.
Subdivision	*Basidiomycotina*
	The sexual spores are basidiospores borne externally on a specialized cell, the basidium. Nearly all the larger fungi, such as the mushrooms, bracket fungi, puffballs, stinkhorns, earthstars and bird's-nest fungi are classified in this group, which also includes two important classes of parasitic fungi, the rusts and smuts.
Subdivision	*Deuteromycotina*
	Fungi in this group lack a sexual stage. The majority are microscopic moulds important as pathogens or common in soil.

puffballs, stinkhorns and allies) or the Ascomycotina (the morels, cup fungi, truffles and allies). Both these groups are distinguished on the basis of the formation of a particular type of sexual structure, the basidium and the ascus respectively.

Within each of the major subdivisions the fungi are grouped together according to an hierarchical system of Classes, Orders, Families, Genera and Species, with appropriate intermediate categories where necessary. The exact details of this system need not concern us here, with the exception of the Species, which is the basic unit of classification. As such it is the category which really concerns the mushroom collector; for instance, the many different types of fungi illustrated in the reference section of this book are all considered to be separate species, and given a name on this basis. The idea of a species is superficially simple, being a population of individuals which are essentially alike and can be distinguished from other species by one or more clear-cut differences. In practice, however, the species may be difficult to define, and there is sometimes disagreement as to what constitutes a clear-cut difference. It is important to

realize that all populations of organisms exhibit a certain range of variation, and the degree to which such variation can extend before a new species is defined is in some cases not clear. Nevertheless, the species is the important unit in terms of describing and naming organisms, and the occurrence of problematical intermediate forms is to be expected as evolution is a continuing process.

Once a species has been described and defined it must be given a name. The system of nomenclature used by biologists dates from 1753 when the Swedish botanist Linnaeus first applied it to the plant kingdom. Each species is given two Latin names, referred to as a binomial. For example, the Shaggy Ink Cap is known to science as *Coprinus comatus*. The first of these names indicates the genus, *Coprinus*, while the second part refers to the species *comatus*. This binomial system has two great advantages over other types of names. In the first place it is universally applied throughout the world so that biologists know what fungus is referred to irrespective of their native language. Secondly, the binomial itself is a type of scientific shorthand which indicates the immediate relationships of the species concerned. To return to the above example, the generic name *Coprinus* places the particular species in a group with all the other Ink Caps, so wherever we are in the world if we see the name *Coprinus comatus* we immediately know that the fungus concerned is an Ink Cap, with the general characteristics of that genus but with some specific features of its own.

For this system of nomenclature to be of lasting value it is important that it should not be changed all the time. To ensure stability there is a set of rigid rules laid down in the International Code of Botanical Nomenclature. Whenever a new species is described and named a certain procedure has to be adopted to validate the name. This procedure involves preserving a *type specimen* of the new species in an herbarium, so that future authors can if necessary refer back to the original type collection to discover what the original idea of the species involved. The new species should also be described in the scientific literature. From time to time a species may be described and named by a particular author, only for it to be discovered at some later date that the same fungus had already been named by a previous author. In cases such as these a rule of priority operates, with the first correctly validated name being retained. Although the constraints imposed by the International Code help to stabilize nomenclature, changes in names are still to some extent inevitable as classification is a continuing rather than static process, and the exact limits of particular groups are sometimes redrawn. This is frequently the case at the level of the genus, with species being transferred from one to another as new evidence becomes available of details of anatomy and spore ornamentation.

Identification

In most instances fungi can only be identified if they are fruiting. Exceptions to this rule include *Chlorosplenium*, which stains the wood in which it lives a characteristic green colour, and certain wood-rotting fungi which cause the development of symptoms specific to particular species. In the vast majority of cases, however, the presence of mycelium merely indicates that a fungus is active in the habitat and until it fruits, which may not be for days, weeks or even years, one can only guess at its identity.

As described elsewhere, the larger fungal fruiting bodies may be formed by species of Ascomycotina or Basidiomycotina. In most instances for any given fruiting body it is relatively easy to tell which of these groups is involved, but there are some difficulties and it may be necessary to demonstrate microscopically whether asci or basidia are being formed. It is, for example, relatively easy to spot a saucer-shaped cup fungus or an agaric with cap and gills, but club-shaped and spherical fruit bodies can cause problems even for the expert.

For both the Ascomycotina and the Basidiomycotina it is important that a number of field observations are made to support any subsequent investigations in the laboratory or kitchen. It is necessary to know where the fungus was growing, what it was growing on and whether it was solitary or part of a troop or ring. It is also useful to make a brief description of some of the macroscopic features of the fruit body in the field as certain structures such as rings and colours can be lost or altered during transport to the laboratory.

More detailed investigations usually begin with a description of the gross morphology of the fruit body. This includes the determination of the whereabouts of the fertile layer, known as the hymenium. It may also be useful at this point to try to discover something about the mechanics of the fruiting body, and especially the means of spore release and dispersal. This often helps us to understand the functioning of the whole structure.

If we are dealing with an Ascomycotina then it is very likely that a microscopic mount of the asci will be helpful in determining several important features of the fungus. This mount may be made in water or iodine and can merely consist of a small piece of the hymenium dug out with a needle and squashed into the mounting medium. If this preparation is examined under high-power objective, about ×40, then we can see the form of the asci and the shape and colour of the spores. Cylindrical, straight-sided, asci are formed by the Discomycetes, i.e. the cup fungi and their close allies, whereas the Pyrenomycetes have club-shaped asci, which often possess thicker walls than those of the Discomycetes. The colour, shape and any cross walls in the spores are often used to decide to which genus the fungus belongs. If it is a

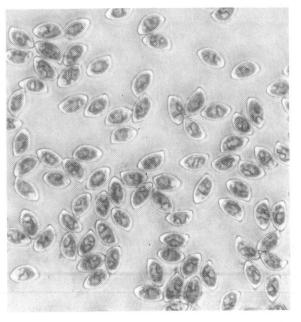

Far left: ring and gills help toward an immediate identification of many fungi
Left: for identification of spores the microscope is necessary. These are the smooth, ellipsoid basidiospores of Pholiota squarrosa, normally pale brown but in this case stained with iodine

cup fungus then there will probably be sterile hairs present among the asci, and these may be coloured. They are also an important taxonomic character, though their use is beyond the scope of this book.

The Discomycetes form a hymenium in which the asci are spread out on an exposed surface which may cover the concave surface of a disc-shaped fruit body or the convoluted outer surface of a saddle or cone-shaped structure. In all instances the degree of convolution is such that the spores can still be shot directly away from the surface of the fruiting body. By contrast the Pyrenomycetes produced their asci in chianti-bottle-shaped spore cases, termed perithecia, and these may be scattered singly on the substrate or aggregated into complex structures which contain numerous individual perithecia. The arrangement of the perithecia and the morphology of complex fruiting bodies are important characters which can be determined using a hand lens or a low-powered (×20) dissecting microscope. In addition many of the Pyrenomycetes live on wood and here a knowledge of the host timber can simplify a search for a name of the fungus.

As regards the Basidiomycotina, the general form of the fruiting body is often extremely important in assigning the fungus to a group. The structure of the fructification is also important as is the whereabouts and arrangement of the spore-producing layer, or hymenium.

If the fungus is a bracket-like fruiting body then it is useful to know if it is annual or perennial and what it is growing on. The form of the hymenium, whether it covers a flat surface, spines, gills or pores is important. In some instances the final determination to generic level involves a knowledge of the way in which the fruiting body is constructed. It is, however, often difficult even for professionals to determine this.

Mushroom-like fruiting bodies are somewhat easier to deal with. All the features of the fruiting body can yield useful information and a systematic study of the cap, gills, pores and stipe is often necessary. The cap should be examined to determine its size, its colour, both when young and if possible when it is old, and its consistency. The outermost layer of the cap, the cuticle, is frequently a valuable guide to the identification of many species. Details of its construction can be examined only by using a microscope but a low-power (×100) will give most of the information required. A sliver of the cap is sliced off, using a razor blade, and mounted in water. At the edges of this you can see the type of cells making up the outer layer and they can usually be characterized as globose or sausage-shaped. Other features of the cuticle can be determined by eye or by feel. It may be dry, greasy, viscid, glutinous or simply moist. It may be peeled off easily or difficult to remove. The upper surface may be smooth, polished and shiny, minutely hairy and velvety, very hairy and shaggy or scaly. The edge of the cap, termed the margin, should be described as regular or wavy, incurved or not, smooth or rough and striate or otherwise. If there is a veil present, and it is important to examine young specimens to be certain, then this can add further useful information. In particular it may be cobweb-like or form an intact sheet of tissue and after it has broken its remains may or may not hang down at the margin forming teeth or filaments. The flesh of the cap should also be examined to see if it has a distinct colour, smell or taste. This latter is discovered by nibbling a small piece which is kept in the front of the mouth for about a minute to see if any sensation develops. Spit out the masticated remains.

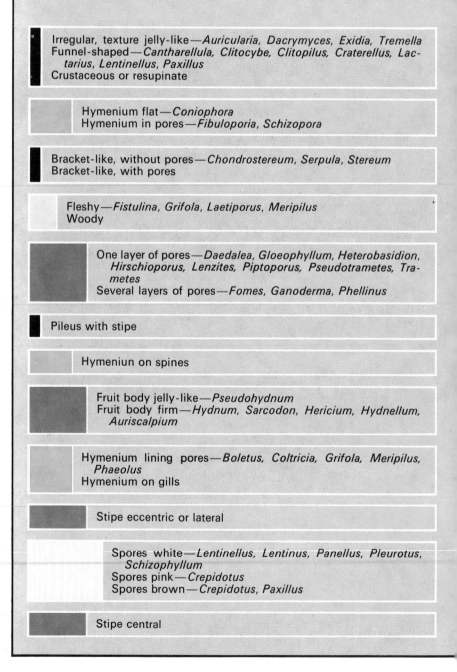

Identification Points
Basidiomycotina (except Gasteromycetes)

A key is provided only for the Basidiomycetes because there are relatively few large Ascomycetes and their difference in form is so obvious as to make identification comparatively easy. Similarly, Gasteromycetes are excluded because their form is so distinctive.

The key is merely a short-cut to placing a specimen in the appropriate genus. To use it, start at the top left corner and work downwards. The first group of characters concern the shape and type of fruit-body and are aligned at the left of the key. For ease of use they are colour-coded with the same shade, in this case black. Having decided which type of fruit-body you are dealing with move on to the next set of characters, which are slightly indented and coded with a different colour. By employing the same downwards and inwards approach at each level of characters, you eventually arrive at the name of a genus, or group of genera. These can then be looked up in the Reference Section to identify the species. As an example, suppose the specimen is a bracket fungus with pores. You then have to decide if it has a fleshy or woody fruit-body. If woody, it may have either a single layer of pores when sectioned, or several layers. If there are several layers it is one of three genera, *Fomes*, *Ganoderma* or *Phellinus*.

Irregular, texture jelly-like—*Auricularia, Dacrymyces, Exidia, Tremella*
Funnel-shaped—*Cantharellula, Clitocybe, Clitopilus, Craterellus, Lactarius, Lentinellus, Paxillus*
Crustaceous or resupinate

Hymenium flat—*Coniophora*
Hymenium in pores—*Fibuloporia, Schizopora*

Bracket-like, without pores—*Chondrostereum, Serpula, Stereum*
Bracket-like, with pores

Fleshy—*Fistulina, Grifola, Laetiporus, Meripilus*
Woody

One layer of pores—*Daedalea, Gloeophyllum, Heterobasidion, Hirschioporus, Lenzites, Piptoporus, Pseudotrametes, Trametes*
Several layers of pores—*Fomes, Ganoderma, Phellinus*

Pileus with stipe

Hymeniun on spines

Fruit body jelly-like—*Pseudohydnum*
Fruit body firm—*Hydnum, Sarcodon, Hericium, Hydnellum, Auriscalpium*

Hymenium lining pores—*Boletus, Coltricia, Grifola, Meripilus, Phaeolus*
Hymenium on gills

Stipe eccentric or lateral

Spores white—*Lentinellus, Lentinus, Panellus, Pleurotus, Schizophyllum*
Spores pink—*Crepidotus*
Spores brown—*Crepidotus, Paxillus*

Stipe central

Spores white

Ring plus volva—*Amanita*
Volva only—*Amanita*
Ring only—*Armillaria, Lepiota, Oudemansiella*
No ring or volva

Parasitic on other mushrooms—*Nyctalis*
Latex produced from broken gills—*Lactarius*
Gills brittle—*Russula*
Gills waxy—*Hygrophorus, Hygrocybe*
Gills thick and distant—*Laccaria, Omphalina, Oudemansiella*
Gills sinuate—*Calocybe, Lepista, Melanoleuca, Tricholoma, Tricholomopsis*
Gills decurrent—*Cantharellus, Cantharellula, Clitocybe, Hygrophoropsis, Lactarius, Leucopaxillus, Omphalina*
Gills delicate—*Marasmius, Mycena*
Gills adnate or free—*Collybia, Cystoderma*
Gills adnexed—*Flammulina*

Spores pink

Volva only—*Volvariella*
No volva

Smells of fish—*Macrocystidia*
Gills free—*Pluteus*
Gills adnate—*Leptonia*
Gills sinuate—*Entoloma, Lepista, Nolanea*
Gills decurrent—*Clitopilus*

Spores brown

In alder or willow swamps—*Naucoria*
Gills deliquescent—*Bolbitius*
Pileus convex or umbonate, fibrillose or scaly, gills clay-brown, terrestrial—*Inocybe*
Gills decurrent—*Gymnopilus, Paxillus*
Gills sinuate—*Hebeloma*
Gills adnexed, ring, robust, with pileus surface powdery—*Phaeolepiota*
Pileus scaly, mostly lignicolous—*Phaeomarasmius, Pholiota*
Partial veil cobweb-like—*Cortinarius, Rozites*
Pileus small, striate—*Galerina*
Gills adnate, ring—*Agrocybe*
Pileus small, conical, with mica-like particles seen under lens—*Conocybe*

Spores purple or black

Gills deliquescent—*Coprinus*
Ring present

Gills free—*Agaricus, Coprinus*
Gills not free, cap slimy—*Stropharia*

No ring

Gills adnate or free—*Paneolus, Psathyrella, Psilocybe*
Gills sinuate—*Hypholoma, Lacrymaria, Psathyrella*
Gills decurrent—*Gomphidius*

The gills or pores can provide valuable clues as to the identity of problem specimens. In particular their method of attachment to the stipe is important and the accompanying diagrams illustrate the major ways in which this is achieved. In addition gills can be described as to their thickness, their texture, whether they are crowded or not and their colour. Sometimes it is also important to discover if the gills all run from the cap margin to the stipe or if there are shorter gills which only partially cover this distance.

Associated with the gills or pores are the basidiospores. These are sometimes critical in determining genera or species. First one must determine the spore colour in mass. This can be done by making a spore print, preferably on two contrasting colour papers, e.g. black and white. Alternatively you can tap out some spores onto a glass slide and scrape them together to get a small pile. The colour of this mass can then be determined by putting the slide on several different coloured surfaces. Most other spore characters are obtained using a microscope. These include their colour, shape, sizes, any surface ornamentation and their reactions to iodine.

The stipe may be central, eccentric or hardly present at all. Its length may be diagnostic, though in many instances there is considerable variation, possibly due to differences in the habitat from where the specimens came. Of more use is the colour and consistency of the stipe. Consistency tends to be slightly difficult to master, though the terms employed—fleshy, stringy, cartilaginous, leathery and woody—are fairly descriptive. In general the two major types to be looked for are those where the stipe snaps cleanly when bent and others where it can be broken into two only by repeated twisting and pulling. The surfaces of the stipe may be of interest; some stipes are bulbous below and others are extended into a long root-like projection. Obviously one should note the presence of a volva and/or a ring. The flesh of the stipe may be similar to that of the cap but in other cases it has its own characteristics.

Below: making a spore print

MUSHROOMS A-Z

The shorter entries relate to those species considered to be of comparatively minor importance and/or lesser distribution than the more detailed entries.

Ascomycetes

This large and diverse group is characterized by the formation of club-shaped cells or *asci*, within which the *ascospores* are formed. These asci are normally formed within an *ascocarp*, or fruiting body, but some Ascomycetes such as the 'yeasts' and 'leaf-curl fungi' develop asci over the surface of the colony or mycelium. There are three basic types of fruiting body: closed, spherical, ball-like structures; flask or chianti-bottle-shaped structures, known as perithecia; and open disc or cup-shaped structures in which the asci form a dense layer on the inner surface. Representatives of this group can be found growing on the ground, under the surface of the soil, saprophytically on wood, parasitically on flowering plants, and on insects. There are many edible Ascomycetes, although they all contain poisonous chemicals which can be removed by bringing specimens to the boil in large quantities of water.

Above, right: Aleuria aurantia
Below, right: Bulgaria inquinans

Aleuria aurantia
ORANGE-PEEL FUNGUS
This easily recognized, striking species is one of the most common autumnal cup fungi. It is also called the Great Orange Elf Cup.
Fruiting body
Cup-shaped, sometimes irregular, becoming almost flat, large, 1–12cm in diameter. Margin inrolled at first, often splitting. Outer surface pinkish-white, mealy with minute sparkling granules. Flesh white, thin, fragile. *Disc:* deep orange, sometimes orange-red. *Stipe:* very short or absent. *Spores:* white in mass, broadly ellipsoid, coarsely netted with an oil drop and a prominent projection at each end, average size 19.5×10.0 microns. (A micron = 1 millionth of a metre.)
Habitat and distribution
Grows singly or in tufts, which are sometimes dense, on bare soil in open places, on lawns, along paths, new roads, near the stumps of newly-felled trees and on wood chips. Widespread and common in Europe, North America, south-east Australia and New Zealand.
Occurrence
September to January in Europe, September to October in North America.
Culinary properties
It must never be eaten raw, and when boiled it produces a liquid which contains harmful chemicals, and which must be discarded. Tastes pleasant. Smell while drying is said to resemble that of *Cantharellus cibarius*. It is worth trying when gathered in large enough quantities.

Bulgaria inquinans
BLACK-STUD FUNGUS
The Black-stud or India Rubber Fungus is often confused with the common, black, jelly fungus *Exidia glandulosa*, which also grows on oak trees. *Bulgaria inquinans* has a

smooth disc, and is often surrounded by a black zone of spores, whereas *Exidia glandulosa* has a minutely-pimply disc and colourless spores.

Fruiting body
At first globular, gradually spreading to become top-shaped, 1–3cm in diameter, resembling a prune when dry. Outer surface sooty-brown, scurfy. Flesh rubbery. *Disc:* black, smooth, shining, becoming flat, finally concave. *Stipe:* very short or absent. *Spores:* brownish-black in mass, kidney-shaped, smooth, average size 12.5 × 6.5 microns.

Habitat and distribution
Grows in clusters, sometimes in large numbers termed swarms, on the bark of felled deciduous trees, especially oak, less frequently on beech, elm, birch. Common in Europe and North America.

Occurrence
October to November.

Culinary properties
None known.

Calycella citrinum
A very common and widespread fungus which, despite the small size of each cup, can be easily recognized by the bright colour of the whole group. There are several similar species which grow on the stems of herbaceous plants, on acorns, beech mast and hazelnuts.

Fruiting body
Cup-shaped to flat, 0.5–5mm in diameter. Outer surface bright yellow when wet, orange, yellow when dry, smooth, waxy. *Disc:* deep yellow, drying to orange-yellow, slighty concave. *Stipe:* short, relatively thick, rarely more than 1mm long, yellow. *Spores:* white in mass, ellipsoid, smooth, with oil drops at each end, average size 11.5 × 4.0 microns.

Habitat and distribution
Grows gregariously, often in large dense masses, on the wood, or bursting through the bark of decaying branches of deciduous trees. Common in Europe, North America and Australia, it probably has a world-wide distribution.

Occurrence
September to December.

Culinary properties
Too small to be worth considering.

Chlorosplenium aeruginascens
Wood permeated by the mycelium of this fungus turns bright green. The stained timber, known as Green Oak, was highly prized by nineteenth-century craftsmen who used it in the manufacture of 'Tunbridge ware'. These patterned veneers were used to decorate small pieces of furniture and knick-knacks.

Fruiting body
Cup-shaped to almost flat, up to 5mm in diameter. Outer surface blue-green, smooth. Flesh blue-green, thin. *Disc:* blue-green, sometimes becoming yellow. *Stipe:* short, slender, up to 3mm long, 1mm thick. Dark green. *Spores:* white in mass, spindle-shaped, smooth, with a small oil drop at each end, average size 7 × 1.8 microns.

Habitat and distribution
Grows gregariously, or scattered, on fallen branches, rotting logs,

decorticated wood, especially oak, less frequently beech, birch, hazel and other deciduous trees. The green wood is common and the fruiting bodies less so, in Europe, North America, Asia, Australia and New Zealand.

Occurrence
April to November, but chiefly in autumn.

Culinary properties
None known.

Claviceps purpurea
ERGOT
Ergot is the name given to the deadly, monstrous, horn-shaped structure which is often found growing from the flowers of certain grasses and cereals. These sclerotia contain several dangerous poisons which cause a serious disease known as ergotism in humans and cattle. When used in controlled amounts, however, these chemicals can be beneficial. Since the sixteenth century midwives have used it in very small doses to speed

labour in childbirth.

Sclerotium
Spindle-shaped or twisted, longitudinally furrowed, variable in size on different hosts. Crust violet-black, white inside, brittle when dry. Falls to ground when mature.

Fruiting bodies
Develop on fallen sclerotia in the spring. Small, 1–2cm tall, drumstick-shaped, purplish-pink. *Ascospores:* thread-like, finally septate, average size 80.0 × 1.0 microns. *Conidia:* asexual spores, produced in large numbers soon after the germination of the ascospores, secrete a sugary solution, termed 'Honeydew'. Ovoid, average size 5.5 × 3.5 microns.

Habitat and distribution
Sclerotia infect the flowers of wheat, oats, barley, rye, rye grass, timothy, couch. Frequent to common, variable from year to year in Europe, Africa, Asia, North America.

Occurrence
Sclerotia, July to September. Fruiting bodies, April to June.

Culinary properties
Deadly poisonous. In the past grain adulterated by ergots has been accidentally or carelessly ground into flour, causing epidemics of ergotism. There are two forms of

Above, left: Claviceps purpurea
Far left: Calycella citrina
Left: Chlorosplenium aeruginascens

this disease: gangrenous ergotism in which the patient may lose one or more limbs and eventually die; and convulsive ergotism in which repeated convulsions and intense pain end in death after three or four days.

Cordyceps militaris
SCARLET CATERPILLAR FUNGUS

The fruiting bodies of this species can readily be traced to a buried pupa or larva of a butterfly or moth. When cut open, these insects are found to be a solid mass of mycelium. The only part of the insect which remains is the skin. The first *Cordyceps* species to be described was *Cordyceps sinensis* which grows only in Tibet and Szechan and is known as *Hia tsao tom, tchom* in China. It is collected and sold in Tibetan markets, and is exported to China where it is highly prized as a drug.

Fruiting body
Club-shaped, tapering downwards from a slightly swollen, fertile head, 1–4 sometimes 5cm high, up to 5mm thick. Bright crimson to orange-red, waxy, minutely roughened at the top. Flesh red or orange. *Spores:* thread-like, breaking up into part-spores which become slightly barrel-shaped, average size 4.8 × 1.3 microns.

Habitat and distribution
Grows singly on caterpillars and pupae of various species of Lepidoptera, usually buried in soil, in woods, hedge banks, meadows, damp lawns. Frequent to common in Europe.

Occurrence
September to October.

Culinary properties
None known.

Cordyceps ophioglossoides
Fruiting body Club-shaped. *Fertile head:* at first yellow, finally black, rough. Ovoid. *Stipe:* rather stout, gradually enlarges into head. Yellowish-olive, smooth or grooved. **Ecology** Grows singly or in small groups, a parasite on the subterranean fungus *Elaphomyces*. From the ground in pine woods. Occasional to frequent in Europe. September to October.
Inedible.

Cyathipodia macropus
STALKED SAUCER

The fruiting body of this species is like that of a *Peziza* with a long stalk. It is one of the commonest cup fungi in Europe but, because of its dingy colours, it can be difficult to see against a background of woodland litter.

Fruiting body
Fertile head: saucer-shaped, 2–4cm in diameter. Outer surface and margin mouse-grey, with rough hairs. Flesh white, thin. *Disc:* grey-brown, smooth. *Stipe:* long, slender, tapers slightly towards the top, 2–7cm long. Grey, with soft, downy hairs, often pitted. *Spores:* white in mass, ellipsoid to spindle-shaped, smooth, usually with a central oil drop, average size 15.0 × 11.0 microns.

Habitat and distribution
Grows singly, in woods, shady, moist places, especially among nettles. Common and widespread in Europe and North America.

Occurrence
July to October.

Culinary properties
Poisonous when raw, and when boiled produces a liquid which must be discarded as it contains harmful chemicals. It can then be cooked gently in a good stock. One of the officially recognized edible species sold in French markets.

Daldinia concentrica
CRAMP BALLS

Old men from country districts used to keep one or two of these hard, black fungi in their pockets, as they believed them to be a safeguard against cramp. The conspicuous fruiting bodies are often to be found covered with a sooty layer of spores, which are discharged nocturnally and violently, travelling up to 2cm. Spore discharge will continue for some time even if a mature specimen is picked and kept dry. They are said by some to be transported by the Alder wood wasp. Small forms of this species are found on gorse and birch after heath fires. It causes a condition in infected timber commonly known as 'Calico Wood' which is a firm white rot, with dark speckling. There is a report from

Top: Cordyceps ophioglossoides
Far right: Cyathipodia macropus
Right: Cordyceps militaris

experts, but unless its youth and freshness can be guaranteed it should not be gathered for food. Workers in the factories where this fungus is tinned often suffer from eye trouble, caused either by its spores, or by irritant chemicals transmitted by hand.

Fruiting body

Mop-like, up to 12cm high. *Fertile head:* at first chestnut, becoming date-brown to sooty-brown. 3—8cm in diameter. Sub-globose, with brain-like convolutions. Margin is attached to the stipe in 2 or 3 places. Flesh white, hollow, waxy, very thin, brittle. *Stipe:* short, stout, grooved, 5—6cm long, 1—4cm thick. Pale flesh-colour to greyish-lavender, slightly cottony. Flesh pithy, cavernous. *Spores:* white to cream

Left: Daldinia concentrica
Below, left: Disciotis venosa
Below: Gyromitra esculenta

Canada of a specimen, measuring 20cm in diameter, which was growing on the under side of maple floorboards.

Fruiting body

Hemispherical, with a slightly incurved base, 2.5—6cm in diameter. At first reddish-brown, soon becoming black, shiny, with tiny, raised spots. Flesh dark purplish-brown with darker concentric zones, hard. *Spores:* black in mass, ellipsoid to spindle-shaped, smooth, average size 14.5 × 7.5 microns.

Habitat and distribution

Grows on dead branches of deciduous trees, especially ash, less frequently on beech and alder. Common in Europe, North America, and Australia, and known in New Zealand.

Occurrence

January to December.

Culinary properties

None known.

Disciotis venosa

Fruiting body Cup or bowl-shaped, attached by a short stalk. Inner surface brown with fold-like ribs radiating from the centre. Outer surface whitish to cream. Smells of nitric acid or hypochlorite.

Ecology Solitary or gregarious on soil in woods and shady places. Europe and eastern North America. Poisonous if eaten raw but edible if well cooked.

Gyromitra esculenta
FALSE MOREL

Experts have long been puzzled by the haphazard distribution of cases of *Gyromitra* poisoning, although they now realize that toxins are produced as the fruiting bodies mature, and these are especially concentrated in old and decayed specimens. This species, also called the Beefsteak Morel and Elephant's Ears, is highly prized by some

in mass, ellipsoid, smooth, with 2 yellow oil drops, average size 20.0 × 10.5 microns.

Habitat and distribution

Grows singly or in troops, on sandy soils in coniferous woods, on heaths, in mountainous areas. Variable in Europe, becoming more common towards the north, frequent throughout the northern coniferous regions of N. America; known in N. Zealand.

Occurrence

April to May, sometimes June.

Culinary properties

All but young, fresh specimens of this species may be poisonous or even deadly, and they must always be boiled and the resulting liquid strained off, before cooking in the usual way. It is very popular in Eastern Europe, Sweden, Finland and France, where it is processed, canned and exported to Germany and North America in large quantities. The toxins are said to be destroyed by drying and storage. Degradation products are synthesized in ageing fruiting bodies, and these toxins are not destroyed by cooking. Their production may be encouraged by reheating previously cooked dishes. The symptoms caused by *Gyromitra esculenta* are nausea, vomiting and diarrhoea, sometimes followed by jaundice, damage to liver and kidneys, finally coma and death. Recent cases of poisoning have been successfully treated with injections of thioctic acid.

Elaphomyces granulatus
Fruiting body Ovoid, pale yellow-ochre, finely warted. *Flesh:* pale-brown, soon becoming blackish-grey.
Ecology In the surface layers of soil, usually in pine woods, less often in deciduous woods. Locally common in Europe. January to December.
Inedible (once used as an aphrodisiac and in love potions).

Above: Elaphomyces granulatus
Top: Helvella crispa
Bottom: Helvella lacunosa

Helvella crispa
WHITE MORSEL FUNGUS
Collections of this fungus are regarded by many people more as a curiosity than a source of food. It is eaten in large quantities in India and France.
Fruiting body
7–10cm high. *Fertile head:* irregularly folded and lobed, 1.5 to 3cm broad. Under surface pale tan, smooth. Flesh off-white. *Hymenium:* pale greyish-tan, minutely powdery. *Stipe:* stout, usually slightly swollen at the base, 2–4cm long, 1–2cm thick. White or cream, deeply grooved. Flesh hollow or chambered. *Spores:* white in mass, ellipsoid, smooth, 19.0 × 11.5 microns.

Habitat and distribution
Grows singly or gregariously, on damp, rich soil in light places, along paths, deciduous woods. Common in Europe, locally common in eastern North America.
Occurrence
August to November, occasionally in spring in Europe, July to frost in North America.
Culinary properties
The flavour is similar to that of *Morchella esculenta*. It should never be eaten raw, and must be boiled in plenty of water, which must be thrown away before cooking, as for the morels.

Helvella lacunosa
BLACK MORSEL FUNGUS
Although this species; also called Elfin Saddle and Bishop's Mitre, is officially recognized as edible by the French authorities, old and

unfresh specimens develop poisonous deterioration products. It is less common in France than *Helvella sulcata*, with which it is often confused. Some experts consider them to be the same species. Clouds of spores are released by tapping the heads of mature specimens.
Fruiting body
Up to 10cm high. *Fertile head:* saddle-shaped, 2–4cm wide. Lobed, lobes soon becoming convoluted and arched away from the stipe, sharply turned back towards it at their margins. Undersurface dark greyish-black smooth. Flesh dark grey, sometimes with lavender tints, thin. *Hymenium:* dark greyish-black, minutely powdery. *Stipe:* parallel-sided, or slightly swollen towards the base, often bent, 2–4cm long, 1–2cm thick. Grey, tinged with olive, deeply grooved. Flesh hollow or chambered. *Spores:* white in mass, ellipsoid, smooth, average size 15.5 × 11.0 microns.
Habitat and distribution
Grows singly or gregariously, on the ground in deciduous woods, especially on burnt or poor soil, in coniferous woods in mountainous areas. Common in Europe, widespread in North America where it is most abundant along the Pacific coast.
Occurrence
September to October.
Culinary properties
It is particularly recommended that small quantities of this species should be tried before consuming large amounts for the first time. Great care must be taken to gather only fresh, young specimens which are safe to eat. It must never be eaten raw and when boiled produces a liquid which contains harmful chemicals and must be discarded. It should then be cooked in the same way as—although inferior in quality to—*Morchella esculenta*.

Helvella monochella
Fruiting body *Fertile head:* consisting of three or four lobes, shaped like a bishop's mitre, outer surface blackish, inner surface whitish. *Stipe:* up to 10cm tall, white, smooth or slightly roughened.
Ecology Along woodland paths and rides. Uncommon in continental Europe.
Edible.

Leotia lubrica
JELLY BABIES
The fruiting bodies of this fungus closely resemble the rather shapeless, rubbery sweets popularly known as jelly babies and hence their most popular common name. It is also called the Green Slime

folds, 2–4cm high. Yellowish-brown, with black ribs. The lower half is free from the stipe. *Stipe:* cylindrical or slightly swollen at the base, often becoming furrowed with age, 4–8cm long. Off-white to yellow, mealy. Flesh thin, hollow, fragile. *Spores:* cream in mass, ellipsoid, smooth, length variable, average size 25.5 × 16.0 microns.

Habitat and distribution
Grows singly on rich, damp soil, in open woods, copses, shady gardens, grassy places. Occasional to frequent in Europe, rather rare in North America, and is found in Australia.

Occurrence
March to May.

Culinary properties
This fungus must not be eaten raw, and when boiled it produces a liquid which must be strained off because it contains harmful chemicals extracted in cooking.

Morchella conica
In Japan this species is known as *Amigasa-take*. It is very similar to the rare *Morchella elata*, which only grows in mountainous areas.

Fruiting body
Fertile head: conical, with almost straight, longitudinal ridges, connected by short transverse folds, 2–5cm high, 2–5cm thick at the base. At first buff-yellow or very pale ochre, becoming darker with age. Flesh yellowish-olive, thin, fragile. *Stipe:* almost as broad as the fertile head at the apex, narrowing slightly downwards, 3–5cm long. Whitish-yellow to pale brown, mealy. Flesh thin, hollow, very fragile. *Spores:* white in mass, ellipsoid, smooth, average size 19.0 × 13.5 microns.

Habitat and distribution
Grows singly, on rich soil in shady places, in woods, conifer plantations, orchards, in the lowlands and mountainous areas. Occasional in

Left, above: Helvella monachella
Left, below: Leotia lubrica
Below: Mitrophora semi-libera
Bottom: Morchella conica

Fungus, the Gumdrop Fungus and the Slippery Lizard Tuft.

Fruiting body
Up to 6cm high. *Fertile head:* convex, approximately 2cm wide. Greenish-black. Margin lobed, overhanging. Flesh gelatinous. *Stipe:* often slightly inflated at the base, 3–5cm long. Amber, sometimes dotted with green, slimy, minutely scaly. Flesh pulpy, finally hollow. *Spores:* white in mass, narrowly ellipsoid to spindle-shaped, often slightly curved, smooth, becoming 5 to 7 septate when mature, average size 22.5 × 5.5 microns.

Habitat and distribution
Grows gregariously or in clusters, on rich, damp soil, humus, among moss, under ferns, in ditches, in deciduous woods. Common in Europe and North America, and also known in New Zealand.

Occurrence
August to October in Europe, July to frost in North America.

Culinary properties
A small species, but is good food value when it occurs in large enough quantities to be worth gathering.

Mitrophora semilibera
This edible, but thin-fleshed species, is not as succulent as *Morchella esculenta*.

Fruiting body
Fertile head: small, conical, with vertical ridges, joined by horizontal

Europe, widespread in North America and Australia.
Occurrence
May.
Culinary properties
This fungus must not be eaten raw and when boiled produces a liquid, which contains harmful chemicals and which must be strained off.

Morchella deliciosa
Fruiting body *Fertile head:* rounded or ovate cap with elongate grey to blackish pits and lighter coloured ridges. *Stipe:* stout, usually enlarged at the base, whitish or yellowish. Can easily be confused with *Morchella esculenta.*
Ecology In grassy places at the edge of woodland. Uncommon in Europe and North America. Spring. Edible and known in America as the Delicious Morel.

Morchella esculenta
MOREL
This edible species was widely used in the past, when it was dried for use as a flavouring during the winter. Knowing *Morchella esculenta* would grow on burnt ground, the Prussians deliberately lit forest

Right: Morchella deliciosa
Top: Morchella vulgaris
Below, right: Nectria cinnabarina
Below: Morchella esculenta

fires to encourage them. Because these fires sometimes got out of hand, the practice was eventually prohibited by royal decree. In Silesia it was believed that the Devil, in a bad temper, seized an old woman, cut her into pieces and scattered these around the wood. Wherever a piece fell a Morel grew, resembling the old woman in its wrinkled appearance. It is the only fungus eaten by Moslem Indians, all other species being regarded as impure. The mycelium grows well in a culture of earth and apple pulp but it does not fruit. The resulting spawn is well flavoured and is marketed as a powder. Large quantities of Morels are sold in the markets of Bavaria and France.
Fruiting body
Fertile head: rounded, egg-shaped with a honeycomb-like arrangement of pits and ridges, 6—12cm high. Colour ranges from pale yellow-ochre to black, pits tend to be darker than the ridges. Flesh rough, fibrous. *Stipe:* slightly swollen at the base, circular in cross section, may be faintly grooved at the top, sometimes pitted at the base, 6—12cm long. Whitish-yellow, becoming brown with age. Slightly mealy. Flesh hollow, fragile. *Spores:* deep cream in mass, broadly ellipsoid, smooth, length variable, average size 19.5 × 12.5 microns.
Habitat and distribution
Grows singly, sometimes in rings, on rich alkaline soil, in woods, hedges, on banks, in pastures, on sand dunes, disturbed ground, bonfire sites. Variable in Europe, becoming more common towards the south. Common in North America, locally abundant in mountainous areas of India and Pakistan. It is found in Australia.
Occurrence
March to May.
Culinary properties
The Morel must never be eaten raw, and must be thoroughly washed, boiled and the resulting liquid strained off, before cooking as required. In Italy it is often seasoned with mixed herbs, coated liberally with oil and stewed. The resulting juice is thickened with flour, and the dish is served sprinkled with breadcrumbs and garnished with lemon. Morels are also good when stuffed with delicately seasoned chopped meats and baked.

Morchella vulgaris
Fruiting body *Fertile head:* elongate egg-shaped, irregular network of pits and ridges. Dark greyish-brown, sometimes tinged olive. *Stipe:* enlarged, grooved at the base, white to cream, smooth.

Ecology On rich soil in woods, in gardens. Variable in Europe, becoming more common towards the south. March to May.
Edible (good).

Nectria cinnabarina
CORAL SPOT FUNGUS
This very conspicuous fungus attacks fallen branches of all types of tree, it can also be found on soft-fruit bushes. Young, pink fruiting bodies are covered in conidia and have been called *Tubercularia vulgaris.*
Fruiting body
Cushion-like, 3—4mm in diameter. At first pale pink, turning cinammon-red, becoming darker with age. Minutely warted when mature. *Spores:* white in mass, ellipsoid, smooth, with a central cross-wall, length variable, average size 18.5 × 6.5 microns.
Habitat and distribution
Found in dense clusters, bursting through the bark of newly-fallen, hardwood, branches, dead twigs, pea-sticks. Common in Europe.

Occurrence
January to December.
Culinary properties
None known.

Otidea onotica
HARE'S EAR
This large, brightly coloured fungus is uncommon in Europe. It is edible, but difficult to gather in sufficient quantities to be worth cooking.
Fruiting body
Usually elongated on one side, ear-shaped, sometimes almost equal-sided, lobes up to 6cm broad, 3–10cm high. Margin inrolled or flattened. Outer surface yellowish-tan, finely mealy. Flesh white, thin. *Disc:* yellow ochre, tinged with pink. Becomes more pink when dry. *Stipe:* short, white, densely hairy, sometimes wrinkled. *Spores:* white in mass, broadly ellipsoid, smooth, with two oil drops, average size 12.0 × 5.5 microns.
Habitat and distribution
Grows in clusters, on the ground, among litter, in deciduous woods, especially oak. Uncommon in Europe, widespread in North America.

Occurrence
September.
Culinary properties
Tastes pleasant, texture delicate. It must never be eaten raw, and when boiled it produces a liquid which contains harmful chemicals and must be discarded.

Paxina acetabula
VINEGAR CUP
Some experts recognize the small form of *Paxina acetabula*, with the ribs on its stipe scarcely continuing on the underside of the cap, as a separate species, *Paxina sulcata*. *Paxina costifera* is another, similar species, but it fruits in autumn, and has a grey disc and a network of broad ribs on its stipe.
Fruiting body
Deeply cup-shaped, 2–6cm in diameter. Margin wavy, lobed. Outer surface yellow-brown, minutely downy. Flesh white, rather tough. *Disc:* dark amber-brown. *Stipe:* short, stout, 1–1.5cm long. Whitish-clay colour, strongly ribbed, continuing upwards as prominent, forked veins on the underside of the cup. Flesh white, hollow or chambered. *Spores:* white in mass, broadly ellipsoid, smooth, with a very large oil drop, average size 21.0 × 13.0 microns.
Habitat and distribution
Grows singly on calcareous or gravelly soils, in woods, especially oak, on heaths. Uncommon in Europe, common in eastern North America.
Occurrence
April to June, occasionally until August.
Culinary properties
One of the officially recognized edible species sold in French markets. It is poisonous when raw, and produces harmful chemicals when boiled, so this liquid must be thrown away. It can then be cooked slowly in a good stock.

Peziza badia
There are several closely related species with which *Peziza badia* may be confused. These include *Peziza badioconfusa* which has narrower, more finely warted spores, and *Galactinia limosa* which has spores decorated with short ridges, and which grows on bare clay around pools.
Fruiting body
At first closed and globose then expanding to become cup-shaped, up to 8cm in diameter, 2–7cm high. Margin soon becomes wavy. Outer surface brown, often with a purple tinge, mealy. Flesh pale reddish-brown, thin, exudes a watery juice.

Disc: dark liver-brown, with olive tints. *Stipe:* very short or absent, stout, sometimes pitted. *Spores:* white in mass, ellipsoid, netted with short ridges, mostly with 2 oil drops, average size 18.5 × 10.5 microns.
Habitat and distribution
Grows gregariously or in tufts, on the ground in woods, on bonfire sites, along the sides of woodland roads. Widespread and frequent in Europe and North America. It is also found in southern Australia.

Above: Paxina acetabula
Left: Otidea onotica
Bottom: Peziza badia

Occurrence

August to October in Europe, July to October in North America.

Culinary properties

It must first be boiled in water and the resulting liquid thrown away as it contains harmful chemicals. Meaty, but lacking in flavour. When finely chopped it can either be stewed slowly, or quickly fried in hot butter until crisp.

Peziza vesiculosa
EARLY CUP FUNGUS

When they grow in dense clusters, the fruiting bodies of this fungus often become distorted due to mutual pressure. The spores escape like clouds of dust when the ripe cups are disturbed. *Peziza vesiculosa* has often been found growing in large numbers, on damp plaster in bomb-damaged houses.

Fruiting body

At first closed and globose, soon expanding to become irregularly cup-shaped, 2.5–7.5cm in diameter, 2–5cm high. Margin incurved, notched, wavy. Outer surface greyish-fawn, coarsely granular with minute irregular warts. Flesh pale fawn, fragile. *Disc:* yellowish-tan to honey-coloured. The hymenium often separates from the flesh forming a blister in the centre of the cup. *Stipe:* absent. *Spores:* white in mass, ellipsoid, smooth, average size 22.0 × 13.0 microns.

Habitat and distribution

Grows in groups or clusters, on manure heaps, richly manured soil, especially in gardens, on mushroom beds, damp plaster. Widespread and common in Europe and North America, it is also found in southern Australia.

Occurrence

August to April.

Culinary properties

Tastes pleasant, and has a delicate texture. It must never be eaten raw, and when boiled produces a liquid which must be discarded as it contains harmful chemicals.

Below: Peziza vesiculosa
Centre: Pustularia catinus
Top: Rhizina undulata
Far right: Sarcoscypha coccinea

Pustularia catinus

Fruiting body Cup-shaped, margin minutely wavy. Outer surface pale ochre, downy. *Disc:* cream to pale ochre. *Stipe:* short, stout or absent.

Ecology Singly or in clusters on soil in woods, along woodland paths, especially under beech. Frequent in Europe. June to September. Inedible.

Rhizina undulata
DOUGHNUT FUNGUS

This fungus is parasitic on conifers. It enters plantations by way of areas cleared by fire, and then spreads to healthy trees which it can parasitize and kill.

Fruiting body

At first disc-shaped, becoming cushion-shaped and irregularly lobed, 1–8cm in diameter. Under surface yellowish-white with numerous white, root-like structures. Flesh reddish-brown, very tough, fibrous. *Hymenium:* upper surface, dark brown to black with a pale margin, undulating. *Spores:* white to very pale brown in mass, spindle-shaped, minutely rough, contain 2 or more oil drops, they have a prominent projection at each end, length variable, average size 31.0 × 9.5 microns.

Habitat and distribution

Found on debris in coniferous woods, especially after bonfires. Common in Europe, uncommon in North America.

Occurrence

June to October.

Culinary properties

None known.

Sarcoscypha coccinea
SCARLET ELF CUPS

This beautiful fungus adds a splash of colour to the drab winter woodland scenery. It was formerly well known to country folk as Moss Cups. In Scarborough, England, it used to be gathered, arranged with moss and leaves, and sold as a table decoration.

Fruiting body

Cup-shaped, with an inrolled margin, 2–6cm in diameter. Outer surface whitish-yellow, downy. *Disc:* scarlet, occasionally white. *Stipe:* short, stout, 1–2cm long. Whitish-yellow, downy. Attached to substrate by a mass of white, downy mycelium. *Spores:* white in mass, ellipsoid, smooth, usually with a group of oil droplets at each end, length variable, average size 28.0 × 13.0 microns.

Habitat and distribution

Grows singly or in groups of two or three, on decayed branches of deciduous trees and bramble stems,

lying on, or partly buried in, humus. Widespread and locally common in Europe and North America. It is also found in Tasmania.

Occurrence
December to March in Europe, April to May in North America.

Culinary properties
This species is poisonous when raw, and must be boiled and the liquid discarded as it contains harmful chemicals. Tastes pleasant, and is worth trying if it can be collected and cooked in large enough quantities.

Spathularia flavida
Fruiting body *Fertile head:* flattened, forms broad flange around upper part of stipe. Yellow, often wrinkled. *Stipe:* round, whitish-yellow.
Ecology Singly on the ground in coniferous woods. Variable in Europe, becoming more common towards the south. August to October.
Edibility unknown.

Terfezia leonis
Fruiting body Sub-globose or pear-shaped, 3–12cm diameter, surface smooth, whitish or cream, with a faint smell of cherry laurel. Internally the fruit-body is several-chambered, asci are large and globose, ascospores coarsely warted. *Stipe:* short, obconical.
Ecology In mountain pine and cedar forests, in fields, and marine sandy places. Southern Europe, north Africa.
Edible. It is called 'leonis' after the old Spanish kingdom of Léon.

Trichoglossum hirsutum
SHAGGY EARTH TONGUES
Collections of this species can be distinguished from other similar species by their downy stipes.
Fruiting body
Fertile head: flattened, spindle-shaped, up to 1.5cm long, 5–7.5mm wide. Sooty-brown to black, dry. *Stipe:* cylindrical, up to 6cm long, 2–3mm thick, dark sooty-brown to black, densely velvety. *Spores:* dark brown in mass, elongate, spindle-shaped, smooth, normally 15 septate when mature, average size 125.0 × 7.0 microns.
Habitat and distribution
Grows in clusters, on acid grassland, among *Sphagnum*. Frequent to common in Europe, North America, West Indies, south-east Australia.
Occurrence
August to November.
Culinary properties
None known.

Tuber aestivum
SUMMER TRUFFLE
Summer Truffles were collected and marketed commercially in southern England until the 1930s. According to a professional truffle hunter, most truffles found were under beeches, the rest were under

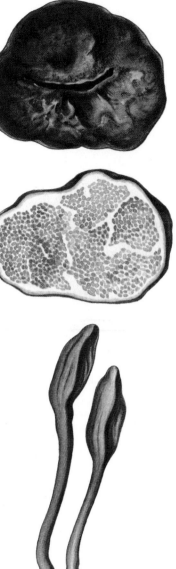

Top: Terfezia leonis
Left: Trichoglossum hirsutum
Below, left: Spathularia flavida
Below: Tuber aestivum

cedar, hazel, hawthorn and sycamore.

Fruiting body

Irregularly globular, 2–7 sometimes 9cm in diameter, bluish-black, glistening when fresh, brownish-black when dry. Covered with large, hard 5 to 6 sided pyramidal warts. Flesh at first yellowish-white, becoming brown and marbled with numerous white veins when mature. *Spores:* white in mass, ellipsoid, netted, size variable, average size 3.0 × 22.5 microns.

Habitat and distribution

Subterranean, 12–50cm deep, in calcareous soil, mostly under beech. Said to be rare in Europe, but this is uncertain as they are difficult to find, becoming more common towards the south.

Occurrence

June to October.

Culinary properties

Smell slight but characteristic. Not regarded as highly as *Tuber melanosporum* but they are good when sliced, boiled and sprinkled with salt.

Tuber melanosporum
PERIGORD TRUFFLE

Pliny described truffles as 'calluses of the soil', while Plutarch explained their existence as the result of the combined action of thunder, rain and the warmth of the sun on the soil. In the sixteenth century they were believed by some to be a product of the semen of rutting deer. By the early nineteenth century, biologists believed that they were a sort of gall produced by oak roots. Later in the century the famous theory of the 'truffle fly', which stung the roots of oak trees causing a gall-like truffle to grow, was put forward by several influential biologists. It was widely believed, and arose from the accurate observation, that clouds of flies were often to be seen hovering close to the soil in areas known to be rich in truffles. Tulasne explained that the flies are attracted by the scent of the truffles, as are other animals. The female flies lay their eggs in the fungus, and then continue their flight. The centre of the 'truffle industry' is Perigord in south-west France, where they grow profusely in the light, porous, clay marl, which overlies limestone. Truffle hunters use specially trained dogs or sometimes pigs to locate these subterranean fungi.

Fruiting body

Globular, 2–10cm in diameter. Black or reddish-black, covered with 6-sided, fluted warts. Flesh violet-black with white veins, veins turn red when exposed to the air. *Spores:* dark brown in mass, ellipsoid, spiny, average size 32.5 × 28.5 microns.

Habitat and distribution

Subterranean, occurs in clusters 5–20cm deep, in calcareous soil, in oak woods, occasionally under beech, hazel. Difficult to locate without a trained dog or pig. Europe, south of the English Channel.

Occurrence

Autumn and winter.

Culinary properties

Smells strong and agreeable. They are delicious when boiled, roasted, cooked in oil, wine or honey and served in a white sauce made from the cooking liquor.

Tuber magnatum

Fruiting body Irregularly top-shaped and resembling a knobbly tuber, 3–15cm in diameter, yellowish to clay colour with darker scurf, flesh soapy, rosy-white to grey with whitish marble-like veins, smells of garlic or cheese.

Ecology Grows buried in soil beneath oaks and other broadleaved trees. Southern Europe and especially the area around Piedmont, and hence its common name—the White or Piedmont Truffle. Autumn or winter.

Edible and highly prized. Commercially important and expensive to buy.

Tuber rufum

Fruiting body Globular or irregularly lobed, foxy-red, surface finely cracked. Flesh firm, at first white with cream veins, becoming red-brown. Tastes nutty, smell unpleasant in old specimens.

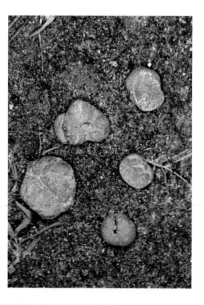

Far right: Tuber rufum
Bottom right: Tuber magnatum
Below: Tuber melanosporum

Ecology In rich soil of deciduous and coniferous woods. Fairly common in Europe. July to August, less frequent in spring. Edible.

Verpa bohemica

Fruiting body *Fertile head:* shaped like an inverted cone, 1–2cm wide at the base, with longitudinal anastomosing folds, pale to dark yellow-brown. *Stipe:* white or cream coloured becoming pale tan, 6–8cm long, hollow or loosely filled.

Ecology On soil in woodlands. Infrequent in North America and Continental Europe. Found in early spring, which gives it the name of the Early Morel.

Edible, but some people are adversely affected by it.

Verpa digitaliformis

Fruiting body *Fertile head:* resembles a thimble on a finger, slightly wrinkled or folded, connected to the stipe at the apex, 0.5–2.5cm wide at the base, yellow-brown to brown. *Stipe:* cylindrical, 5–10cm long, whitish, becoming hollow.

Ecology Open deciduous woodland, under hedges, sand dunes and gardens. Infrequent in North America and Europe. Spring. Inedible.

Xylaria hypoxylon
CANDLE SNUFF FUNGUS

This fungus has a luminous mycelium. In dark places, such as on the underside of logs, in hollow trees or under leaves, abnormally long

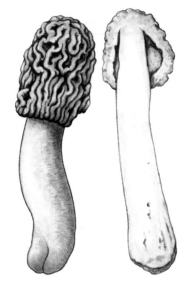

fruiting bodies are produced. These will grow towards a source of light and can be made to twist and turn by altering the direction of the light.

Fruiting body
Usually forked, antler-like, 3–8cm high. Tips at first white with powdery conidia, becoming black and rough with the tips of protruding perithecia when these mature. Flesh white, tough, corky. Unbranched forms with pointed tips only form perithecia. *Stipe:* black, felty. *Spores:* black in mass, smooth, slightly bean-shaped, average size 18.5 × 5.5 microns.

Habitat and distribution
Grows in dense masses on stumps and decorticated fallen branches of deciduous trees, especially sycamore, ash and beech. Common in Europe and North America.

Occurrence
January to December. Conida in spring, perithecia later.

Culinary properties
None known.

Xylaria polymorpha
WOOD CLUB FUNGUS

A small form of this species is found on gorse and birch after heath fires. Abnormal growths, due to insufficient light, are sometimes found in hollow trunks or on the underside of logs. As in the case of *Xylaria hypoxylon*, it is thought by some people to have a luminous mycelium. It is also called Dead Man's Fingers and Devil's Fingers.

Fruiting body
Irregularly club-shaped with a short cylindrical stipe, up to 8cm high. Covered with light-brown, powdery conidia when young. Black, dull, somewhat wrinkled, with the tips of perithecia protruding out in mature specimens. Flesh white, tough. *Spores:* black in mass, spindle-shaped, smooth, average size 26.0 × 7.0 microns.

Habitat and distribution
Grows gregariously or in clusters, on rotting stumps, dead branches, buried wood, especially beech. Common in Europe, North America and Australia. Also occurs in New Zealand.

Occurrence
January to December.

Culinary properties
None known.

Above: Xylaria polymorpha
Left: Xylaria hypoxylon
Far left: Verpa bohemica
Bottom: Verpa digitaliformis

Basidiomycetes

All members of this group, which contains the greater proportion of the larger fungi, produce spores on the tips of projections, termed sterigma, which stick up from club-shaped cells, known as basidia. There are several important subdivisions, which are individually described below.

Class Gasteromycetes

The fruiting bodies of this group, the Stomach Fungi, remain closed during spore formation and maturation. The spores are shed by a variety of interesting mechanisms. None of this class is especially important, either to its surroundings or to Man. They are mostly terrestrial fungi, although a few grow on wood or dung. Young specimens of the more fleshy members are edible, but this group includes many small, dry, inedible species.

Bovista nigrescens

The old, brown fruiting bodies of this species being blown about by the wind, are a common sight in autumn. When nestling in grass, young white specimens bear an irritating resemblance to golf balls.

Fruiting body

Almost spherical, 3–6cm in diameter. White, smooth at first, this outer skin cracks and flakes off, leaving the tough, shining, blackish-brown inner skin. Spores

Top: Calvatia excipuliforme
Right: Bovista nigrescens
Centre: Bovista plumbea
Bottom, right: Calvatia utriformis

disperse, through an irregular, torn mouth at the top during the time it is blown around after being detached. Gleba: at first white, then olive, finally purplish-brown, soft. Spores: brown in mass, spherical to ovoid, smooth, with a long stalk, average size 5.5 microns in diameter.

Habitat and distribution

Found sporadically, among grass in pastures, on downs, heaths, sand dunes, in Europe and eastern North America.

Occurrence

January to December.

Culinary properties

Smells fruity, tasteless when raw. Young, white fleshed specimens are delicious when cooked. They should be peeled before cooking.

Bovista plumbea

The smooth, white, young fruiting bodies of this very small fungus

resemble table-tennis balls. Its web-like basal mycelium is not rooting, and mature specimens are often loosened from the soil and blown about by the wind, thus ensuring that the spores are widely distributed.

Fruiting body

Small, almost spherical, 1–3cm across. Outer skin smooth, white, soon flakes off. Inner skin lead-coloured, smooth, shining, Spores disperse, through a small, rounded apical opening, following the detachment of the fruit body. Gleba: at first white, then clay-coloured, finally olive-brown, soft, loose. Spores: brown in mass, ovoid, smooth to minutely rough, with a long pointed stalk, average size 5.0 × 3.8 microns.

Habitat and distribution

Grows singly or gregariously, in grass, on light sandy soils, in pastures, meadows, on heaths, sand dunes, in open woodland. Common in Europe and North America.

Occurrence

August to November.

Culinary properties

Highly recommended.

Calvatia excipuliformis

A common puffball, this species is large enough to be worth gathering for food. It is recognized by its shape and well-developed, sterile base.

Fruiting body

Pestle or club-shaped, the rounded head narrows gradually into the long, sterile, stem-like base, 8–20cm high, 2–10cm across at the top. At first whitish with spiny warts which are split at the base and united at the top. These soon fall off, leaving the brown, smooth or downy inner wall which breaks away in patches at the top, liberating the spores. Gleba: at first white, then yellow, finally olive brown. Spores: olive in mass, spherical, warted, average size 4.5 microns in diameter.

Habitat and distribution

A fairly common species of woods,

heaths, pastures, in Europe and eastern North America.

Occurrence

August to November.

Culinary properties

They should only be eaten while the flesh is white.

Calvatia utriformis
MOSAIC PUFFBALL

The dried fruiting bodies of this fungus were once widely used by country folk as styptics. Pliny classified this species with the cup fungi and they were not generally recognized as puffballs until the mid-nineteenth century. In mature specimens the outer layer of skin flakes off at the top, exposing the fragile inner layer which soon breaks away, liberating the spores. When all the spores are dispersed the remarkably persistent sterile base can remain in place for several months, or it becomes free and is blown about by the wind.

Fruiting body

Large, top or pear-shaped, tapering to a short, stout, stem-like base, 6–12cm in diameter. At first white, finally cinnamon-brown. Outer layer woolly, soon becomes scaly,

then cracked into star-shaped areas. Lower half sterile, separated from spores by a distinct membranous diaphragm. *Gleba:* at first white, turning yellow, finally olive-brown as the spores mature. Very fragile and powdery. *Spores:* dark olive in mass, spherical, smooth, average size 4.5 microns in diameter.

Habitat and distribution
Common on downs, calcareous and sandy pastures, sand dunes of northern Europe and northern and mid-western North America. It is found in the cooler temperate areas of Australia, and also occurs in New Zealand.

Occurrence
July to November in Europe, August to November in North America.

Culinary properties
Only young, white-fleshed specimens should be eaten. They used to be sold in some North American markets, but were slow to become popular.

Clathrus ruber
In appearance this is one of the most attractive fungi, but its very strong, unpleasant smell keeps ad-

mirers at a respectable distance.

Young fruiting body or Egg
Conspicuous, white, attached at the base by white cord-like mycelium. At first smooth, later shows a network of marks. The fruiting body bursts the egg as it expands, leaving the remains as a cup surrounding the base.

Mature fruiting body
An open lattice-work, globular, red, paler at the base, outer surface ribbed. Flesh thick, spongy. *Gleba:* olive-brown, foul smelling, covers the inner surface of the open network. *Spores:* olive-brown in mass, ellipsoid, smooth.

Habitat and distribution
Grows singly in garden borders, on heaps of leaves, on undisturbed soil under hedges, in woods. Common after rain in Europe, southwards from the south coast of England, rare in North America.

Reported in Jamaica, the Bahamas, Puerto Rico.

Occurrence
Late summer and autumn.

Culinary properties
None known.

Crucibulum laeve
This is a widespread but exclusively temperate species, which has not yet been found in the tropics. It produces two forms of peridioles: those that are small and pale are usually found in dry areas; and large and strongly coloured peridioles which usually occur in specimens from warm, wet regions. Crowded groups of cups are often found growing on a basal pad of mycelium. A double fruiting body may be formed when the walls of two cups touch. New fruiting bodies are known to have grown from within the remains of old specimens, arising from a 'pad' of living mycelium inside the base. The new fungus is at first completely encased within the old one.

Fruiting body
At first globular, greyish to dirty-cinnamon, expanding to bell or cup-shaped, 3–7mm high, 4–8mm wide. Top closed by a two-layered membrane. Outer surface ochre to tawny, downy, becoming brownish-tan or grey, almost smooth when mature. Inner surface silvery-grey to white, smooth, shining. The membrane withers and peels off at maturity exposing the small, circular, lens-shaped peridioles, 1–2mm in diameter. Attached to the cup by cords, covered with a thick white tunica which frequently ruptures. *Spores:* colourless, ellipsoid to ovoid, smooth, size variable, average size 8.5 × 4.0 microns.

Habitat and distribution
Grows in crowded groups on sticks, twigs, decaying wood, driftwood, bark of living trees, on dead bramble stems, fern fronds, rotten sacking, old matting, manure, rare on soil. Common in temperate areas of Europe, North America, South America, Japan, Australia, New Zealand.

Occurrence
September to March in Europe, July to November in North America.

Culinary properties
None known.

Left: Clathrus ruber
Below: Cyathus olla
Bottom: Crucibulum laeve

Cyathus olla
Although this fungus grows well in damp, shady places, it can withstand drought, and is abundant under tussocks of vegetation on the arid Peruvian plain. It is the most common European *Cyathus* species, and one of the most abundant in North America. The North American

form grows in groups on a solid mass of hyphae and soil, known as an emplacement. Very variable in shape and size, this species can be recognized by the fine texture of the fruiting body wall, and by the irregularly shaped peridioles.

Fruiting body
At first with incurved margin, expanding to trumpet-shaped, with a narrow base and wide flaring mouth, 8–12mm high, 7–10mm broad at the top. Outer surface at first tawny brown, minutely downy, finally becoming greyish-brown, smooth. Inner surfaces dark greyish-brown to silvery-brown, smooth, shining. The cup contains 6–8 large irregular, silky-grey peridioles, 2–3mm in diameter. Each attached to the cup by a strong whitish cord. *Spores:* colourless, ovoid to broadly ellipsoid, smooth, average size 12.0 × 7.0 microns.

Habitat and distribution
Grows singly or in small groups, on soil, straw, twigs, fir cones, felled wood, planks, in gardens, fields. Common in Europe, south of Sweden, North America, South America, South Africa, Iran, Australia. Also occurs in New Zealand.

Occurrence
March to November.

Culinary properties
None known.

Below: Cyathus striatus
Far right: Geastrum quadrifidum
Right: Geastrum fornicatum

Cyathus striatus

This species can be distinguished from other birds nest fungi by its beautifully shining, furrowed inner surface and its hairy exterior. It is frequently attacked by the parasitic fungus *Hypocrea latizonata*, which forms a broad whitish band of vegetative hyphae causing the development of abnormal fruiting bodies. The coarse-textured, brown mycelium readily grows and produces fruiting bodies in culture. Some metabolic products of the mycelium are weak antibiotics, known as cyathins.

Fruiting body
At first rounded, expanding to a cut off, inverted cone, 8–12mm high, 6–8mm broad. The tops of young specimens are closed by a thin, whitish, smooth membrane. Outer surface at first tawny becoming darker brown, covered with coarse, shaggy hairs. Inner surface varied in colour from pale grey to almost black, smooth, shining, fluted. The membrane withers away at maturity exposing 10–12 circular, flattened, grey peridioles, 1.5–2mm in diameter. Each attached to the cup by a strong elastic cord. *Spores:* colourless, ellipsoid, smooth, with a distinct projection at one end, average size 19.0 × 9.0 microns.

Habitat and distribution
Grows gregariously, usually in clusters, on dead wood, fence posts, stumps, twigs, fir cones, dead leaves, fern fronds, stubble. Common and widespread in temperate areas of Europe, North America, Central America, India, China, Japan.

Occurrence
March to November.

Culinary properties
None known.

Geastrum fornicatum

Small groups of this fungus are reminiscent of small manikins. It was first described in 1688 by G. Seger, who called it *Fungus anthropomorphos*, and his published drawing of two or three specimens included one with a human profile.

Fruiting body
5–10cm high when expanded. *Outer skin:* splits into two layers. The inner layer divides in 4 straddling rays, whose tips remain attached to an equal number of smaller lobes on the margin of the outer layer which remains as a membranous cup on the ground. Rays, dark brown, fleshy, become peeled or worn away exposing the whitish-tan fibrous tissue. *Inner fruiting body:* spherical or urn-shaped, with a distinct stalk. Dark brown, minutely

velvety. Apical pore, large, elevated, fibrous, lacerated, wrinkled. *Spores:* blackish-brown in mass, globose, distinctly warted, average size 3.8 microns in diameter.

Habitat and distribution
This species has a world-wide, but rather erratic, distribution. Rare to occasional in grass on the borders of deciduous woods.

Occurrence
April to November.

Culinary properties
Not recommended.

Geastrum quadrifidum

This species is easily confused with

Geastrum fornicatum, which is actually much larger.

Fruiting body
2–3cm across, approximately 3cm high when expanded. *Outer skin:* purplish-brown, with 4 straddling rays, the tips stuck in the substrate. Flat weft of mycelium between ray tips. *Inner fruiting body:* ovoid, flattened, with a distinct stalk. Lead-grey, powdered with minute glistening particles. Apical pore with a definite edge. *Spores:* dark, smoky purplish-brown in mass, globose, distinctly rough, average size 5.5 microns in diameter.

Habitat and distribution
A widespread, locally frequent, species of coniferous woods, of Europe, North and Central America, Japan, New Zealand.

Occurrence
August to October.

Culinary properties
Not recommended.

Geastrum rufescens

This is probably the most common British earthstar. Groups of unexpanded fruiting bodies, which are usually buried under forest debris, look rather like miniature cottage loaves. Expanded specimens recognized by their small size, and by the sessile inner fruiting body which nestles in the cup-like outer layer.

Fruiting body
At first globular, 3–6mm in diameter when expanded. *Outer skin:* splits into 6–9 rays. Rays curl back and bend underneath the fruiting body. Undivided portion forms a cup round the base of the inner fruiting body. Outer surface pale brown, inner surface yellow to watery-brown. *Inner fruiting body:* almost spherical, sessile, smooth, cinnamon-buff. With an apical, slightly elevated, fringed mouth. *Spores:* deep brown in mass, globose, warted, size 5.0 microns in diameter.

Far left: Geastrum rufescens
Left: Geastrum triplex
Bottom, left: Geastrum velutinum
Bottom, right: Mature Geastrum striatum

Habitat and distribution
Grows in groups or colonies, on the ground around old stumps in conifer, oak or beech woods. Widespread and locally common in temperate forests of Europe, North and Central America, Japan, Australia.
Occurrence
July to November.
Culinary properties
Unopened specimens have a fruity smell. Not recommended.

Geastrum striatum
Fruiting body At first globular. *Outer skin:* irregularly split into 6–12 dark brown, fleshy rays. *Inner fruiting body:* lead-grey to blackish-brown, stalked, with a distinct collar. Mouth, furrowed, beak-like.
Ecology Deciduous woods, heaths, sand dunes. Occasional in Europe. January to December. Inedible.

Geastrum triplex
COLLARED EARTHSTAR
The unexpanded fruiting bodies of this species look just like onions. Late in the year, old dry specimens are sometimes blown about by the wind and collect in ditches. The spores are dispersed through the apical pore by the action of rain-drops striking inner fruiting body.
Fruiting body
At first globular, sharply pointed at the top. Up to 10cm across when expanded. *Outer skin:* splits into 5–7 pointed rays, which become curled underneath the fruiting body. Rays at first flesh-coloured, thick, becoming cracked across. Later dark brown, horny. *Inner fruiting body:* almost spherical, sessile, pale brown, surrounded by a basal cup. Apical pore becomes lacerated, surrounded by a more or less definitely outlined, broadly conical, silky area. *Spores:* brown in mass, globose, spiny, average size 5.5 microns in diameter.
Habitat and distribution
A locally common species on rich soil, and around rotten stumps in deciduous woods, especially beech, or warm temperate areas of Europe and North America. Also occurs in New Zealand.
Occurrence
August to October.
Culinary properties
Not recommended.

Geastrum velutinum
This species is apparently absent from Europe, although further research may correct this impression. The unexpanded fruiting bodies are attached, at the base, to an obvious mycelial web, by a well-developed, mycelial cord.

Fruiting body
At first globular or ovoid, 3–4cm in diameter when expanded. *Outer skin:* splits into 5–7 buff to pale brown pointed rays, which remain expanded and flattened on the substrate, or become curled underneath the fruiting body. *Inner fruiting body:* almost spherical, sessile, 1–1.5cm across. Buff to dark brown. Apical pore surrounded by a distinct silky, convex zone. *Spores:* light brown in mass, globose, distinctly warted, average size 3 microns in diameter.
Habitat and distribution
A common woodland species, which grows on leaf mould in the warm temperate forests of North and South America, West Indies, Africa, Australia, New Zealand.
Occurrence
Summer and Autumn.
Culinary properties
Not recommended.

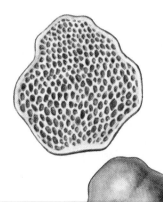

Hymenogaster tener

Fruiting body Small, irregularly ovoid, lobed. Silvery-white, shining, reddish where bruised. *Gleba:* at first white, finally pinkish-grey. Glebal chamber empty, easily visible. Smells pleasant.

Ecology Usually on calcareous soils, beneath humus or leaf litter of deciduous woods, especially oak. Frequent to common in Europe. January to December.

Edibility unknown.

Top: Hymenogaster tener
Right: Langermannia gigantea
Far right: Lycoperdon ericetorum
Bottom: Lycoperdon echinatum

Langermannia gigantea
GIANT PUFFBALL

There have been many stories told about this unusually large fungus. Specimens weighing up to 18 kilogrammes are not uncommon, and there is an unconfirmed report of one weighing 100 kilogrammes. In New York State in 1877 an extremely large fruiting body was reported to have been mistaken for a sheep. The Giant Puffball was known to the Ancient World, and was probably *Pezis* as described by Theophrastus. Country folk made good use of this fungus, most commonly as a styptic. As can easily be imagined, this fungus was soon found to be a useful source of food, although only young, white-fleshed specimens are safe to eat, and each one must be checked for infestation by worms and maggots.

Fruiting body

Large, rounded sometimes flattened, usually grooved at the base, attached by thick, cord-like, mycelial strands, 15–40cm or more across. At first greyish-white becoming yellow, finally brown in old, dry specimens. Outer surface at first downy, soon becoming smooth. Sterile base very small, or absent. When mature the outer skin cracks and breaks away at the top, leaving the brittle inner skin exposed. This collapses permitting the dispersal of the mature spores. *Gleba:* at first white and firm, then yellow, finally olive-brown. Spore mass compact, powdery, dry. *Spores:* olive-brown in mass, spherical, minutely warted, average size 4.0 microns in diameter.

Habitat and distribution

It is found in the same places year after year, sometimes growing in rings, on rich soil, in open woodland, orchards, meadows, gardens, along roadsides, railway embankments, beside drainage ditches. Locally common in Europe and north-eastern North America.

Occurrence

August to September in Europe, August to October in North America.

Culinary properties

Young, white-fleshed specimens are deliciously cheesy and crumbly. A large fruiting body can be kept and sliced for several days. Giant Puffballs have been included on menus for state occasions.

Lycoperdon echinatum
SPRING PUFFBALL

This rather uncommon species is recognized by its spiny, hedgehog-like appearance.

Fruiting body

Globular, narrowing downwards to a small, slender, sterile base, 3–6cm

broad. At first creamy-white, soon becoming brown. Decorated with well-developed, persistent spines, arranged in groups of 3 or 4, free at the base, joined at the tips, surrounded by mealy warts, which give a netted appearance to old, weathered specimens when the spines have dropped off. The spores disperse through a small, torn, apical mouth. *Gleba:* at first white, then yellowish-olive, finally dark purplish-brown. *Spores:* dark olive-brown in mass, spherical, warty, often with a long pedicel, average size 5.5 microns in diameter.

Habitat and distribution

Found growing on rich soil in deciduous woods, glades, pastures, especially under beech. Variable in Europe becoming more common towards the south, apparently rare, but probably locally frequent in North America, east of the Rocky Mountains.

Occurrence

Spring to autumn in Europe, August to November in North America.

Culinary properties

Well flavoured and tender when cooked.

Lycoperdon ericetorum

This is the smallest British puffball, and like all the others, it is edible

when the flesh is white. If it can be found only in small quantities, it can be added to other fungus dishes. It grows in very poor soil and often occurs where nothing else will.

Fruiting body

Small, globose to pear-shaped, narrowed at the base to a thin cord-like root, 1–3cm across. At first white to whitish grey, scurfy, finally pale yellowish-brown, smooth, shining. Sterile base absent. Spores are dispersed through a small apical pore in mature specimens. *Gleba:* at first white, then yellow, finally brownish-olive. *Spores:* brownish-olive in mass, spherical, smooth, with a large oil drop, average size 3.8 microns in diameter.

Habitat and distribution

Grows in tufts or scattered, on poor sandy soils, on heaths, poor pasture-land, hedge banks. Frequent in Europe, common in eastern North America.

Occurrence

August to November in Europe, June to October in North America.

Culinary properties

Individual specimens are small, but they can usually be found in quantities large enough to be worth gathering.

Lycoperdon molle

This is an uncommon species of coniferous woods, where it grows among moss, especially *Polytrichum*.

Fruiting body

Rounded or pear-shaped, with a stem-like, sterile base, 3–4.5cm high, 2–5cm across. Colour varies from white to light brownish-grey. Outer skin covered with short, separate, erect, hair-like spines, these become flattened towards the base. The spines become worn away in mature specimens, leaving the pale-brown, shiny inner skin. *Gleba:* at first white, turning yellow, then olive, finally purplish-brown or dark olive-brown. *Spores:* dark brown in mass, spherical, finely warted, average size 4 microns in diameter.

Habitat and distribution

Widespread, but not abundant, in coniferous forests, less frequent on heaths, in Europe and North America east of the Rocky Mountains.

Occurrence

August to November in Europe, September to November in North America.

Culinary properties

A rather small species, but well flavoured, and holds its body when cooked.

Lycoperdon perlatum
DEVIL'S TOBACCO POUCH

The fruiting bodies of this species vary greatly in shape and size, and are sometimes attached in pairs to white mycelial cords. These may grow to a great length and so enable the fungus to spread in a remarkable manner. When ripe, the spores can be seen puffing from the apical pore, in dark satanic-looking clouds. In the past they were used as styptics by country folk. They often confuse golfers, as a fruiting body looks very much like a golf ball from a distance. Mushroom lovers know them as Poor Man's Sweetbread, because of their fine texture and flavour.

Fruiting body

Top-shaped, or rounded at the top with a stem-like sterile base, 4–7cm high, 3–5cm across. At first white finally dirty yellowish-brown. Decorated with long fragile warts, surrounded by granules. The warts soon fall off leaving a net-like pattern. Spores are dispersed through a small protruding apical pore. *Gleba:* at first white, firm, then greenish-yellow, finally olive-brown, powdery. *Spores:* olive-brown in mass, spherical, minutely rough, average size 4 microns in diameter.

Habitat and distribution

Grows singly, gregarious, often in tufts, occasionally in rings, on humus rich soil, in open woods, glades, pastures. Common in Europe, North America and Australia. It probably has a world-wide distribution.

Occurrence

July to December in Europe, July to October in North America.

Culinary properties

The strong smell of radish disappears when cooked. Fruiting bodies mature rapidly, and are not often

found with the white flesh, which is much sought after by enthusiasts. They are excellent when sliced and fried in batter or egg and bread-crumbs, or when stewed gently in milk and a white sauce made from the liquor.

Lycoperdon pyriforme
WOOD OR STUMP PUFFBALLS

This is the only British puffball which grows on wood. The fruiting bodies form very large clusters on rotten stumps and logs, growing from intricately branched mycelial strands. Sometimes a collection of this species is found growing on soil, but when the mycelial strands are followed they are always attached to buried wood. Old specimens are very persistent and are often found in good condition in early spring, when the snow has melted.

Above: Lycoperdon perlatum
Bottom, left: Lycoperdon molle
Below: Lycoperdon pyriforme

Fruiting body
Pear-shaped or rounded with a slight hump at the top, narrowing downwards to a short, fluted, sterile base, 3—5cm high, 2—4cm across. At first white, coarsely mealy, soon becoming greyish or yellowish-brown, smooth. Spores disperse through a small, irregular mouth at the top. *Gleba:* white at first, then greenish-yellow, finally deep olive-brown. *Spores:* deep olive-brown in mass, spherical, smooth, average size 4.3 microns in diameter.

Habitat and distribution
Grows in very large dense clusters, sometimes of several hundred individuals, on deciduous logs, stumps or buried wood, on the edge of old sawdust heaps. Common in Europe and North America, and found in New Zealand, it has a world-wide distribution.

Occurrence
August to November in Europe, July to November in North America.

Culinary properties
Tastes and smells slightly acrid, a little lemon juice or sherry improves the flavour. Becomes intensely bitter when the flesh is slightly tinged with yellow.

Lysurus gardneri
Young fruiting body Globular, white, soft, leathery, attached by white mycelial strands.
Mature fruiting body *Cap:* of five to seven red-brown fingers at first pressed together, conical, finally diverging, slightly incurved, wrinkled with a central longitudinal groove. *Gleba:* coating fingers, olive-brown. *Stipe:* tall, cylindrical, hollow, white. Smells slightly foetid.
Ecology On well-manured ground, undecomposed horse manure, in gardens, greenhouses. A tropical species introduced into temperate areas of Europe and North America, where it appears in hot, dry summers. Common in Australia, New Zealand.
Edibility unknown.

Melanogaster variegatus
RED TRUFFLE
Collections of Red Truffles were sold in the markets of southern England, and were preferred to *Tuber aestivum* by some people.
Fruiting body
Irregularly globular, tuberous, 1—4cm in diameter. At first yellow-ochre, finally dull reddish-brown, becoming black where bruised. Cuticle felty. Attached to soil by elaborately branched rhizomorphs. *Gleba:* consists of thick-walled chambers, at first whitish-yellow, finally bright orange, filled with purple-black mass of spores. *Spores:*

Above: Lysurus gardneri
Centre, right: Melanogaster variegatus
Below, right: Mutinus caninus
Below, far right: Mutinus elegans

black in mass, ellipsoid, smooth, with distinct hyphal cup, average size 3.5 × 8.5 microns.
Habitat and distribution
Grows in tufts of five or six fruiting bodies, mostly on the surface of the soil, but buried under litter of deciduous trees, especially beech. Frequent in Europe and eastern North America.
Occurrence
January to December.

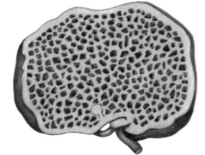

Culinary properties
Tastes sweet, smell reminiscent of bitter almonds, it can be used as an alternative to truffles.

Mutinus caninus
This is similar to *Phallus impudicus*, but is smaller, more brightly coloured, and has a milder smell. The tropical species, *Mutinus bambusinus*, differs in having a bright red cap which tapers into an acute purplish-red point, and which measures half the total height of the fruiting body.

Young fruiting body or egg
Whitish-yellow, 1—2cm in diameter, pear-shaped or ovoid, attached by white cord-like mycelium at the base. Splits into 2 to 3 lobes as fruiting body expands, remains as a volva at the base of the stipe.
Mature fruiting body
Cap: dark green, soon becoming orange-red, colour fading downwards. 2—2.5cm high, up to 2.5cm thick. Pointed, fused to the top of the stipe. *Gleba:* dark green, sticky, smells faintly faecal, soon disappearing. *Stipe:* almost cylindrical, slender, tapering slightly towards the base, 10—12cm long, 1.3cm thick. White, often flushed pink or orange, wrinkled. Flesh spongy, hollow. *Spores:* pale yellowish in mass, ellipsoid, smooth, average size 4.5 × 1.8 microns.
Habitat and distribution
Often found in groups, in woods, among dead leaves, on and around old stumps, on rotting sawdust. Common in Europe, locally common in eastern North America.
Occurrence
July to November in Europe, August to October in North America.
Culinary properties
Egg gelatinous, rather firm. Good when sliced and fried.

Mutinus elegans
Young fruiting body Ovoid, whitish-brown to pinkish-flesh.
Mature fruiting body *Cap:* at first olive-brown, soon becoming orange-red. Pointed, fused to the top of the stipe. *Stipe:* narrows towards the top, raspberry-red, becoming paler at the base.
Ecology On rich soil in woods, gardens. Warm temperate areas of Europe, introduced into gardens in cooler regions.
Edibility unknown.

Phallus hadriani

Young fruiting body Egg-shaped, white, becoming pink to deep violet when exposed to the air.

Mature fruiting body *Cap:* almost conical, honeycombed, Olive-brown, slimy. *Stipe:* tapers towards the perforated apex, white, spongy. Smells faint and sweetish.

Ecology On sand dunes, among dune grasses, in gardens, pastures. Variable in Europe, rare, becoming more common towards the south. July to January.

Edibility unknown.

Phallus impudicus
STINKHORN

The objectionable smell as well as the distinctive appearance of this species are so characteristic that it cannot be confused with any other. It is, in fact, more frequently smelt than seen. Quite often the young fruiting bodies, commonly known as 'eggs', have been mistaken for real ones and the mystery surrounding their origin led to the belief that they were witches' or devil's eggs. In central Europe country folk used the fruiting bodies to treat gout, rheumatism and epilepsy, and also in love potions and aphrodisiacs. It is claimed to be successful in the treatment of skin and internal cancer, but was formerly regarded as a cause of cholera and typhoid epidemics. It is still used in the treat-

ment of cattle in France and Germany. A vertical section through the 'egg' shows the cap fully formed, whereas the base of the stipe is very short and compact. The stipe expands very rapidly on emerging from the egg, increasing in length by approximately 7.5cm in one hour. In a bell jar, it has been observed to attain full size in one and a half hours. Viable spores of *Phallus impudicus* have been found in the excreta of flies and birds. The spores can germinate inside some flies, the resulting mycelial strands spreading out from the cadavers.

Young fruiting body or egg

Egg-like, 3–4cm in diameter, white, elastic to touch, attached by white cord-like mycelium.

Mature fruiting body

Cap: conical, attached to stipe at the apex, 4.5–11cm high, 3–5cm in diameter. At first dry, velvety, dull olive green, almost immediately becomes slimy and smelly. Flies, snails and some birds rapidly eat the mucous, leaving the white honeycomb surface. *Gleba:* dark olive green slime. *Stipe:* tapers at top and bottom, perforated at the top, 10–20 cm long, 1–2cm thick. White. Volva at the base contains a brown gelatinous material which surrounded the fruiting body inside the 'egg'. Flesh spongy, hollow. *Spores:* dark olive-green in mass, ovoid, average size 4.0 × 12.0 microns.

Habitat and distribution

Grows singly or in troops, in deciduous woods, often on and around rotting birch, near rhododendrons, in gardens, in cemeteries. It is adversely affected by atmospheric pollution. Common in Europe and North America west of the Mississippi, but rare in eastern North America. It is found in south-east Australia.

Occurrence

July to November.

Culinary properties

The mature fungus is inedible due to its obnoxious smell. It was thought by some to be poisonous when flies were seen to die after licking the evil smelling gleba. The eggs are eaten on the Continent, and are regarded as a delicacy in parts of Germany, where they are used in sausage and also sold as a type of 'truffle'. They are good when fried. The Chinese regard *Lysurus myoksin*, a similar species to *Phallus impudicus*, as a great delicacy and a cure for gangrenous ulcers.

Pisolithus arrhizus

Fruiting body A solid, partly sunken stem-like base supports the globose or pear-shaped head which is 5–15cm in diameter, ochraceous to blackish-brown, almost smooth, Skin flakes off to reveal the spore mass which is contained in a several chambers separated by distinct walls. Spores yellow, becoming black as they mature.

Ecology On ground in sandy or gravelly places, conifer woods and cultivated fields. Frequent in south-eastern and Pacific north-west North America and southern Europe. Elsewhere is sporadic, being introduced with forest trees. The *Pisolithus* associated with various species of *Eucalyptus* is probably a separate species.

Edible when young and used as an aromatic flavouring.

Far left: Phallus hadriani
Top: Phallus impudicus
Below: Pisolithus arrhizus

Rhizopogon luteolus
FALSE TRUFFLE

This species is probably more common than is generally believed. It is difficult to find and inedible. Mature specimens burst open irregularly thus allowing the spores to escape.

Fruiting body

Egg-shaped, 2–8cm in diameter. Dirty white to honey-yellow, finally olive-brown. Cuticle leathery, cracked, densely covered by brown thread-like strands. *Gleba:* consists of cells or cavities, at first white, finally dirty olive-yellow. Cavities are usually empty, small ones can become filled with spores. *Spores:* white to pale tawny-yellow, ellipsoid or irregularly bent, smooth, average size 4.0 × 10.5 microns.

Right: Rhizopogon luteolus
Above, centre: Rhizopogon rubescens
Above, right: Scleroderma citrinum
Below, right: Scleroderma verrucosum

Habitat and distribution

Grows in groups, partly buried in sandy soil of coniferous woods, under conifers on heaths. Variable in Europe and North America, becoming more common towards the north. It probably has a worldwide distribution.

Occurrence

September to November.

Culinary properties

Not recommended.

Rhizopogon rubescens
FALSE TRUFFLE

In Japan, where it is regarded as a delicacy, this fungus is known as *Sho-ro.* Sho-ro hunters use bamboo rakes to dig out the sandy soil around Red Pines where it is known to grow.

Fruiting body

Irregularly globular, rather like a potato tuber, up to 8cm long, 4cm wide. White at first, bruising pink, becoming yellow, then finally brown with age and when dried. Almost smooth, but with some channels, ridges and depressions. Portions of fruiting bodies below soil are covered in dark brownish-black rhizomorphs. *Gleba:* consists of small irregularly flattened cavities. At first pure white, turns pink when cut, brown in mature specimens. *Spores:* pale brownish-yellow in mass, oblong to ellipsoid, smooth, average size 2.5 × 6.5 microns.

Habitat and distribution

Grows in clusters, partly, sometimes completely buried in sandy soil, always under conifers, in woods, along river banks, roads, paths, in sand dunes. Occasional in Europe, widespread and locally common in North America, common in the pine forests of Japan.

Occurrence

Late summer to late autumn.

Culinary properties

Highly flavoured when cooked, texture firm, rather like the Perigord Truffle. Highly esteemed in Japan, usually in soups.

Scleroderma citrinum
COMMON EARTHBALL

The Common Earthball is widely used in Continental Europe as a substitute for the Perigord Truffle, and it is served in exclusive restaurants in Eastern Europe. A cheap 'truffle' sausage, incorporating *Scleroderma aurantium,* is very popular in some areas. It is said by some to be poisonous when eaten in large quantities, but perfectly safe when used with discretion.

Fruiting body

Rounded or pumpkin-shaped, sessile, 4–6cm in diameter. Outer surface dirty olive-yellow, soon becomes cracked into distinct areas, often beautifully arranged. Fruiting body wall thick, firm, white, turns pink when cut, when mature breaks open irregularly to release the spores. *Gleba:* at first grey, solid, becoming purple-black, marbled with whitish threads, finally powdery. *Spores:* blackish-brown in mass, spherical, with a small-meshed network, average size 9.5 microns in diameter.

Habitat and distribution

Often grows in tufts, on the ground, especially on peaty and sandy soil, around birch or conifers, in open woodland, on heaths, in pastures, along roadsides. Common in Europe and Australia and northern North America, found only in the mountains in the south.

Occurrence

June to November.

Culinary properties

Has a strong taste and smell which remains unless well stewed or fried. Specimens must be peeled and the base cut away before cooking. A single withered fruiting body will embitter a whole dish.

Scleroderma verrucosum

This rounded thin-walled fungus is smoother than *Scleroderma aurantium.* Specimens have been known to be sliced, darkened and sold as Perigord Truffles or used instead

of them in pâté de fois gras and other traditional French dishes.

Fruiting body

Almost spherical, flattened at the top, with a thick, stem-like base, 2–7cm across. Ochre or dingy brown, warty scaly, soon becoming smooth. Fruiting body wall thin, fragile when dry, cracks irregularly to form a rather large opening. *Gleba:* white at first, finally amber-brown, powdery. *Spores:* amber-brown in mass, spherical, warty to spiny, average size 12.0 microns in diameter.

Habitat and distribution

Found occasionally on rich, sandy soil, in deciduous woods, in Europe, eastern North America, and Queensland, Australia.

Occurrence

July to November in Europe, June to October in North America.

Culinary properties

Only fresh, white fleshed specimens should be eaten. A bitter taste develops as the spores mature. Harmless but worthless.

Sphaerobolus stellatus

The spore dispersal mechanism of this small, star-shaped fungus has fascinated botanists since it was first discovered in 1729. The force

exerted by the sudden inversion of the inner cup shoots the spore ball for a distance of up to 3 metres. A slight sound can be heard when the projectile is discharged. The mechanism has been compared to that of cannon and other pieces of military equipment, and indeed Buller called it the *Sphaerobolus* gun.

Fruiting bodies

At first showing as small yellowish-white spheres, 2mm in diameter, immersed in white cottony mycelium. Later they split from the apex forming 5–8 orange, pointed rays,

exposing the central, spherical, orange-yellow, spore containing ball, immersed in a slimy liquid. At maturity the two layers of the stellate cup are joined together only at the points of the rays. Suddenly the inner cup turns inside out and the ball is catapulted out with force, landing several metres away. *Spores:* white in mass, ovoid, smooth, average size 4.0 × 8.5 microns.

Habitat and distribution

Grows in large numbers on rotten wood, sticks, leaves, old sawdust, sacking, less frequently on dung. Common in Europe, eastern North America, Trinidad, Venezuela and south-eastern Australia and also found in New Zealand. It probably has a world-wide distribution.

Occurrence

January to December in Europe, May to September in North America.

Culinary properties

None known.

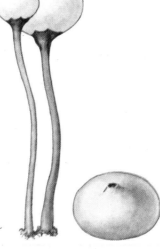

Tulostoma brumale

At first glance this fungus looks like a small puffball but if the surrounding sand is dug away, a slender stem is found, growing vertically downwards and ending in a tuft of mycelium. The ball-like head has been found poking through gaps in stone walls and pavings.

Fruiting body

Head: spherical with a minute projecting mouth, 1–2cm in diameter. At first clay-brown, thin outer skin peels off, finally whitish-grey. *Gleba:* rusty-brown. *Stipe:* buried, long, slender, narrows slightly towards the top, fits into a socket at the base of the head, 2–5cm long. Brown, fibrillose to scaly, wearing away to expose a paler layer underneath. *Spores:* pink in mass, spherical, warty, average size 4.5 microns in diameter.

Habitat and distribution

A rare, possibly locally frequent species, of calcareous sand dunes, dry banks, old walls, between stone paving sets, in Europe, eastern North America, south-east Australia.

Occurrence

May to February.

Culinary properties

Not recommended.

Tulostoma fimbriatum

Fruiting body A globular head on a long ridged stipe. Outer skin reddish-brown, soon peeling off but remaining as fine flakes at the base of the head and on the stipe. Inner skin pale brown, velvety, with a cone-shaped, apical mouth, surrounded by a fringe of fine hairs.

Far left: Sphaerobolus stellatus
Centre: Tulostoma brumale
Left: Tulostoma fimbriatum
Below: Vascellum pratense

Ecology Singly or in small groups on damp firm soil. Frequent in warm temperate areas of Europe. November to December.
Edibility unknown.

Vascellum pratense

Fruiting body Urn- or top-shaped, at first covered with small

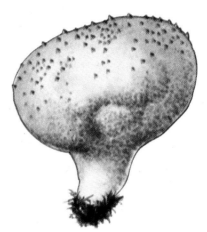

white spines which soon disappear, opening by a well-defined rather large mouth which continues to enlarge. Spore mass white then becoming dark olive, clearly separated from the sterile base of the fruit body which occupies about one third of the whole.

Ecology Among grass on lawns, pastures, and golf courses, Common in Europe and on the pacific coast of North America. Summer and autumn. Frequently forms rings in the grassland.

Edible when young.

Class Hymenomycetes
The members of this group usually have well-developed fruiting bodies which produce basidia and spores on a layer known as the hymenium. This layer is usually exposed from the earliest stage of development, or becomes exposed as the fruiting body matures.

The Jelly Fungi
These are divided into three main groups—the Tremellales, the Auriculariales and the Dacrymycetales.

The gelatinous fruiting bodies of the species in the Tremellales order are frequently white or brightly coloured, especially yellow or orange. All the members of this order grow saprophytically on wood.

The members of the Auriculariales group have fruiting bodies which are gelatinous but with a more definite shape than is found in the Dacrymycetales and the Tremellales. Most of these species are saprophytic on wood, although one or two members are parasitic on living trees. Edible, but can be tough unless they are cooked with care.

All the members of the Dacrymycetales grow saprophytically on wood. The fruiting bodies are gelatinous, but very diverse in shape and size, ranging from very small, dot-like structures to erect, branched, antler-shaped forms.

Top: Calocera cornea
Below: Auricularia auricula
Below, right: Calocera viscosa

Auricularia auricula
JEW'S EAR
Myth and legend have connected this species with Judas Iscariot, who is supposed to have hanged himself upon an elder tree, after betraying Jesus Christ to the Pharisees. It is said that in consequence this tree, which became known as the Judas tree, frequently bears a growth which strongly resembles a human ear. This became known as Judas's Ear, becoming corrupted through time to 'Jew's Ear'. A species known as *Ki-kurage* in Japan is sold in grocery stores, and is widely used

to add an agreeable texture to other food. It is exported to China in amounts exceeding those consumed by the Japanese. China also imports great quantities of this fungus from Tahiti. This Oriental species may not be *Auricularia auricula*, but a close relative, *Auricularia polytricha*. It is extensively used in Chinese cookery, making excellent soup and vegetable dishes. In China it is successfully cultivated on oak saplings and wooden palings. *Auricularia auricula* is eaten only occasionally in Europe. In old herbals it is known as *Fungus sambuci*, being prescribed as a poultice for inflamed eyes, and when boiled in milk, or soaked in beer or vinegar, as a gargle.

Fruiting body
Gelatinous, ear-shaped, liver-brown, translucent when moist, 3–10cm broad. Shape irregular in old specimens. Outer (upper) surface slightly greyish, velvety. Dries out to a hard black lump. *Hymenium:* (under surface) veined, forming irregular depressions. *Stipe:* absent, fruiting body laterally attached. *Spores:* white in mass, smooth, cylindrical, curved, average size 18.0 × 7.0 microns. Order Auriculariales.

Habitat and distribution
Grows singly or gregariously, often in overlapping tiers, mostly on elder, less frequently on oak and other deciduous trees in Europe where it is common. In North America it is uncommon, and grows on many different trees; it is found in south-eastern Australia. Is generally believed to have world-wide distribution.

Occurrence
January to December, especially October and November.

Culinary properties
It is very nutritious but rather tasteless. The flesh becomes very tough if cooked too quickly, and it should never be fried or sautéed. It is best sliced and stewed in milk or stock for several hours. It is especially good in soup.

Calocera cornea
Fruiting body Erect, club-shaped or awl-shaped, occasionally forked near the top. Yellow to orange-yellow, firm, gelatinous, sometimes longitudinally wrinkled. Order Dacrymycetales.

Ecology Gregarious or in small tufts, on fallen branches of deciduous trees, especially ash, oak, lime, elm. Common in Europe, North America, Central and South America, Australasia, Asia, parts of Africa. January to December. Edibility unknown.

Calocera viscosa
STAGHORN FUNGUS
This brightly coloured fungus is often mistaken by beginners for a bright yellow species of *Clavaria*. Also called the Yellow Antler Fungus and the Sticky Coral Fungus, it can be distinguished by its tough, elastic texture, slimy surface and by the fact that it grows on coniferous stumps.

Fruiting body
Erect, repeatedly dichotomously branched, like a stag's horn, with a long rooting base, 3–8cm high. Bright golden-yellow, slimy when moist. Becoming orange and horny when dry. Flesh yellow, tough, flexible, cartilaginous or gelatinous. *Hymenium:* smooth, covers the whole surface of the fruiting body. *Spores:* white to yellow in mass, ovoid, smooth, average size 9.8 × 4.0 microns. Order Dacrymycetales.

Habitat and distribution
Grows in tufts on and around old conifer stumps, especially in mountainous areas. Common in Europe and northern North America. It is known in Asia, Japan, Pakistan, Tibet, Tasmania.

Occurrence
September to April.

Culinary properties
None known.

Dacrymyces stillatus

This fungus forms small, gelatinous pustules on dead wood, which are conspicuous in wet weather. In extremely wet conditions the fruiting bodies become very soft and seem to dissolve. When it is dry, they shrivel up and become minute dark orange smears, which will revive during the next rainfall. Asexual spores are commonly produced in accompanying, but separate, fruiting bodies, or they can sometimes be mixed with basidia on the same structure.

Fruiting body

Gelatinous, cushion-shaped or drop-like, 2–5mm broad. Flesh transparent. Sometimes two types of fruiting body are produced, the first orange with asexual arthrospores only. The second yellow, often rather wrinkled, with basidia, producing basidiospores. *Hymenium:* covers the outer surface. *Spores:* yellow in mass, cylindrical, slightly curved, smooth, 3 septate, average size 13.5 × 5.5 microns. Order Dacrymycetales.

Habitat and distribution

Grows in large confluent masses, on decayed wood, dead branches of various trees, worked coniferous wood, usually old pine boards, wooden rails, fence posts. Common in Europe. Reports are doubtful from North and South America. It is known from Central America, Asia, Japan, New Zealand, South Georgia (Antarctica).

Occurrence

January to December but only after rain.

Culinary properties

None known.

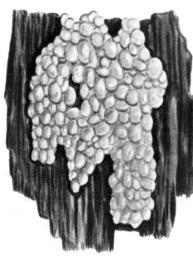

Exidia albida

This common fungus forms translucent, undulating masses on the bark of deciduous trees.

Fruiting body

Gelatinous, contorted, brain-like, often lobed, 3–10cm broad. Whitish-grey, sometimes tinged with red, becoming dingy brown when dry. Flesh tough, horny when dry. *Hymenium:* on the surface away from the wood, powdery. *Spores:* white in mass, spherical, smooth, average size 9.5 microns in diameter. Order Tremellales.

Habitat and distribution

Common on branches of deciduous trees especially copper beech in parts of Europe and birch, sugar maple and hickory in North America. Widespread in the deciduous forests of Australia.

Occurrence

September to April in Europe, summer in North America.

Culinary properties

Has a slight, sweet, woody taste, makes a pleasant dish.

Exidia glandulosa
WITCHES' BUTTER

This jelly fungus is usually found hanging from the underside of fallen logs. It is recognized by its comparatively large size, its colour and its warted hymenium.

Fruiting body

Gelatinous, variable in shape, contorted brain-like, rounded or flattened, sometimes pendant. Olive-black, rather woolly on the side next to the wood. *Hymenium:* covers the surface away from the wood, warty, rough, often wavy or folded. Black and glistening when dry. *Spores:* white in mass, cylindrical, curved, smooth, average size 13.5 × 4.5 microns. Order Tremellales.

Habitat and distribution

Often grows in crowded groups, on decaying stumps, logs, fallen branches of deciduous trees, especially oak and copper beech. Common in Europe, it is known from Australia.

Occurrence

January to December, especially October to December.

Culinary properties

Not recommended.

Pseudohydnum gelatinosum
QUIVERING SPINE FUNGUS

This extremely beautiful fungus is translucent with a blue tinted upper surface and white spines. It could be mistaken for one of the 'Hedgehog Fungi', *Hydnum* species.

Fruiting body

Gelatinous, tongue or fan-shaped, often slightly lobed, lateral, 2–6cm broad. Pearl-grey with steel blue tints, shading into violet. Finally brownish. Minutely downy on the upper surface. Flesh translucent, soft, thick. *Hymenium:* on spines on the underside, white, somewhat translucent. Conical, straight, shorter near the margin. *Stipe:* if present lateral, fairly thick, pearl-grey, hairy. *Spores:* white in mass, broadly ovoid to globose, smooth, average size 6.0 × 5.0 microns. Order Tremellales.

Habitat and distribution

Grows on conifer stumps, trunks, sometimes on the ground among coniferous debris, on sawdust. Variable in Europe, apparently becoming more common towards the south. Widespread, but uncommon in North America. It is known from Australia.

Occurrence

September to November in Europe, September to October in North America.

Culinary properties

It is delicious when stewed, served hot or cold.

Top: Exidia albida
Far left: Dacrymyces stillatus
Bottom: Exidia glandulosa
Below: Pseudohydnum gelatinosum

Tremella mesenterica

This fungus is very variable in shape; it looks rather like a blob of butter, and is usually recognized by its colour. It is highly regarded by some experts and would seem to be well worth experimenting with.

Fruiting body

Gelatinous, contorted, brain-like, folds may be flattened, 2–10cm broad. Orange-yellow, slimy when moist, dark orange, hard and shrivelled when dry. *Hymenium:* covers the whole surface of the fruiting body. Powdered with white spores in mature specimens. *Spores:* white in mass, broadly ellipsoid to pip-shaped, smooth, very variable in size, average size 7.5 × 6.5 microns. Order Tremellales.

Habitat and distribution

Grows on dead branches, twigs of deciduous trees, on gorse, broom, ivy. Common and widespread in Europe and North America. It is also found in parts of Australia.

Occurrence

January to December, especially October to December in Europe, June to first frosts in North America.

Culinary properties

Has a slightly sweet, woody flavour, resembles lumpy custard when cooked.

Tremiscus helvelloides

Fruiting body Fan-shaped or somewhat lobed, 3–12cm tall, attached by a short stalk, pink to rose coloured, gelatinous, shining, viscid, smells of moss. Order Dacrymycetales.

Ecology In groups or tufts on ground under conifers, especially in mountains. Frequent in North America and continental Europe. Edible. Can be eaten raw when young, later it needs cooking.

Order Aphyllophorales

This large and very diverse order is characterized by the tough consistency of the fruiting bodies of most species. These fruiting bodies range in form from thin, crust-like structures to large complex, brackets. The club-shaped Fairy Clubs, the Hedgehog fungi, which have their hymenium on downward projecting teeth on the lower side of the stalked cap, and the delicious Chantarelles, which have fold-like hymenium, are also members of this very diverse group of fungi. At present the taxonomy of the polypores is in a state of flux.

Albatrellus confluens

Fruiting body Numerous caps form a dense tuft up to 35cm across. Caps are irregular in shape, with lobed margins, up to 10cm wide, surface cracked, smooth, rose-yellow becoming brownish. Tubes decurrent to the base of the stipe, white becoming yellowish, short, firmly attached to flesh. *Stipe:* short, becoming fused at the base to form a massive structure, smooth, scurfy, whitish with pink tinge towards base. Flesh whitish, thick, brittle, bitter taste and smelling of almonds. **Ecology** Conifer woods. Europe. June to November.

Flesh edible if first blanched. Caution should be exercised when it is first tried.

Albatrellus pes caprae

Fruiting body *Cap:* sub-circular or irregular, 3–12cm wide, sometimes deeply divided by a groove forming a cloven hoof shape, margin undulate, dingy brown to pinkish-brown becoming brown, cover-

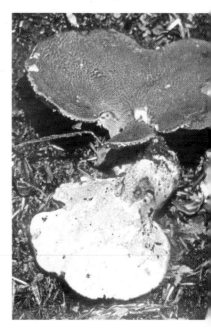

ed with brownish filaments or scales. *Pores:* decurrent, whitish to yellowish, large, angular openings, *Stipe:* central, eccentric or even lateral, thick, 3–8cm long, whitish to brown. Flesh-white or greenish.

Top: Tremella mesenterica
Right: Albatrellus pes caprae
Bottom right: Albatrellus confluens
Below: Tremiscus helvelloides

Ecology Solitary or in tufts on ground in deciduous and conifer woods. Continental Europe and North America.
Edible when young.

Albatrellus ovinus

This is an unusual polypore in that it is centrally stalked and grows on the ground. It could be confused with *Boletus* species, but can be easily distinguished from them by its tubes, which are not easily separated from the firm, somewhat woody flesh.

Fruiting body
Cap: at first white, becoming

brownish-yellow, finally tinged olive. 5–10cm in diameter. Irregularly convex, or depressed. Margin sometimes lobed. Cuticle smooth, then scaly cracked. Flesh yellowish-white, firm, fragile. *Tubes:* short, irregularly decurrent. *Pores:* at first white, finally lemon-yellow, or when bruised. *Stipe:* small, usually central, occasionally eccentric, short, thick, curved, 2cm or more thick. White becoming yellowish-brown. *Spores:* white to yellow in mass, ovoid, smooth, average size 3.8 × 3.3 microns.

Habitat and distribution
Grows on the ground in coniferous woods in mountainous areas. Frequent in Northern Europe, Alps and Jura des Vosges, as yet there is no record of it from the United Kingdom, it may occur in Scotland. Rare in eastern North America.

Occurrence
September to frost.

Culinary properties
Smells agreeably of almonds. Young specimens are good when eaten raw but they can be used to good effect in cooked dishes.

Auriscalpium vulgare

This dainty little fungus is easily recognized when spotted, but frequently does not show up clearly against the dark background in coniferous woods.

Fruiting body
Cap: dark brown, margin at first yellowish-chestnut. Kidney-shaped or semicircular. Margin sometimes lobed. Cuticle hairy. Flesh thin, tough, leathery. *Gills:* at first flesh coloured finally grey-brown, thin, tough, crowded. *Stipe:* lateral, erect, slender, 4–7cm long, date-brown or black, hairy especially at the base. *Spores:* white in mass, ovoid, smooth, 4.8 × 3.8 microns.

Habitat and distribution
Grows singly or in small groups on old, fallen pine cones. Common in the coniferous forests of Europe and North America.

Occurrence
All year round, especially autumn.

Culinary properties
Not recommended.

Bjerkandera adusta

Fruiting body Downy, with fawn or greyish-fawn zones, margin white at first. Semi-circular to bracket-shaped, sessile, sometimes extended downwards behind. *Pores:* minute, white then greyish-black.

Ecology On trunks, stumps, fallen logs of deciduous trees, especially beech. Common in Europe. January to December.
Edibility unknown.

Left: Bjerkandera adusta
Far left: Albatrellus ovinus
Bottom: Auriscalpium vulgare

Cantharellus cibarius
CHANTARELLE

This is one of the most popular of the edible fungi. It is sold by the basketful in Japan, where it is known as *Shiba-take*, and is gathered and eaten on a large scale in China. It is also sold in French and German markets. In Europe generally, *Cantharellus cibarius* has been drastically overpicked in the woods near urban areas. Country folk traditionally cut the fruiting bodies into strips, dry them and

store them in bags, usually hanging these in a warm, dry place. In some areas dried specimens are ground into a powder for use as a flavouring. There are several varieties of this species, which are distinguished by exact colour variations, size and habitat. For example, var. *brunescens* has a dark ochre, streaked cap, and smells strongly of peaches. Var. *umbrina* is found under cedars and sequoias, has a brownish-fawn cap, and yellowish flesh in the stipe. Specimens of *Cantharellus cibarius* can be very similar to the odourless *Hygrophoropsis aurantiaca* which has no culinary value. It can also be confused with the poisonous *Clitocybe illudens*.

Fruiting body
Cap: a striking apricot-yellow, 3—10cm in diameter. At first top-shaped, finally depressed in the centre. Margin incurved at first, becoming wavy. Cuticle like chamois leather when moist. Flesh yellow, paler when dried. *Gills:* apricot-yellow, fold-like, decurrent, irregularly branched, often uniting to form a network at the top of the stipe. *Stipe:* continuous with the cap, 5cm long, 2cm thick. Pale apricot-yellow, smooth. Flesh solid. *Spores:* white in mass, ellipsoid, smooth, average size 9.0 × 5.0 microns.

Habitat and distribution
Grows singly or in groups, in deciduous woods especially under beech and oak, under conifers in mountainous areas. Common, but possibly becoming less so in Europe, North America, Japan, and China.

Occurrence
July to December in Europe, June to October in North America.

Culinary properties
Sometimes smells of apricots as it dries, flavour excellent, slightly peppery. Needs long slow cooking as it can be tough. It is improved if shredded and soaked in milk overnight, before cooking. Can be dipped in egg and breadcrumbs and fried, or added to omelettes. Rich in vitamins A and D, and in the pigment carotene.

Cantharellus cinereus
Fruiting body Small. *Cap:* brownish-grey. Deeply, irregularly funnel-shaped, with a wavy margin. *Gills:* powdery grey, rib-like, irregularly branched. *Stipe:* grooved.
Ecology In tufts around stumps of deciduous trees. Occasional in Europe.
Edibility unknown.

Cantharellus infundibuliformis
Experts disagree about the food value of this fungus. It is very

tough, often dry and fibrous, and has a bitter taste. The variety *lutescens* is an entirely yellow form of *Cantharellus infundibuliformis*, which can be very variable in colour.

Fruiting body
Cap: colour varies from dark-brown to dingy yellow when moist, greyish when dry. 2—5cm in diameter. At first broadly convex, becoming deeply funnel-shaped when mature. Margin incurved, then becoming wavy. Cuticle slightly woolly when dry. Flesh yellow, tough. *Gills:* at first yellow, then becoming greyish-lilac. Decurrent, vein or fold-like, blunt, irregular, branched. *Stipe:* relatively long, wavy, often grooved or compressed, sometimes slightly swollen at the base, 2—7cm long, 5—10mm thick. Deep yellow, smooth. Flesh hollow. *Spores:* white to very pale yellow in mass, broadly ellipsoid to sub-globose, smooth, average size 10.3 × 7.5 microns.

Habitat and distribution
Grows gregariously, often in clusters, on acid soils in coniferous and deciduous woods, especially in mountainous areas. Common in Europe and North America.

Occurrence
July to January in Europe, August to November in North America.

Culinary properties
Tastes bitter, smells faintly aromatic. Not recommended by some experts, but is probably worth gathering when found growing in profusion.

Chondrostereum purpureum
VIOLET CRUST
This species is well-known as the cause of 'silver-leaf' in fruit trees. It is also a problem in beechwoods

in Continental Europe. The spores germinate during autumn in cracks and wounds in the bark. Infected trees are weakened by a rot, and it is dangerous to use this timber in positions where strength is needed. Infection can be controlled in managed woodland by the prompt clearing of timber after felling and by painting exposed wood with fungicidal compounds.

Fruiting body
Either lies flat on a horizontal surface, with the hymenium on the outer side, or forms small brackets on a vertical surface. *Cap:* whitish-grey. 1—3cm broad. Bracket-shaped, margin, scalloped or lobed. Cuticle woolly or hairy. Flesh thin, leathery. *Hymenium:* at first lilac or brownish purple, soon becoming discoloured, dirty-grey, smooth. *Stipe:* absent. *Spores:* white in mass, ellipsoid or slightly sausage-shaped, size vari-

Top: Cantharellus infundibuliformis
Right: Chondrostereum purpureum
Below: Cantharellus cibarius
Bottom: Cantharellus cinereus

able, average size 7 × 2.8 microns.
Habitat and distribution
Often grows in overlapping tiers on the trunks of deciduous trees, especially plum, apple and other fruit trees and beech, on dead trunks, stumps. Common in Europe, North America, Australia.
Occurrence
January to December.
Culinary properties
Inedible.

Clavaria argillacea
FIELD OR MOOR CLUB FUNGUS
The small greenish-yellow fruiting bodies of this species are a common sight on heaths and heather moors, where they often grow in profusion.
Fruiting body
Unbranched, club-shaped, blunt or rounded at the top, often slightly flattened, with a distinct yellow stipe, 3–8cm high. Pale greenish-yellow to dirty yellow. Flesh yellow,

very fragile. *Spores:* white in mass, oblong, smooth, average size 10.0 × 5.0 microns.
Habitat and distribution
Grows in groups, among moss, on peaty ground, heather moors, heaths, in open coniferous woods. Common in Europe, and is found in Australia.
Occurrence
July to November.
Culinary properties
Taste reminiscent of tallow, inedible.

Clavaria vermicularis
Fruiting body Densely tufted, fertile head scarcely distinguishable from stipe, elongate to worm-like, upright, rarely branched, brittle, pure white becoming yellowish-brown at tips, 3–10cm tall and up to 1.0cm wide. Slight smell of iodine.
Ecology Among grass and moss in meadows, more rarely in wood-

lands. Common in Europe and eastern and central North America. Late summer and autumn.
No culinary interest.

Clavariadelphus fistulosus
Fruiting body Large, fragile, narrowly club-shaped, often wavy or twisted. At first yellow, becoming date-brown.
Ecology On fallen branches, twigs, leaves of deciduous trees especially beech, alder, oak. Uncommon in Europe. August to February. Edible.

Clavariadelphus pistillaris
This massive, broadly club-shaped fungus is among the largest of this group of species. It is edible and

popular in Poland, Russia and Germany, but care must be taken when gathering it for food, because specimens attacked by *Hypomyces*, a parasitic fungus, develop a bitter taste.
Fruiting body
Unbranched, pestle to club-shaped, narrowing towards the base, 10 to 15 sometimes 30cm high, 2–6cm thick at the top. Yellowish-tan, later becoming a reddish-brown especially towards the base, and where touched. Cuticle minutely velvety, often wrinkled, becoming cracked on the top of large specimens. Flesh white, at first firm, becoming loose and cottony in the centre. *Spores:* pale yellow-ochre in mass, ovoid to pip-shaped, smooth, average size 13.5 × 7.5 microns.
Habitat and distribution
Grows singly, sometimes in small groups, on the ground in deciduous woods, especially under beech. Occasional to frequent in Europe, widespread in North America, and is also found in south-eastern Australia.
Occurrence
September to December in Europe, August to September in North America.
Culinary properties
Tastes and smells mild, can be enjoyable if cooked with care.

Clavulina cristata
WHITE CORAL FUNGUS
This species can be found growing in many different shapes and colours, the crested branches being rather like moose horns. It sometimes grows parasitically on the Ascomycete *Helminthosphaeria*, in turn its base is often blackened by the growth of a parasitic mould. It is regarded by some as a variety of the very similar *Clavaria cinerea*.
Fruiting body
Irregularly branched from a short, stout base, 3–8cm high. Branches flattened towards the top, with crested tips. Colour varies from pure white to pinkish-white to grey. Flesh white, tough. *Spores:* white in mass, broadly ellipsoid to globose, smooth, with a central oil drop, average size 8.5 × 6.8 microns.
Habitat and distribution
Grows singly, or in groups, lines or tufts, on the ground in deciduous and coniferous woods, especially along woodland paths, under hedges, especially in hilly and mountainous areas. Common in Europe and eastern and central North America, and has been found in certain parts of south-eastern Australia.

Above: Clavariadelphus pistillaris
Top, centre: Clavaria vermicularis
Left: Clavaria argillacea
Bottom: Clavariadelphus fistulosus

Occurrence
June to December.
Culinary properties
Fresh specimens are acceptable when finely chopped and stewed slowly for at least one hour. Old, dry fruiting bodies are tough and leathery.

Below: Clavulina rugosa
Right: Clavulina cristata
Far right: Coniophora puteana
Centre: Coltricia perennis
Bottom, right: Coriolus hirsutus
Bottom, left: Clavulinopsis corniculata

Clavulina rugosa
Fruiting body   Tall, simple, club-shaped with longitudinal wrinkles or irregularly branched, thickened towards blunt apex. Whitish-grey, tinged with yellow. Flesh is brittle to the point of being fragile.
Ecology   Grassland, along woodland paths, in hilly regions. Common in Europe and North America, east of the Rocky Mountains, reported from Australia. August to December.
Edible (fresh specimens only).

Clavulinopsis corniculata
Fruiting body   Forms a densely branched tuft on a very short, downy base. Branches bright yellow, base white. Flesh tough.
Ecology   Grasslands, along grassy woodland paths. Common in Europe. April to December.
Edible (when fresh).

Coltricia perennis
Fruiting body   *Cap:* with alternating tawny, rusty-brown zones, minutely velvety, margin wavy, split. Funnel-shaped, leathery. *Pores:* rusty-brown with a silky sheen, minute. *Stipe:* swollen towards the base, deep rust-brown, velvety.
Ecology   On sandy soil, bonfire sites, in woods, on heaths, especially under conifers. Common in Europe. January to December.
Edibility unknown.

Coniophora puteana
In Britain, *Coniophora puteana* and *Serpula lacrymans* are responsible for 90 per cent of the decay in internal woodwork. It causes localized damage in damp conditions, where floorboards lie directly on damp concrete, or in roof timbers that are periodically wet from leakages. When found growing out of doors, its presence can be recognized by its fruiting bodies, but these are apparently infrequent on internal timber. Indoors, the mycelium can be seen on the surface of infected wood, covering quite a large area with tree-like branching. At first these branching strands are white or yellowish-brown, rapidly darkening to almost black, thus discolouring the infected wood, until finally it is so black that it sometimes appears to be charred. The rotten wood cracks along the grain, and at right angles to it, although this perpendicular cracking is not as extensive as in wood rotted by *Serpula lacrymans*. In the days of sail, it was an important

cause of damage to wooden ships.
Fruiting body
A thin, crust-like, easily peeling skin. Irregularly spread over, and closely pressed onto the substrate, with the hymenium on the outer surface. 2–60cm in diameter. Sterile margin cream, paper-thin, tears easily, sometimes with a fringe of thin, spidery mycelium. *Hymenium:* at first yellow, gradually changing to olive-brown or olive green as the spores mature. Smooth, becoming irregularly warty in mature specimens. *Spores:* olive-brown to rusty in mass, broadly ellipsoid, smooth, average size 12.0 × 7.5 microns.
Habitat and distribution
Grows on dead coniferous and deciduous wood in forests, and on structural timber. Common in Europe.
Occurrence
January to December.
Culinary properties
Inedible.

Coriolus hirsutus
This saprophytic fungus causes a rot indistinguishable from that caused by *Coriolus versicolor*.
Fruiting body
Cap: uniform yellowish-brown or greyish-brown. 3–5cm broad. Semicircular, flattened, zoned. Cuticle coarsely hairy. Flesh white,

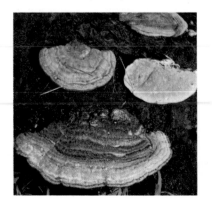

thin, tough, flexible when fresh. *Tubes:* white, very thin. *Pores:* pale grey, becoming dirty-yellowish-brown. *Stipe:* absent. *Spores:* white in mass, cylindrical, smooth, average size 7.0 × 2.5 microns.

Habitat and distribution
On the trunks and newly-fallen branches of deciduous trees. Occasional to frequent in Europe, it is found in Central American and northern South America.

Occurrence
June to March.

Culinary properties
Inedible.

Coriolus versicolor

This attractive fungus causes a fibrous rot in felled timber, fences, posts and in pit props. It can be found on external structural woodwork, and is quite common on hardwood sills that have become damp. The white mycelial strands can often be seen on buried portions of garden stakes, causing damage below the level of the soil. The caps are very variable in colour, being paler when found growing in the shade. Some of the colour variants have been given varietal names. For example, var. *nigricans* is an entirely greyish-black form. Symmetrical, well-shaped specimens are sometimes made into costume jewellery such as brooches.

Fruiting body
Cap: usually with multicoloured concentric zones, of yellow, brown, grey, greenish-grey or black, with a paler margin. 3–5cm across. Semi-circular, flattened, with a wavy surface. Margin thin, often waved or lobed. Cuticle velvety with satiny concentric zones. Flesh white, tough, thin, continuous with the walls of the tubes. *Tubes:* white, very short. *Pores:* white to dirty-yellow, smooth, round, becoming angular and torn, usually small, but

variable in size. *Stipe:* absent. *Spores:* white in mass, cylindrical, smooth, average size 6.5 × 2.5 microns.

Habitat and distribution
Grows in large tiered groups, on stumps, fallen branches and seasoned timber of deciduous trees, especially oak. Common in Europe, it is found in Venezuela, Equador and Panama, and also occurs in New Zealand.

Occurrence
January to December.

Culinary properties
Inedible.

Craterellus cornucopioides
HORN OF PLENTY

Clusters of this fungus are not always easy to see when growing on dark soil or among dead leaves. When found it is unmistakable,

looking at first sight like old, dirty, black leather. It is best used in a powdered form as a flavouring in soups and stews. It is sometimes called the Trumpet of Death.

Fruiting body
Cap: dark brown to blackish-brown when moist, dull brown when dry. 5–12cm in diameter. Funnel-shaped, often hollow to the base. Margin scalloped or wavy. Cuticle scaly. Flesh membranous or leathery, tough when moist, brittle when dry. *Hymenium:* on lower surface, ash-grey to pinkish-brown. Smooth or radially wrinkled. *Stipe:* usually short almost absent, continuous with the cap, black. *Spores:* white to very pale salmon-pink in mass, ellipsoid, smooth, average size 14.0 × 8.5 microns.

Habitat and distribution
Grows singly or in dense troops, among dead leaves on the ground in deciduous woods, especially under beech, less frequently under hornbeam or oak. Common in

Europe, in the deciduous forests of eastern North America, Queensland, Australia, and is found in Panama.

Occurrence
August to November in Europe, July to September in North America.

Culinary properties
Tastes slightly bitter, smells faintly but pleasantly aromatic. It has an uninviting appearance, but it is highly regarded by some experts. The flesh turns black when cooked. Blends well in casseroles and risottos. In the Neopolitan area of Italy, it is cut into thin slices, boiled in milk, the pieces are then beaten and fried in oil. In Scandinavia it is usually cooked in a casserole with plenty of butter. An ideal species for drying, whole dry fruiting bodies are quickly reconstituted when soaked in water, or they can be ground into a powder and used as a seasoning. It may also be successfully pickled.

Corticium evolvens

Fruiting body Crust-like or resupinate, more rarely shelf-like, rounded warted patches, margins slightly hairy, white becoming faint ochre-coloured.

Ecology On newly-dead branches of deciduous and conifer trees. Very common in Europe. Can be found the whole year around.
No culinary interest.

Daedalea quercina
MAZE FUNGUS

This saprophytic fungus, which is also called Mazegill, is especially common on oak stumps, felled logs and converted timber. It is occasionally found in houses, but more frequently in out-buildings and on window frames, causing a brown, cubical root. The mycelium continues growing on the same stump or log for many years, forming new fruiting bodies each year. In the past bee-keepers used smouldering lumps of this fungus to drive

Below: Corticium evolvens
Left: Craterellus cornucopioides
Far left: Coriolus versicolor
Bottom: Daedalea quercina

bees from the hive. It was once used for grooming horses.

Fruiting body
Cap: grey to pale greyish-brown. 5–30cm across. Bracket-shaped, semi-circular, to almost hoof-shaped. Concentrically zoned, furrowed, sometimes radially wrinkled. Margin blunt. Flesh pale wood-colour or pale red-brown, corky, hard, extending down into the walls of the tubes. *Tubes:* pale wood-colour, up to 2.5cm long. *Pores:* pale wood-colour, rounded at the margin, elongated, wavy and maze-like further away, walls thick. *Stipe:* attached by a broad base. *Spores:* white in mass, ellipsoid to pip-shaped, smooth, length variable, average size 6.3 × 2.8 microns.

Habitat and distribution
Grows on dead wood attached to living trees, on stumps, converted timber, mostly oak, but sometimes on chestnut, beech and other hardwoods. Common in Europe and North America.

Occurrence
January to December.

Culinary properties
Inedible.

Below: Fibuloporia vaillantii
Bottom, right: Fistulina hepatica

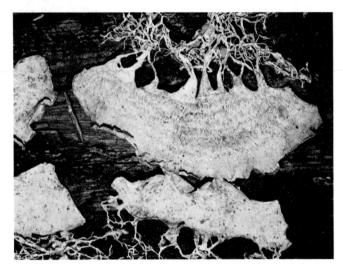

Fibuloporia vaillantii
This saprophytic fungus grows on felled and converted softwood timber. It flourishes in very damp and dark conditions, and is a cause of serious wood decay, especially down coalmines, and in leaking buildings. Stalactite-like growths can sometimes be seen hanging from the roof-timbers of damp mines. White sheets of mycelium form on the surface of the infected wood. The mycelial strands are finer than those of *Serpula lacrymans* and remain white. *Fibuliporia vaillantii* requires more moisture, for its development than *S. lacrymans* and can also withstand a higher temperature, but it produces a similar type of rot.

Fruiting body
Spreads on the substrate, with the hymenium on the outside. White or pale cream, with a white margin. 20–30cm across, thick and pad-like or skin-like, soft. Margin cottony, tasselled. *Tubes:* vary in length with the thickness of the fruiting body, 3–10mm long. *Pores:* angular, large 0.5–1.0mm across, may become torn and tooth-like when growing on a vertical surface. *Stipe:* absent. *Spores:* white in mass, smooth, ellipsoid, average size, 6.0 × 3.5 microns.

Habitat and distribution
Grows on coniferous wood, in woods, damp mines and buildings. Common in Europe, it is also found in Australia.

Occurrence
January to December.

Culinary properties
Inedible.

Fistulina hepatica
BEEFSTEAK FUNGUS
The flesh of this fungus looks and feels like red meat—it is also called the Ox-tongue Fungus—but has an insipid flavour and texture when cooked, and is a very poor imitation of the real thing. It is, however, one of the officially recognized edible species sold in French markets. In the olden days, when people believed that trees were enchanted, the tongue-like fruiting bodies of this fungus were thought to belong to gallant knights, and were never picked, in case their owners should return and claim them. Infected timber is not weakened at first, and turns a rich brown colour with attractive patterns. This is known as Brown Oak and in the past was highly prized for decorative work, being easy to carve yet strong. *Fistulina hepatica* finally causes a brown, cubical rot in infected trees. It is the cause of hollowing in many oak trees, and may be one of the main factors causing the stag-headed condition often seen in old oaks. In Britain, it is much more common than it is in the better managed forests of Europe.

Fruiting body
Cap: reddish-brown to liver coloured. 5–30cm wide. Hoof, tongue or bracket-shaped. Cuticle rough, usually movable on a gelatinous layer underneath. Flesh red, yields a reddish juice when cut, fibrous, veined, pliant. *Tubes:* crowded, but separate from each other. *Pores:* yellow, becoming flushed with pink, dingy in old specimens, round, minute. *Stipe:* lateral, short or absent. *Spores:* pinkish-brown in mass, almost spherical or egg-shaped, smooth, average size 4.5 × 3.5 microns.

Habitat and distribution
Parasitic on living deciduous trees, especially oak, and on sweet chestnut in the south. Frequent to common in Europe, locally common in eastern North America.

Occurrence
August to November.

Culinary properties
Young specimens have a very astringent taste. When cooked slowly and well flavoured with onion or garlic and herbs, it is a very poor imitation of stewing beef. It is widely used as a tenderizer on steak. Sometimes it is boiled, discarded and the stock used in soups and gravies. Some enthusiasts recommend that it should be boiled, sliced and covered in vinegar. It can also be sliced and served raw.

Fomes fomentarius
TRUE TINDER FUNGUS
Fomes fomentarius is the earliest fungus known to have been used by man. It was discovered in the excavation of an 8,000 BC Early Mesolithic lakeside camp at Star

year, they form almost the whole thickness of the fruiting body. *Pores:* off white, then dirty cinammon, very small, round, thick walled. *Stipe:* absent, fruiting body broadly attached to the tree. *Spores:* white in mass, ellipsoid to spindle-shaped, smooth, average size 16.5 × 5.8 microns.

Habitat and distribution
In the United Kingdom it grows only on birch, elsewhere it can be found on most types of deciduous tree. Common in Europe, is restricted to the Scottish Highlands in Britain and is frequent in N. America.

Occurrence
January to December.

Culinary properties
Inedible.

Fomitopsis pinicola
Fruiting body Reddish-brown, shiny, margin paler. Bracket or hoof-shaped, sessile. Flesh corky, firm. *Pores:* at first pale yellowish-white, finally brown, a new layer added to the underside each year.

Carr, Yorkshire. Some specimens were found still adhering to birch stems. In other cases the flesh had been stripped off, and as they were found close to lumps of iron pyrites and flints, were probably used as tinder by these primitive hunters. Hippocrates called it Amadou, and mentioned that it was used to cauterize wounds. Pliny named it *Aridus fomes fungorum.* Two methods of preparing this fungus have been described. The softest, downiest portions are cut off, and are stewed or soaked for a time in hot water. They should then be beaten with a mallet and rubbed until they are as soft as fine leather.

The resulting material was used as a styptic on wounds, and is still used for minor cuts in the more remote areas of Central Europe. Until comparatively recent times it was used in dentistry, for drying out the cavities in teeth before filling. Woodcutters of Bohemia and southern Germany used the suede-like material produced in this way for the manufacture of various articles of dress, as well as picture frames, tobacco pouches and other fancy goods. The tougher pieces of the fungus are treated in a different manner. They are soaked for a time in a mixture of hot water and urine, or ashes, then beaten until they become soft, and soaked again in a solution of saltpetre, or salt, ashes and saltpetre, to increase their inflammability. This material was used as tinder, as it readily catches light from a spark, and will go on

glowing for a long time. One of its many uses was for lighting the fuses of old guns. About a hundred years ago, in eastern Canada, very rotten wood, rich in the mycelium of this species, was known as 'punkwood' or 'touchwood' and was widely used as tinder. At the height of its use, 50 tonnes was said to be harvested each year from the Thuringian forests in Germany.

This species is a parasite which attacks the sapwood of deciduous trees. It was formerly confused with *Ganoderma applanatum,* and was thus thought to be common in Britain. It is now known to be very rare, growing only in Scottish Highlands, whereas in Europe it is one of the commonest polypores. The fruiting bodies are perennial, and the tubes become stratified in old specimens, a new layer being developed on the underside each year. Each layer may produce crops of spores for four successive years. As this fungus is commercially useful, it is rarely left to attain old age, but some specimens have been found in Europe with 25 to 30 layers, and there is a record of a bracket with 50 layers from North America.

Fruiting body
Cap: pale brown to greyish-black, fawn to brown on the margin. Up to 50cm across. Hoof-shaped, concentrically furrowed, with a blunt margin. Cuticle at first slightly downy. Flesh tawny, felty to compact. *Tubes:* rusty brown, a new layer added to the underside each

Ecology On conifers, sometimes on deciduous trees. Causes a red heart-rot. Common in Europe and N. America. January to December. Inedible.

Ganoderma applanatum
ARTIST'S FUNGUS
For many years this species, which is also called the Flat Tinder Fungus, was confused with *Fomes fomentarius,* which is now known to be rare in Britain. The *Ganoderma* can be recognized by its hard, brown, rather knobbly crust, and its deep brown flesh. The fruiting bodies produce a phenomenal quantity of brown spores, which frequently collect like powder on the tree trunk or lower fruiting bodies.

Top, left: Fomes fomentarius
Above: Fomitopsis pinicola

Often an abnormal form or variety is found, which shows, when broken open, each layer of tubes separated by a thin whitish layer of flesh. Designs drawn with a pointed implement on the fresh white pore surface turn brown and are reasonably permanent. *Ganoderma applanatum* causes a white butt-rot and eventually kills the trees it attacks.

Fruiting body
Cap: dull red-brown, margin paler, whitish-grey then brown, often becoming cocoa-brown from deposited spores. 5–30cm wide. Bracket-like, rather flat, with low, concentrically-zoned, humps. Margin rounded. Cuticle waxy, crust-like, very hard in old specimens. Flesh brown, corky-hard, thick. *Tubes:* red-brown or cinammon, often obscurely stratified. *Pores:* at first whitish, becoming cinnamon when rubbed or with age, small. *Stipe:* absent. *Spores:* cocoa-brown in mass, ovoid, flattened at one end, thick walled, net-like pattern on surface but smooth, average size 10.3 × 6.3 microns.

Habitat and distribution
Grows singly or in overlapping tiers on the trunks of ageing deciduous trees, especially beech or poplar, in mountainous areas.

Above: Ganoderma applanatum
Top: Ganoderma lucidum *(the specimen shown is immature, with the kidney-shaped cap yet to appear)*
Far right: Grifola frondosa
Right: Gloeophyllum saepiarium

Frequent to common in Europe and North America. It is found in Trinidad, Venezuela, Columbia and Panama.

Occurrence
Fruiting bodies perennial, January to December.

Culinary properties
Inedible.

Ganoderma lucidum
Fruiting body Dark chestnut-brown, shining, with concentric furrows. Kidney-shaped to circular with a longish lateral stipe. *Pores:* at first off-white, finally dull brown.
Ecology Usually at ground level on stumps of deciduous trees, caus-

ing white rot. Occasional to frequent, widespread in Europe. January to December. Edibility unknown.

Gloeophyllum saepiarium
In the British Isles this fungus is a serious cause of decay in conifers, but is rare on structural timber. In Continental Europe it grows commonly on softwood fencing, bridge timbers and telegraph poles. It will attack timber which is fully exposed to the sun, growing actively in wet weather but remaining dormant when it is dry. The fruiting bodies appear approximately five months after the spores germinate, causing a brown-red rot, with cracks separating the annual rings.
Fruiting body
Cap: at first rusty-brown, finally becoming blackish-brown to chestnut, margin paler, more yellowish.

3–6cm across. Bracket-shaped. Margin broad, cuticle warty, hairy at first, zoned, finally scaly. Flesh brownish-yellow, corky, tough. *Hymenium:* gill-like, irregularly forked, firm. *Stipe:* absent. *Spores:* white in mass, cylindric, slightly curved, smooth, average size 9.5 × 3.5 microns.

Habitat and distribution
It grows on coniferous trees, on stumps and logs, and on structural timber on the Continent. Common throughout Europe.

Occurrence
January to December.

Culinary properties
Inedible.

Grifola frondosa
HEN OF THE WOODS
In Japan this fungus is likened to the waving hands and kimono

sleeves of dancing girls and it is called *Mai-take*, which literally means 'dancing mushroom'. Elsewhere it is compared, more prosaically, to a squatting hen, with feathers spread protecting her chicks. It was known to the classical world and was sold in Roman markets. Very large tufts are sometimes found and there are records of specimens weighing up to 3 kilogrammes. The perennial mycelium of this species persists in the roots and trunk base of infected trees, where it causes a white heart rot. The mycelium spreads into the surrounding earth and forms soil-binding masses. Some experts separate *Grifola intybacea* from *G. frondosa* on the basis of its darker and greyer caps. Other classifiers describe these grey specimens as the variety *intybacea*.
Fruiting body
Arises from a thick stipe which

repeatedly divides. The spatulate caps at the end of each branch form a densely layered tuft, up to 30cm broad. *Cap:* colour varies from yellowish-brown to dark grey-brown, with dark radiating streaks, often with a paler margin. 4–6cm wide. Narrowly fan-shaped to semi-circular, flattened. Margin often wavy. Cuticle wrinkled, with radiating fibrils. Flesh white, at first soft, becoming tough, fibrous. *Tubes:* white, short, decurrent. *Pores:* white to yellowish, very small, irregular, usually toothed in old specimens. *Stipe:* thick, smooth, white, richly branched, end of each branch gradually merges, laterally, with a cap. *Spores:* white in mass, ellipsoid, smooth, size 6.0 × 4.3 microns.

Habitat and distribution
Grows in large dense tufts at the base, or on the ground near,

deciduous trees, especially oak and hornbeam. Variable in Europe, becoming more common towards the south. More common in North America than in Europe. Common in Australia.

Occurrence
September to frost.

Culinary properties
Smells mealy and is reminiscent of mice. Young caps make a delicious aromatic dish if cooked with care. Mature specimens must be chopped finely, and need long, slow cooking. This produces a well-flavoured gravy. The Japanese either eat it fresh or preserve it in salt.

Hericium coralloides
This beautiful species is unfortunately very rare. It is highly recommended by experts.

Fruiting body
At first pure shining white, becoming yellow with age. Up to 35cm across. Made up of dense interlacing branches, each tapering to a point. *Spines:* grow from one side of each branch, awl-shaped, 6–10cm long, hanging in clusters, like tassels. *Stipe:* thick, trunk-like. *Spores:* white in mass, globose, smooth, average size 4.5 microns in diameter.

Habitat and distribution
Grows in tufts, on dead trunks and branches of deciduous and coniferous trees, especially beech and Douglas fir. Widespread, but rare, in Europe, North America, Australia and New Zealand.

Occurrence
October to November in Europe, August to first frosts in N. America.

Culinary properties
Young specimens are good when

stewed, or when cooked in butter with black pepper and a little nutmeg, and served in a white sauce.

Heterobasidion annosum
ROOT FOMES
This very common parasite is one of the most important causes of heart rot in conifers, killing many young trees, especially Norway Spruce. In

damp conditions it continues to grow on structural timber, and especially pit props. It is not a conspicuous fungus; the fruiting bodies grow at ground level, around the bases of trees and on soil banks, and are often obscured by litter. The spores germinate, either on newly cut stumps or in cracks or wounds in the bark at the base of living conifers. The mycelium then spreads along the roots to nearby standing trees. This fungus can have an indirect effect on the flora of a dense coniferous forest if it kills several adjoining trees. When these infected trees fall they leave a gap in the canopy, which admits sufficient light to allow flowering plants to grow.

Fruiting body
Usually bracket-like, rarely lying flat on a horizontal surface. *Cap:* bright reddish-brown, with a white margin. 2–4cm across. Bracket-shaped, shell-shaped or irregular. Cuticle, thin, hard, crust-like, irregularly bubbly, often concentrically grooved. Flesh whitish, at first leather, finally hard, woody. *Tubes:* become stratified, each layer 5 to 8mm thick, older tubes becoming filled with hyphae. *Pores:* white at first, then creamy, round to oval, somewhat irregular. *Stipe:* absent. *Spores:* white in mass, broadly ellipsoid to subglobose, smooth, average size 5.0 × 4.0 microns.

Habitat and distribution
Grows in overlapping tiers at the base of coniferous trees. Common in Europe, Central and North America, Australia, mountainous areas of India.

Occurrence
January to December.

Culinary properties
Inedible.

Left: Heterobasidion annosum
Bottom: Hericium coralloides

Hirchioporus abietinus

This saprophytic fungus forms small, attractive shelves on coniferous wood, causing a yellow, crumbling rot. It also decays worked timber, in damp conditions, especially down coalmines.

Fruiting body

Usually small brackets, rarely flat on the substrate with the hymenium on the outer surface. *Cap:* whitish-grey or greenish-grey, often tinged violet, especially on the margin. 1—3cm broad. Caps often united laterally to form a narrow shelf, 7.5cm or more wide. Shell-shaped, zoned. Cuticle downy with adpressed hairs. Flesh brown or purplish-brown, thin, tough, leathery, elastic even when dry. *Tubes:* lilac, very short. *Pores:* lilac,

Top, right: Hydnellum zonatum
Right: Hirchioporus abietinus
Bottom: Hydnum repandum

unequal, often angular. *Spores:* white in mass, ellipsoid, curved, pointed at one end, smooth, average size 7.5 × 5.0 microns.

Habitat and distribution

Grows in overlapping tiers, on dead trunks, stumps, fallen branches of conifers, especially where the trees have been killed by fire. Common in Europe and America.

Occurrence

January to December.

Culinary properties

Inedible.

Hydnellum zonatum

When growing in dense clusters, the fruiting bodies of this fungus often grow together and become joined. The flesh is very tough, and is not improved by cooking, but the resulting juices make a well flavoured gravy.

Fruiting body

Cap: reddish-brown with paler concentric zones, and margin. 3—6cm in diameter. Funnel shaped, uneven. Margin wavy, sterile underneath.

Cuticle silky, becoming radially wrinkled. Flesh thin, tough. *Spines:* brown with grey tips, becoming rust in mature specimens. Decurrent, short, slender. *Stipe:* short, slender, parallel-sided, with a tuberous base. Brown, cottony. *Spores:* dark brown in mass, subglobose, warty, average size 5.5 × 4.5 microns.

Habitat and distribution

Often found growing in dense clusters, on the ground or from fallen branches, in deciduous or coniferous woods. Rare to occasional in Northern Europe, locally abundant in eastern North America.

Occurrence

September to November.

Culinary properties

Flesh does not become tender when cooked, but it yields a pleasant flavour to the cooking liquor.

Hydnum repandum
WOOD HEDGEHOG

This very popular edible fungus, the Hedgehog Mushroom or Wood Urchin, is frequently sold with Chantarelles in Italy, where it is known

as *Steccherinos*, meaning little hedgehogs. It is one of the officially recognized edible species sold in French markets.

Fruiting body

Cap: pale yellow to pinkish-buff. 5—10, sometimes 15cm in diameter. At first convex, then flattened and irregular, or depressed. Margin incurved, often lobed. Cuticle smooth, often slightly cracked. Flesh white, firm, rather brittle. *Spines:* pale cream, conical, unequal in length, up to 5mm long, decurrent. *Stipe:* short, stout, often eccentric, 5—12 cm long, 1—4cm thick. Creamy white, slowly stains yellow where bruised. Flesh white, solid. *Spores:* white in mass, subglobose, smooth, average size 7.8 × 6.5 microns.

Habitat and distribution

Grows in groups, often in rings, on grassy banks in deciduous woods, especially under beech, under conifers in mountainous areas. Common in Europe and North America. It is found in Tasmania.

Occurrence

August to November in Europe, July to November in North America.

Culinary properties

It should be boiled to remove the bitter taste, which can also be improved by soaking in milk. Cut into strips or sliced, it is said to be as delicious as oysters after slow cooking for one hour in a closed vessel. Try it dipped in egg and breadcrumbs, fried and served with fried onions. The Wood Hedgehog dries well.

Inonotus hispidus

Fruiting body At first yellowish-brown, then dark rust, finally blackish-brown, shaggy hairy. Bracket-shaped, sessile. *Pores:* exude drops. *Spores:* yellowish-brown.

Ecology On trunks of deciduous

strong winds. *L. sulphureus* was responsible for a great deal of decay in wooden ships, when the logs used in the construction had been cut from infected trees, and it is still a problem today in modern lifeboats, barges and yachts. Iso called the Chicken Mushroom.

Fruiting bodies
Form large masses of closely overlapping caps, 30—40cm across, growing from a common tuber-like stipe. *Cap:* at first orange-yellow, fading to pale whitish-tan. 10—20cm broad, bracket-shaped, flattened, somewhat irregular. Margin wavy. Flesh at first yellow, soon becoming white, thick, spongy, fragile and very light when dry. *Tubes:* sulphur-yellow, short. *Pores:* at first bright sulphur-yellow, fading

trees, especially apple, ash. Attacks through wounds in bark, causes a spongy, white heart-rot. Common in Europe. May to February. Edibility unknown.

Hymenochaete rubiginosa
Fruiting body Bracket-like or flat on substrate with hymenium on the outer surface. At first dull yellowish-brown, downy, finally dark chestnut to black. Often zoned, warty. Flesh tough. *Hymenium:* rusty-brown, minutely rough. Grows in thickness each year.
Ecology In large overlapping groups which persist from year to year, on decaying trunks, stumps, branches of deciduous trees, especially oak, copper beech. Frequent in Europe. On hard-wood posts in Australia. January to December. Edibility unknown.

Laetiporus sulphureus
SULPHUR SHELF
This fungus is a dangerous enemy to all trees in both cool temperate regions and the tropics. It attacks the most durable timber, even oak, and is one of the few fungi to be found on old yew trees. In Mediterranean areas it is a serious pathogen on chestnuts. The spores germinate in wounds or cracks in the bark at the base of the tree. Sometimes the mycelium may live in the wood for several years before the fruiting bodies appear. It causes a red-brown cubical rot in the heart wood, the cracks becoming filled with tough washleather-like sheets of mycelium. Infected trees may survive for many years, with fruiting bodies appearing on the trunk each season, but they gradually become hollow, and are liable to fall in

with age, rounded finally becoming angular. *Stipe:* lateral, very short or absent. *Spores:* white in mass, ovoid to pip-shaped, smooth, average size 6.5 × 4.5 microns.
Habitat and distribution
Grows in many overlapping, tufted layers, at the base of deciduous and coniferous trees. Common in Europe, North America, Venezuela, Australia, South Africa.
Occurrence
May to November in Europe, June to September in North America.
Culinary properties
Smells strong, but quite pleasant, tastes slightly acrid. Only young, knob-like, caps, or the edges of newly-expanded caps are tender. It is good when fried in egg and breadcrumbs, or cooked gently in butter and served on toast with a white sauce. In stews and patties it can replace the meat. It is particularly delicious when boiled, cooled, sliced and served with salad.

Top, left: Inonotus hispidus
Above: Laetiporus sulphureus
Left: Hymenochaete rubiginosa

Lenzites betulina

At first glance, this species could be mistaken for *Coriolus versicolor* but it is distinguished by the gill-like plates on its undersurface.

Fruiting body

Cap: white to grey, sometimes tinged with brown. 4—8cm broad. Semicircular, flattened, zoned. Margin sometimes wavy. Cuticle hairy to woolly. Flesh white, thin, soft at first, becoming corky. *Tubes:* white to yellowish-white, elongated to form gill-like plates, often branched, walls thick. *Stipe:* absent. *Spores:* white in mass, cylindrical, smooth, average size 5.0 × 2.3 microns.

Habitat and distribution

Often grows in overlapping tiers, on stumps and stout branches of deciduous trees especially birch, sometimes beech. Occasional to frequent in Europe, common in the mountainous areas of eastern North America. It is found in Australia.

Occurrence

January to December.

Culinary properties

It has a nutty flavour, and a gummy texture. Young specimens are pleasant when eaten raw.

Top right: Phaeolus schweinitzii
Right: Merulius tremullosus
Below: Lenzites betulina
Bottom: Meripilus giganteus

Meripilus giganteus

This is one of the largest of the bracket fungi, forming large dense tufts around the base of oak and beech trees. Its gastronomic qualities are highly regarded by enthusiasts on the Continent.

Fruiting bodies

Form dense tufts of separate caps and stipes, up to 1m across, which are united in a tuber-like base. *Cap:* leather-brown to date-brown, with a creamy-yellow margin. 10—20cm wide. Semi-circular to fan-shaped, zoned. Margin wavy or lobed. Cuticle separates into scurfy scales. Flesh white, turns black where bruised or cut, thin, rather brittle at first, then becoming tough. *Tubes;* white, very short, decurrent. *Pores;* white, turn black where bruised, round, very small. *Stipe:* short, lateral, broadens at the top and merges with the cap. *Spores:* white in mass, broadly ellipsoid to pip-shaped, smooth, average size 5.5 × 4.5 microns.

Habitat and distribution

Grows in dense, layered tufts at the base of deciduous trees, around stumps, on roots, especially oak and beech. Common in Europe and North America.

Occurrence

July to January.

Culinary properties

Smells rather like sour cherries. Young tender caps are good when stewed and make delicious gravy. Old specimens are tough.

Merulius tremullosus

A rather attractive fungus, it is recognized by its translucent woolly cap and gelatinous flesh.

Fruiting body

Flat and spreading with the hymenium on the outer surface. The top edge becoming broadly free and bent over to form a bracket. *Cap:* pale greenish-white, somewhat translucent, with a pink margin.

1—4cm broad. Bracket-shaped. Margin toothed or fringed. Cuticle woolly. Flesh white, thin gelatinous. *Hymenium:* orange-buff to pink, with a network of folds or veins forming shallow, elongated pores, which radiate from the point of attachment of the fruiting body. *Spores:* white in mass, sausage-shaped, smooth, average size 4.5 × 1.0 microns.

Habitat and distribution

Often in groups, with brackets superimposed in tiers. On rotten stumps, trunks, inside hollow, deciduous trees. Occasional to frequent in Europe, common in Eastern North America.

Occurrence

September to March in Europe, October to November in North America.

Culinary properties

Tastes slightly woody, rather tough, and only worth gathering for food in the absence of anything better.

Phaeolus schweinitzii

Fruiting body Dark brown, margin at first yellow, densely downy. Bracket-shaped. *Pores:* greenish-yellow, brown where bruised. *Stipe:* absent or short, thick, brown, downy.

Ecology Often in groups, usually at ground level, on stumps and roots of conifers. Causes a brown cubical butt rot, especially of pines. Frequent to common in Europe. August to December.
Edibility unknown.

Phellinus igniarius
FALSE AMADOU

The fruiting bodies of *Phellinus igniarius*, which is also known as Willow Fomes, are perennial, each year producing a fresh layer of tubes on the underside. Old fruiting bodies are extremely tough and they may have 20 to 30 layers of tubes. It causes a white heart rot in infected

trees, and makes the felled timber unsaleable.

Fruiting body

Cap: at first rust, then blackish-grey, with a whitish-grey margin. 5–25cm wide. Bracket or hoof-shaped, concentrically furrowed, usually radially and irregularly cracked. Cuticle slightly downy in young specimens. Margin thick, rounded. Flesh rusty-brown, zoned, very hard. *Tubes:* brown, up to 1cm long, often stratified, older tubes becoming filled up with white mycelium. *Pores:* whitish-grey, hoary in young specimens, finally cinnamon. Minute, round, long remaining closed. *Stipe:* absent. *Spores:* white in mass, globose, smooth, average size 6 microns in diameter.

Habitat and distribution

Grows on the trunks of deciduous trees, especially willows and poplars. Widespread and locally common in Europe and Australia.

Occurrence

January to December.

Culinary properties

Inedible.

Phellinus pomaceus

In the past the fruiting bodies of this species were used by country folk to make poultices for the treatment of swollen faces. The fungus was ground down on a nutmeg grater, heated in the oven, then applied. It is a common fungus on old plum trees, in which it causes a heart rot.

Fruiting body

At first brown, finally grey, margin grey, then cinnamon. 2–6cm across. Cushion-shaped or irregularly spread, sometimes hoof-shaped. Margin rounded, velvety at first. Cuticle concentrically furrowed, becoming cracked. Flesh light brown, very hard, woody. *Tubes:* cinnamon, approximately 6mm long, stratified

in older specimens. *Pores:* at first with a greyish bloom finally brown, minute, remaining closed for a long time. *Spores:* pale brown in mass, almost globose, smooth, average size 6 × 5.5 microns.

Habitat and distribution

Grows on living, rosaceous, fruit trees, especially hawthorn and plum. Common in Europe and North America.

Occurrence

January to December.

Culinary properties

None known.

Far left: Phellinus igniarius
Centre: Phellinus pomaceus
Left: Phellinus robustus

Phellinus robustus

Fruiting body Hoof-like, long-lived bracket, 10–30cm wide and up to 30cm thick, brown upper surface, flesh and tubes reddish-brown.

Ecology On oak. Continental Europe. Can be found the whole year around.
Inedible.

Piptoporus betulinus
RAZOR STROP FUNGUS

Until World War I, the Razor Strop Fungus or Birch Fungus was a feature of many country homesteads. Bee-keepers used lumps of smouldering fruiting body to drive the bees from a hive. Before matches came into general use, a piece would be kept smouldering, in a tin with restricted ventilation, and was carried into the fields by farmworkers, to make a fire to cook their lunch. A valuable antiseptic could also be made, by heating the fungus slowly with charcoal, in a closed tin, until the fumes stopped escaping. Thin pencil-sized pieces were used as fuses for firing charges when blowing up tree stumps. These were known as 'quick touch' if they were dipped in saltpetre, and 'slow touch' if left untreated. In the early

Top, left: Piptoporus betulinus
Top, right: Polyporus squamosus
Below: Polyporus brumalis
Far right: Polyporus varius
Below, far right: Pseudotrametes gibbosa

nineteenth century, the pore surface was widely used as a razor-strop. It grows exclusively on birch, causing a brown, powdery rot and eventually killing infected trees.

Fruiting body

Cap: greyish to pale watery brown. 5–30cm across. Kidney-shaped or shell-shaped, convex, with a hump at the back. Cuticle smooth, thin, separating. Margin thick, incurved, projects beyond the pore surface. Flesh white, thick, firm, at first quite moist, becoming dry and corky with age. *Tubes:* white up to 1cm long, becoming separated from the flesh in old specimens. *Pores:* white, becoming slightly discoloured with age, minute, rounded with thick walls. Frequently rough with numerous needle-like projections. *Stipe:* absent or very short, in the form of a slight boss. *Spores:* white in mass, sausage-shaped, smooth, average size 4.8 × 1.8 microns.

Habitat and distribution

It grows in large numbers, usually very crowded together, on birch. Common in Europe and northern North America. It is found in Australia.

Occurrence

January to December, especially in summer and autumn.

Culinary properties

Very young specimens are of fair quality.

Polyporus brumalis

Fruiting body *Cap:* at first deep brown, downy, becoming paler, smooth. Margin hairy, often wavy or lobed. Convex, finally depressed. *Pores:* whitish to yellowish. *Stipe:* central, sometimes eccentric, often wavy or curved upwards from base, grey, chestnut towards the base.
Ecology On stumps, trunks, branches of deciduous trees, often on buried wood. Frequent in Europe. January to December.
Edibility (unknown).

Polyporus squamosus
DRYAD'S SADDLE

Specimens of this handsome and often very large fungus have been found weighing up to 20 kilograms and measuring up to two metres around the edge. Its fruiting bodies decay more easily than those of other polypores, and have usually disappeared by the beginning of the winter. The mycelium continues to grow inside an infected tree or piece of timber for several years and fruits each autumn. Abnormal growths, resembling miniature stag's horns, are produced in continuous darkness, but normal caps will develop if these structures are stimulated by as little as one hour of light.

Fruiting body

Cap: pale yellow-ochre, with concentrically arranged dark brown spots. 10–35cm in diameter. Kidney-shaped to circular, spreading horizontally. Cuticle with large, thin, feathery scales, closely pressed onto it. Flesh white, at first soft, finally tough, comparatively thin. *Tubes:* yellowish-white, decurrent, up to 1cm long. *Pores;* white, becoming dirty yellow, at first minute, then large, angular, torn. *Stipe:* lateral to eccentric, short, stout, several joined at the base, up to 7.5cm long, 2–5cm thick. Whitish-cream, with a black base. Flesh white, hard. *Spores:* white in mass, ellipsoid, smooth, with a slight projection at one end, length variable, average size 12.5 × 4.5 microns.

Habitat and distribution

Grows in tufts on trunks, stumps, old timber of deciduous trees, especially elm, ash, pear. Common in Europe, uncommon in east and central North America. It is found in Australia. Propagation is helped by small beetles found in fruit body.

Occurrence

April to December in Europe, May to November in North America.

Culinary properties

Smells strong, unusual, suggestive of uncooked tripe to some. A tough toadstool, which is only palatable when finely shredded and stewed slowly.

Polyporus varius

Fruiting body *Cap:* colour varies from yellow-ochre to cinnamon, often with dark brown radiating lines. Tongue, shell-shaped or circular, finally depressed. *Pores:* cream becoming grey. *Stipe:* central or eccentric, short, cream, becoming black, downy towards the base.
Ecology On stumps, trunks, fallen branches of deciduous trees.

Common in Europe. January to December.
Edibility unknown.

Pseudotrametes gibbosa

This very common polypore causes an active white rot in old beech stumps.

Fruiting body

Broadly attached. *Cap:* whitish to greyish, often with greenish patches of algal growth. 8–15cm across. Bracket-shaped, zoned. Margin rounded, often wavy. Cuticle densely downy. Flesh white, corky, tough. *Pores:* dirty white, radially elongated, 3–5 times longer than wide, thick walled. *Stipe:* absent. *Spores:* white in mass, cylindrical, smooth, average size 5.0 × 2.3 microns.

Habitat and distribution

Grows in overlapping tiers, on the stumps of deciduous trees, especially beech. Common in Europe.

Occurrence

August to March.

Culinary properties

Inedible.

Pycnoporus cinnabarinus

Fruiting body Bright orange-red, fading to dull orange-yellow, slightly warty, faintly zoned. Bracket-shaped, sessile. *Pores:* deep blood-red, minute.

Ecology In overlapping tiers or rows on trunks of deciduous trees,

especially birch, beech. Occasional in Europe, more common towards the south. Widespread in Australia. July to October.
Edibility unknown.

Ramaria botrytis

Care must be taken not to collect the bitter *Ramaria formosa* in mistake for this edible species. It is a popular food in parts of North America and Europe, and it is sold in Japanese markets, where it is called *Nedzumi-take*. Individual fruiting bodies should be carefully inspected before being cooked, as they are often worm infested.

Fruiting body

Large, compound, densely branched, 5–15cm high, 20–30cm across. Branches swollen at the tips and divided into several small branchlets, they spring from a stout, massive base, 3–4cm high, up to 6cm thick. Dingy yellowish-brown or tan, red to purplish at the tips. Flesh white to yellow, moist, firm, brittle, wine-red in branchlet tips. *Spores:* pale yellow in mass, ellipsoid, faintly longitudinally striate, otherwise smooth, average size 15.0 × 5.0 microns.

Habitat and distribution

Often found growing in arcs or rings, on acid, rich soil in deciduous woods, under conifers in mountainous areas, often under rhododendrons. Occasional to frequent in Europe, widespread in North America, most abundant towards the south-east and along the Pacific coast. Widespread in Australia.

Occurrence

August to November.

Culinary properties

Tastes mild, acid in old specimens, smells fruity but faint. Fresh young specimens are compact, meaty and tender, with a good flavour. The large fleshy base and main branches require longer cooking than the fragile tips.

Ramaria flava
YELLOW CORAL FUNGUS

Old specimens of this edible species may be confused with the bitter purgative *Ramaria formosa*, which is 2–4cm taller.

Fruiting body

With many short branches from a large, fleshy base, 10–20cm high, 6–15cm thick. Branches cylindrical, erect, crowded, divided at the tips into tooth-like points. Base white, becoming reddish-brown when bruised or with age, branches bright sulphur yellow, becoming brown with age. Flesh white, soft, elastic. *Spores:* yellow in mass, ellipsoid, finely warted, average size 12.0 × 5.0 microns.

Habitat and distribution

Grows singly, on the ground, occasionally on very rotten wood, in open deciduous woods, especially beech, in open coniferous woods in mountainous areas. Occasional to frequent in Europe, common in North America, widespread on gravelly soil in Australia, and is found in Colombia.

Occurrence

September to October in Europe, July to September in North America.

Culinary properties

The flesh is tender and delicious,

Above: Ramaria botrytis
Left: Pycnoporus cinnabarinus
Below: Ramaria flava

but specimens growing on wood tend to be tough, stringy and astringent.

Ramaria formosa
BEAUTIFUL CORAL FUNGUS

This species of *Ramaria* is poisonous to some people, while others can sample it in small amounts, without ill effects. It can easily be collected by mistake instead of the edible species *botrytis* and *flava*.

Fruiting body

Large, densely branched from a short, stout base, 10–25cm high. Branches elongated, erect, divided at the ends into thin straight branchlets. Pinkish-buff at the base, salmon-pink branches with yellow or pinkish-yellow tips. Flesh pale pink, finally becoming ochreous, turns brownish-black where bruised, fragile. *Spores*; ochre in mass, ellipsoid to ovoid, rough, average size 13.0 × 4.3 microns.

Habitat and distribution

Grows in large tufts, rows or rings, on the ground in deciduous woods, especially beech, under conifers in mountainous areas. Rare in Great Britain, frequent in Europe, widespread and common in North America, and is found in eastern Australia.

Right: Ramaria formosa
Top, right: Sarcodon imbricatum
Bottom, right: Schizophyllum commune

Occurrence

July to November.

Culinary properties

Inedible due to its unpleasant, bitter taste, which leaves a persistent, rasping sensation in the throat. Causes violent diarrhoea.

Sarcodon imbricatum
SCALY PRICKLE FUNGUS

This large species is recognized by its dark, overlapping, tile-like scales, which are said by some to resemble a hawk's plumage. Only young specimens should be gathered for food, as old ones develop a bitter taste.

Fruiting body

Cap: dull greyish-brown. 5–15cm in diameter. At first convex, becoming slightly depressed in the centre. Cuticle with woolly scales, overlapping concentrically from the centre. Flesh dingy white or buff, thick, firm, brittle. *Spines:* whitish-grey to grey-brown. Decurrent, short, blunt, mostly of equal length, very fragile in old specimens. *Stipe;* swollen at the base, 2–7cm long, 2–5cm thick. Greyish-white to pale brown, smooth, slightly felted at the base. Flesh solid. *Spores:* dark reddish-brown in mass, globose, warty, average size 6 microns in diameter.

Habitat and distribution

Grows in groups, occasionally in rings, in sandy soil of coniferous or deciduous forests, especially oak. In mountainous and lowland areas. Variable in Europe becoming more common towards the north. Common in northern North America, and in the Rocky Mountains.

Occurrence

September to November in Europe, July to September in North America.

Culinary properties

Old specimens often have a slightly bitter taste. Smells pleasantly spicy. Has a very fine, delicate flavour, after being boiled and the liquor strained off. It is good when dipped in egg and bread crumbs and fried with onions. Dries well, and can be ground into a powder and used as a flavouring.

Schizophyllum commune
THE SPLIT GILL

Although the species occurs naturally in Europe, it is especially common on hardwood logs imported from the tropics. It does not cause serious decay, but its presence reduces the value of the timber. The longitudinal splitting and curling of the gills appears to be an adaptation for the protection of its spore-producing structures in drought conditions, and explains one of its common names. Another, the Fan, derives from its overall shape. When dried specimens are moistened, the gills straighten out and soon begin to develop and shed spores. There are records of dried fruiting bodies reviving after several years. Geneticists have frequently

used this fungus to study the processes of reproduction in fungi.

Fruiting body

Cap: brownish-grey when moist, whitish-grey when dry. 1–4cm in diameter. Fan-shaped or kidney-shaped. Margin incurved, somewhat lobed. Cuticle downy. Flesh brownish when moist, white when dry, thin, tough, pliant. *Gills:* greyish-violet, radiating from the point of attachment of the cap. Longitudinally split, the edges rolled back in dry weather, straight when wet. *Stipe:* absent, or narrowed behind into a stipe-like base. *Spores:* pale pink in mass, cylindrical, smooth, length variable, average size 5.0 × 1.3 microns. Similar to *Shizophyllum commune* are some of the lignicolous *Panellus* genus.

Habitat and distribution

Grows gregariously or scattered, on trunks, dead branches, newly felled logs, stacked timber of deciduous trees, sometimes on coniferous wood in mountainous areas. Variable in Europe and North America, becoming more common towards the south. Common in Australia, South Africa, central and northern South America.

Culinary properties

Inedible.

Serpula lacrymans
DRY ROT

The fruiting bodies of this fungus arise from thick strands of whitish-grey mycelium, by which it spreads from one source of wood, across and even through alien substrates, to another. These strands will continue to grow through mortar, brick, cracks in stone for as long as the originally infected wood continues to give nourishment, or until they are unable to extend further, due to lack of support, for instance, when they reach an exterior wall, or end of a joist. It flourishes in damp, unventilated conditions, and will grow from just above the freezing point of water to about 25°C. Because of this it is not a significant nuisance in tropical areas, as it is in cooler, temperate regions, being particularly bad in the wooden houses of Arctic Europe. As it stops growing well below human body temperature, the widely held belief that it is pathogenic to man has been disproved. However, a respiratory allergy can be caused by the inhalation of air containing a high concentration of spores, and of course, the dank conditions in which the fungus thrives are injurious to health.

Fruiting body

Usually lies flat on a horizontal surface with the hymenium on the outer side, occasionally forms brackets on a vertical surface. Indefinite in size, from 2cm to 1m broad, mature fruiting bodies up to 1cm thick. Brown or rusty-cinnamon, honeycomb-like, with a thick, white, downy margin. *Hymenium:* covers the honeycomb-like surface. The hymenial folds become elongated into tooth-like projections in bracket-shaped fruiting bodies. *Spores:* bright orange-yellow in mass, ellipsoid, smooth, average size 9.5 × 5.5 microns.

Habitat and distribution

Very common on structural timber of buildings, mines and ships, in damp, badly ventilated conditions, in temperate areas of Europe, North America, Asia, Australasia.

Occurrence

All the year round.

Culinary properties

None known.

Sparassis crispa
SPONGE FUNGUS

It is impossible to confuse this species with any other. Perfect specimens resemble huge rosettes —hence the common name Cauliflower Fungus—and fruiting bodies weighing several pounds are not rare. Unfortunately it is becoming rather uncommon due to the destruction of old forests.

Fruiting body

Dense, rounded, cauliflower-like mass of flat, lobed branches, 25–35cm across. At first cream, then yellow, the edges of the branches become brown with age. Flesh waxy, brittle. *Spores:* pale yellow ochre in mass, broadly ellipsoid to pip-shaped, smooth, average size 6.0 × 4.5 microns.

Habitat and distribution

Forms large masses at the base of pine stumps, occasionally inside hollow stumps. Frequent in Europe, rather rare in eastern North America. It is found in Australia.

Occurrence

August to November.

Culinary properties

Tastes mild, faintly nutty. The flesh becomes tough in old specimens. One fruiting body is enough for a meal, and very large ones can be kept fresh in a bowl of water, stored in a cool, dark place. It makes good soups and casseroles. Is good as a flavouring in omelettes and soufflés. Dries well when broken into small pieces. Whole dried specimens make pretty ornaments.

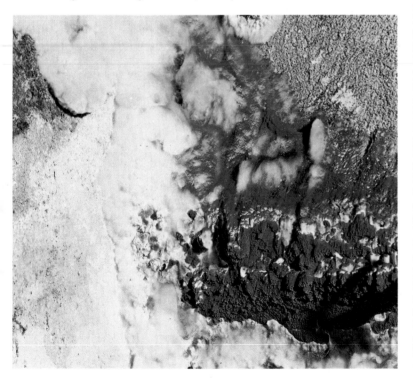

Above: Sparassis crispa
Bottom, left: Serpula lacrymans

Stereum hirsutum

The shape of this fungus varies according to where it grows. It is normally bracket-shaped, but is funnel-shaped when it grows on a horizontal surface, such as the top of a stump. When it fruits on the underside of a log, it lies flat with the hymenium on its outer surface. It is an important cause of decay in felled oaks left lying on the ground and is naturally important as an agent in the saprophytic decomposition of fallen branches and trunks of many broadleaved trees.

Fruiting body
Cap: colour varies from yellow to grey. 1—4cm broad, bracket-shaped, often irregular, zoned. Often with several brackets joined laterally. Margin waved or lobed. Cuticle coarsely hairy. Flesh thin, tough, leathery. *Hymenium:* at first bright yellow-ochre, finally becoming dull grey, smooth or somewhat uneven. *Stipe:* absent. *Spores:* white in mass, ellipsoid, flattened on one side, smooth, average size 6.0 × 3.0 microns.

Habitat and distribution
Grows in tiers, on stumps, logs, fallen branches, felled and worked wood of deciduous trees. Common in Europe and Australia, it is found in Venezuela.

Occurrence
January to December.

Culinary properties
Inedible.

Below: Stereum hirsutum
Centre, top: Stereum rugosum
Centre, bottom: Thelephora palmata
Far right: Thelephora terrestris

Stereum rugosum

Fruiting body Lies flat on substrate with hymenium on the outer surface, margin upturned. *Hymenium:* pinkish-buff becoming grey, blood-red, bleeding, where cut or bruised.

Ecology On stumps, fallen branches, trunks of living deciduous trees. Common in Europe, found in Australia. January to December. Edibility unknown.

Thelephora palmata

Fruiting body Erect, with many flattened branches from a slender stipe. Purplish-brown, paler towards the top. *Smell:* foetid or of garlic.

Ecology In clusters on ground in coniferous woods, especially under pine. Occasional to frequent in Europe, reported from Australia. August to November. Edibility unknown.

Thelephora terrestris

The dark colour of this fungus blends with that of the surrounding soil and dead leaves, thus making it difficult to see. It is a menace in young pine plantations, where it strangles seedlings. In North America it also attacks young maple trees. This species can, under certain conditions, form mycorrhiza with pine trees.

Fruiting body
Erect, or sometimes spread over the substrate, with only a small upturned margin. *Cap:* chocolate-brown to blackish-brown with a paler margin. 3—8cm broad. Fan-shaped, irregularly funnel-shaped or circular. Margin fringed. Cuticle with shaggy radiating scales. Flesh brown, thin, tough, fibrous. *Hymenium:* pale cocoa-coloured, wrinkled or granular. *Stipe:* absent. *Spores:* dark brown in mass, angular, warted, average size 8.5 × 6.8 microns.

Habitat and distribution
Grows in often large, dense clusters, on the needle cover in pine plantations, on roots, twigs, branches, trunks of conifers, on heaths. Common in Europe, on maple in North America.

Occurrence
July usually August to December.

Culinary properties
Inedible.

Vuilleminia comedans

This inconspicuous fungus is present everywhere in woods, and is most easily recognized on branches of living trees, between the rolled-back bark and the wood.

Fruiting body
A thin crust beneath rolled-back bark. Dull flesh-coloured. *Spores:* white in mass, cylindrical, curved, average size 18.0 × 6.3 microns.

Habitat and distribution
On dead branches and young stems of deciduous trees. Common in Europe, it is known in Australia.

Occurrence
January to December.

Culinary properties
None known.

The Agarics

The classic mushroom-like fungi order. It includes species which grow on the ground, on dung, on wood, and on other toadstools. Saprophytes, a few parasites and many fungi which form a special mycorrhizal relationship with tree roots are included amongst the diverse species grouped in the Agaricales. Many of the species are edible, a few are dangerously poisonous, and some cause hallucinations. The fleshy or cartilaginous fruiting bodies of this group are generally stalked, with a cap which bears a hymenium on its underside. This spore-forming layer may line tubes or gills and is responsible for the production of huge numbers of spores from a single fruit body.

Agaricus arvensis
HORSE MUSHROOM

This is a very large mushroom, found in open grassland and closely related to *A. sylvicola* from which it differs in having no basal bulb. It was occasionally cultivated accidentally in the days when 'virgin' spawn was used in mushroom beds.

Fruiting body

Cap: white, bruising and becoming yellow with age, 8–15cm, or even up to 20cm diameter, at first convex then expanded. Cuticle silky fibrillose, shining, smooth. Flesh permanently white, thick and firm. *Gills:* at first whitish then grey, never pink, finally blackish-brown. Free, rather narrow, generally broader towards stipe, crowded. *Stipe:* equal or slightly thickened towards base, 5–12.5cm long, up to 3cm thick. White, staining yellowish, smooth, hollow, sometimes fibrous. Prominent ring, rather large and thick, exterior surfaces often radially

cracked. *Spores:* purplish-brown in mass, ellipsoid, smooth, average size 8 × 5.5 microns.

Habitat and distribution

Grows in pastures, also on cultivated land, lawns, near cow and goat sheds and hayricks, more rarely in clearings in woods. It is found frequently in Britain, Europe and North America, east of the Rocky Mountains. It occurs in New Zealand.

Occurrence

July to November.

Culinary properties

Sweetish taste, smells rather strongly of aniseed; meaty and delicious when young, too tough to serve as food when old. One of the officially recognized species sold in French markets.

Agaricus augustus
THE PRINCE

This is one of the most desirable edible mushrooms. It is large with a cap not unlike that of *Lepiota procera*, but differing in the fineness of its scales and lack of a pronounced umbo. Successive crops can be produced if a site where it is known to grow is kept watered. It usually grows in groups.

Fruiting body

Cap: yellowish-brown or whitish, dries yellow, with very delicate hazel-brown scales. 10–20cm in diameter. Semi-globose at first, then expanded and convex. Flesh white, may yellow slightly when cut. *Gills:* white at first, never pink, finally brown, free. *Stipe:* rooted deep in soil, tall, cylindrical, 10–20cm high. Scaly before cap expands, then white and smooth with a large, hanging, membranous ring near the top. Flesh bruising

yellowish. *Spores:* chocolate-brown in mass, smooth, ellipsoid. Average size 8.5 × 5.0 microns.

Habitat and distribution

Found occasionally in woods, parks, near compost heaps, in flower beds, on lawns, in orchards, sometimes on verges. In Europe and North America, especially along Pacific coast.

Occurrence

August to November in Europe, June to October in North America, especially in the rainy season.

Culinary properties

Smells strongly of aniseed. It is meaty and of fine flavour but should be cooked as quickly as possible. A good method is to wash, dry and cut into pieces, dust with flour, sauté in butter and serve on toast in its own gravy.

Top, left: Vuilleminia comedans
Centre: Agaricus arvensis
Left: Agaricus augustus

Above: Agaricus
bisporus
Right: Agaricus
bitorquis

Agaricus bisporus
Fruiting body *Cap:* rounded, expanding to become flat, whitish or with brown, radiating fibrils, margin with fragments of ring. *Stipe:* short cylindrical, smooth, flesh-white bruising reddish-brown, with a ring. *Gills:* free, pink then purple-brown, crowded.

Ecology On manure heaps and other sites rich with organic matter. Edible. This is the 'cultivated mushroom' sold in shops in many parts of the world. Some experts recognise two species, *Agaricus bisporus*, which is streaked with brown, and *Agaricus hortensis*, which has a pure white cap. In America these two forms are sold separately. It is, however, likely that they are really the same species with a cultivated form which has been selected over the long period the fungus has been cultivated.

Agricus bitorquis
THE PAVEMENT MUSHROOM
There is a great deal of resemblance between this species and *Agaricus campestris*, from which it is distinguished by its double ring, the lower one sometimes appearing at first sight to be like a volva. Found frequently in towns and cities, forcing its way through hard-packed surfaces, it occurs in similar habitats to that of *Coprinus atramentarius*.

Fruiting body
Cap: whitish, becoming pale buff with yellow (sometimes reddish) patches. 6–10cm in diameter. At first convex, soon becoming flat, with a persistently incurved margin. Cuticle thick, silky, cracking in the centre, not peeling when young, peels easily in old specimens. Flesh white, becoming pinkish with age or when cut. *Gills:* at first pinkish, then cinnamon, finally brownish-black with whitish edges. Free, not quite reaching the stipe, narrow, very crowded and of unequal lengths. *Stipe:* stout, slightly club-shaped, 4–6cm long, 1–3cm thick. White

turning pinkish, with two torn narrow rings, the lower one, like a thin volva, is usually covered with soil and can be damaged during development. *Spores:* purplish-brown in mass, almost globose, smooth, average size 6.0×4.5 microns.

Habitat and distribution
Almost exclusively found in urban areas, it usually grows singly, but may occur in dense clusters on hard packed soil, from cracks in pavements, or along gutters and old driveways. Variable in Europe becoming more common towards the south, frequent in eastern North America and Trinidad.

Occurrence
May to October.

Culinary properties
Tastes and smells rather strong, but agreeable. The flesh is rather tough, and it is not equal to *Agaricus campestris* in flavour, but it is perfectly safe and is highly prized by those who have tried it.

Agaricus campestris
PINK BOTTOMS
This cosmopolitan edible species is very closely related to *Agaricus bisporus*, the 'cultivated mushroom' usually sold in shops. At the button stage it can be mistaken for the deadly *Amanita verna* or Destroying Angel. Therefore, every button should be broken open before cooking. It has been known at least since Greek and Roman times and in seventeenth century French scientific literature, its cultivation from spawn was first described.

Old people in country areas believed that the Field Mushroom would only grow in fields where stallions had grazed. This superstition probably dates back to Roman times and is not without foundation. *Agaricus campestris* is a declining species, its decrease probably being related to the reduced horse population of recent years. Known as *Kallulic-div* meaning the Fairies' Cap in Afghanistan and Central Punjab, it appears in the deserts on camel tracks after rain, when it is gathered and eaten fresh or dried in the sun. *Mokshai*, young dried specimens, are sold in the bazaars of Northern India as medicines. It is collected and eaten in large quantities in China and Japan, but there is no record of it being sold commercially, as it is in France, where it is one of the officially recognized species sold in markets.

Fruiting body
Cap: at first white, later tinged brownish. 4–8cm in diameter. At first hemispherical, finally flattened. Margin extends beyond edge of gills, fringed and torn. Cuticle of fine, radial fibrils, sometimes minutely scaly towards the centre. Flesh white, faintly reddish above the gills, thick and firm. *Gills:* deep pink when young, even in unopened cap, chocolate to blackish-brown when old. Free, crowded, edge even. *Stipe:* short and stout, tapering downwards or slightly bellied, 3–7cm high, up to 2cm thick. Whitish with a narrow ring which soon falls off, bruising brownish when handled, almost smooth.

Solid at first, finally hollow. *Spores:* purplish-brown in mass, smooth, ellipsoid, average size 7.5 × 4.8 microns.

Habitat and distribution
A frequent, universal species, often growing in rings in richly manured meadows and pastures, always away from trees, from sea level to high mountains. In dry conditions it grows on heaps of horse-manure. Temperate areas of Europe, Afghanistan, South Africa, Australia, Northern India, China, Japan, U.S.A. and southern Canada.

Occurrence
August to November in Europe, July to October in North America, especially after rain.

Culinary properties
Tastes and smells agreeable. It is eaten throughout its range. Can be eaten raw or cooked by any method.

Agaricus comtulus
Fruiting body Small. *Cap:* creamy-white, darker in the centre. Convex becoming flat. *Stipe:* thin, with flaring ring near the apex.
Ecology Grassland, near trees. Infrequent in Europe, North America, South Africa. September to November. Inedible.

Agaricus macrosporus
One of the largest agarics, specimens of this fungus can be as big as a dinner plate. Attempts have been made at cultivation, but it is not suitable for marketing on a large scale as it soon exudes a dark-brown, smelly liquid, even when shipped a short distance.

Fruiting body
Cap: white or pale buff, yellow when rubbed; colour changes to golden-yellow—like ripe wheat in dry sunny weather. 12–26cm diameter, globular at first then hemispherical. Margin inrolled often with ragged patches of veil hanging from it. White, thick flesh. *Gills:* at first greyish, never deep pink, finally blackish-brown. Free, broad to narrow, inflated or upward curving, pointed at both ends, crowded. Mostly of one length, many forked from stipe. *Stipe:* stout, cylindrical or inflated towards base, with a large flaring membranous ring. Length hardly exceeds cap diameter. Whitish with concentric white or brown cottony scales below and on underside of ring, which may be tinged salmon when old. Fresh pale pinkish, turns orange when exposed to air. *Spores:* brownish-black in mass, elongate pip-shaped, average size 10 × 6.0 microns.

Habitat and distribution
In pastures on chalky soils. The season and distribution of this species is incompletely known, but it is found in Britain, North America and Europe, where it is reported as being quite common.

Occurrence
September to October.

Culinary properties
Edible with a pleasant anise or almond smell when young, but this quickly becomes unpleasant.

Agaricus silvaticus
This is a beautiful tawny, radially-streaked species of conifer woods.

Fruiting body
Cap: variegated with thin, reddish-brown, scales radiating from a brown centre to the paler margin, 4–8cm in diameter, convex, soon becoming flattened, margin at first incurved. Flesh white, reddens slightly when cut. *Gills:* at first pale to deep pink, finally blackish-brown, free, thin, crowded. *Stipe:* rather long with a slightly bulbous base, length 8–11cm. Somewhat scaly towards base, white, bruising yellowish, becoming brown and hollow with age. Near the apex a distinct spreading white ring, striate above, cottony below. *Spores:* purplish-brown in mass, ellipsoid, smooth, average size 5.5 × 4 microns.

Habitat and distribution
Found in association with conifers, especially where there is a thick layer of needles. Frequent in Australia, Britain and Europe, widespread but not common in North America.

Occurrence
September to November.

Culinary properties
It has an agreeable flavour.

Top, left: Agaricus campestris
Centre: Agaricus macrosporus
Below, left: Agaricus comtulus
Below: Agaricus silvaticus

Top: Agaricus silvicola
Right: Agaricus
xanthodermus
Far right: Agrocybe
dura
Bottom: Agrocybe
erebia

Agaricus silvicola
COMMON WOOD MUSHROOM

This slender woodland mushroom is recognized by its yellowing cap and its distinctive, but fleeting smell of anise. It is edible, but is sometimes mistaken for *Agaricus xanthodermus*, and can easily be confused with poisonous *Amanita* species. Great care must be taken to obtain a correct identification before eating.

Fruiting body

Cap: creamy-white, bruising and ageing yellowish. 6–12cm in diameter. At first rounded or bell-shaped, soon expanding. Cuticle silky, turns brick-red with a few drops of Henry's reagent. Margin at first incurved. Flesh thin, whitish to pale cream. *Gills:* at first greyish-white, tinged flesh colour, never deep-pink, finally blackish-brown. Free, rounded behind, thin and crowded. *Stipe:* long, narrowing upwards from bulbous base, 5–12cm long, 1.5–2.5cm thick. White becoming yellowish with age, smooth, with a double ring hanging laxly from apex. Flesh ageing brownish. *Spores:* purple-brown in mass, smooth, ellipsoid, average size 5.5 × 3.5 microns.

Habitat and distribution

In coniferous, occasionally deciduous woods. Common in Europe, occasional in North America and Australia.

Occurrence

August to December in Europe, August to September and occasionally in spring in North America.

Culinary properties

Tastes and smells spicy, it is not as highly flavoured as *Agaricus campestris*. Is delicious with meats and tomato sauce. Enriches dishes of less strongly flavoured *Lactarius* and *Russula* species. The stipes of older specimens can be tough.

Agaricus xanthodermus
YELLOW STAINER

This is a very dangerous mushroom because of its similarity to various edible species. It can be distinguished by the vivid yellow colour which develops in the flesh at the base of the stipe. For this reason it is important, when collecting mushrooms for food, to have the whole stipe intact. It can be distinguished from *Agaricus silvicola* by the latter's brick-red reaction with Henry's reagent.

Fruiting body

Cap: silky white, greyish-brown towards the centre, turns yellow where scratched, especially on the margin. 5–10cm in diameter. Convex when young, but with a dis-

tinctly flattened top, finally more or less flat. Cuticle does not change colour with Henry's reagent. Flesh white, thick in centre, thin at margin. *Gills:* at first whitish finally purple-brown. Free, variable in width, but not broad compared with thickness of flesh, crowded. *Stipe:* cylindrical with a bulbous base. Up to 7cm long, 1–1.5cm thick. White, smooth and shining with a white, thick-edged ring near the top. Sometimes tinged purplish-brown at apex, eventually becoming brownish lower down. Flesh white, immediately turns bright yellow in the base when cut. *Spores:* purple-brown in mass, smooth, ellipsoid, average size 5.5 × 3.6 microns.

Habitat and distribution

Found in troops on chalk grasslands especially where the grass has been trampled, near beech woods, in meadows or gardens. This species is not uncommon in Britain, but it seems to be rare elsewhere in Europe. It occurs in South Africa and is locally common in Australia.

Occurrence

August to October in Europe, May and June in South Africa.

Culinary properties

Smells like writing ink when raw, produces an unpleasant smell on being cooked. When eaten it can cause alarming symptoms of coma, vomiting and diarrhoea, but with complete recovery within a few days. Some people seem to eat it with no ill-effects.

Agrocybe dura

Fruiting body *Cap:* creamy-white becoming dingy brown, dry. Convex then flat. *Stipe:* with torn, cottony ring near the apex.

Ecology On calcareous soils, roadsides, gardens, cultivated land. Occasional in Europe, common in North America. April to October. Edible (caps only).

Agrocybe erebia

Fruiting body *Cap:* dark brown, slightly slimy with striate margin when wet, dull greyish-brown when dry. *Stipe:* stoutish, with whitish, membranous, grooved ring just above the middle.

Ecology Deciduous woodland, under hedges. Occasional in Europe. Inedible.

Agrocybe praecox
SPRING AGARIC

This species is one of the earliest to appear in spring. It is very plentiful, but it is only gathered for food if there is nothing else available.

Fruiting body

Cap: dull clay-brown when moist, whitish when dry. 3–7cm in diameter. Convex then expanding to nearly flat. Margin incurved at first, with tattered remnants of veil sticking to it. Cuticle smooth, often slightly sticky. Flesh white, medium thick. *Gills:* at first whitish to yellowish-grey, then brownish or rusty. Adnexed, rounded behind, broad with scalloped edges. Very crowded. *Stipe:* rather slender, usually straight, sometimes slightly swollen at the base, 5–8cm long. Whitish, becoming streaked brownish, mealy or smooth, with small, hanging, membranous ring at apex. Flesh yellow-brown. *Spores;* cigar-brown in mass, smooth ellipsoid, with obvious germ-pore, average size 9.5 × 6.0 microns.

Habitat and distribution

Grows singly or in groups in grassy places in woods, under hedges, on

lawns and in gardens. Common in Europe, north eastern North America and South Africa.

Occurrence

May to July, especially after rain.

Culinary properties

Tastes and smells of oatmeal, not highly rated, use caps only.

Agrocybe semiorbicularis

Fruiting body *Cap:* hemispherical becoming convex, yellowish to pale tan, about 2.5cm across, smooth. *Gills:* becoming cinnamon, adnate, crowded. *Stipe:* slender, 6–7.5cm long, lacking a ring, yellowish, smooth and shining, tough.

Ecology Among grass in pastures and by roadsides. Common in

Europe and North America. Early summer to autumn.
Edible.

Amanita aspera

Fruiting body *Cap:* fuscous brown to pallid dirt-brown, densely covered with small, yellow, conical warts. *Gills:* white and sometimes yellow. *Stipe:* base enlarged and covered with warts, yellow above ring and grey below.

Ecology Solitary in deciduous and conifer woodlands. Uncommon in Europe and North America. Autumn.
Poisonous.

Amanita caesarea
CAESAR'S MUSHROOM

Also known as the Royal agaric or Orange amanita, *Amanita caesarea* was highly prized by the Greeks, and by the Romans who called it *Boletus*. A poisoned dish of these mushrooms was used to murder Claudius Caesar, and afterwards Nero used to joke about *Boleti* being the food of the Gods. Great care must be taken to identify this species correctly when gathering it for food, as it can easily be confused with *Amanita muscaria*. It can be recognized by its smooth wart-free cap—though the distinctive warts of the *muscaria* species may be washed off by rain—and by its yellow gills and stipe. It is sold in French markets.

Fruiting body

Cap: bright red or orange, fading to yellow. 10–15cm in diameter. At first hemispherical, becoming flat with a slight hump in the centre. Margin distinctly striate. Cuticle smooth. Flesh white, yellow or orange beneath the cuticle. *Gills;* yellow, free. *Stipe:* parallel-sided or tapering upwards from the slightly swollen base, 12.5–20.5cm long, 2cm thick at the base. Yellow, with darker patches, smooth above the conspicuous, yellow, membranous ring, scaly below. Base enclosed in a large, loose, ovoid, bag-like volva, with a short, secondary volva within. *Spores:* white in mass, ellipsoid, smooth, average size 12.0 × 8.5 microns.

Habitat and distribution

Often forms large rings, occasionally grows in troops, on sandy soil in coniferous woods, sometimes in beech woods. Variable in Europe, locally common south of the English Channel, occasional in the south of North America.

Occurrence

July to September, sometimes October.

Above: Amanita caesarea
Top: Agrocybe semiorbicularis
Far left: Agrocybe praecox
Bottom: Amanita aspera

Culinary properties
Tastes and smells pleasant. Can be cooked by any method, making a very delicate dish. It is highly recommended.

Amanita citrina
FALSE DEATH CAP
The white form of this species, sometimes called var. *alba*, is a very dangerous mushroom, because it can easily be confused with the deadly poisonous *Amanita phalloides* and *A. virosa*. It should never be gathered for food.

Fruiting body
Cap: lemon-yellow, with white or greyish-white patches. 5–9cm in diameter. Hemispherical then flat. Cuticle smooth, shining when dry, with membranous remnants of veil sticking to it. Flesh white, often with a yellowish line beneath cuticle.

Right: Amanita citrina
Top centre: Amanita eliae
Top right: Amanita gemmata
Bottom, right: Amanita fulva
Bottom, centre: Amanita excelsa

With sulphuric acid applied, there is no change. *Gills:* white, cut away next to the stipe, crowded. *Stipe:* tapers upwards from the distinctly bulbous base, 7–8cm long, 8–12mm thick. White, lined above the soft, flaring ring, smooth below with a globular volva, the free edge forming a gutter around the top of the basal bulb. *Spores:* white in mass, subglobose, smooth, in iodine they turn blue-black, average size 9.5 × 8.0 microns.

Habitat and distribution
Grows on light sandy soils, in deciduous or coniferous woods, especially under beech and oak. Common in Europe, widespread and frequent in North America.

Occurrence
July to November in Europe, September to November in North America.

Culinary properties
Smells of raw potato when broken. Inedible due to its disagreeable taste, it is said by some to be poisonous.

Amanita eliae
Fruiting body *Cap:* campanulate to umbonate, 4–13cm diameter, tawny to greyish-ochre, slightly viscid, volva with a few white to yellowish patches. *Gills:* white, free. *Stipe:* slightly enlarged at apex, 10–13cm long, slender, white to tawny, squammulose below the ring.
Ecology Woods and downs beneath trees. Rare. August to October.
Edibility unknown.

Amanita excelsa
Fruiting body *Cap:* rounded, margin entire and without striae, grey to brown, with soft, flattened grey warts. *Gills:* white, crowded, sometimes slightly decurrent. *Stipe:* stout, swollen at base, with a large white striate ring towards the top.
Ecology Solitary in both deciduous and conifer woods. Frequent in Europe. June to October.
Edible but easily confused with the highly dangerous *Amanita pantherina*.

Amanita gemmata
Fruiting body *Cap:* yellow, smooth, slightly viscid, with scattered white warts. *Gills:* white or pale ivory. *Stipe:* white, base bulbous, with thin white ring near top.
Ecology Under Douglas Fir and other conifers and some deciduous trees. Europe and North America. Autumn in America and spring to winter in Europe.
Probably poisonous and as it may hybridise with *Amanita pantherina* it should be carefully avoided.

Amanita fulva
Fruiting body *Cap:* red-brown, smooth, with regularly and deeply grooved margin. *Stipe:* whitish, ring absent, base surrounded by a loose volva. Closely resembles the less common *Amanita vaginata*.
Ecology Deciduous woods and heaths, especially under birch. Common in Europe. May to November.
Edible (excellent).

Amanita muscaria
FLY AGARIC

This brightly coloured, attractive species—the storybook toadstool—is one of the easiest to recognize. It is poisonous, but its appearance is normally so distinctive that it could not be gathered in mistake for an edible species. However, the warts on the cap may be washed off by rain. The primitive tribes of North East Asia chewed *Amanita muscaria* as an intoxicant, very much as we use alcohol. Since mediaeval times, at least until the last war, it was used as a fly-killer, either broken up in milk or the whole cap sprinkled with sugar. Ibotenic acid, one of the toxins present in this species, is a mild insecticide. Practitioners of homeopathic medicine dispense it as a powder, or as a tincture made from the fresh fungus. Fly Agaric is a favourite food of reindeer. In North America, the cap colour varies according to the area in which it grows. The variety *alba*, a white form, is found in the coniferous forests of Michigan, whereas in the east the caps are yellow to orange, and in the west, blood-red. Unexpanded fruit bodies are wholly creamy-white and could be mistaken for puffballs. It would, therefore, be wise to cut open each one to check before cooking. In Australia and South Africa it is found only under the pines which were introduced from Europe, and probably arrived as mycelium on their roots.

Fruiting body

Cap: colour variable yellow to orange to scarlet, with white or yellowish patches. 10–17cm in diameter. At first hemispherical then convex. Margin striate in mature specimens. Cuticle slightly slimy, moist, with fluffy patches of veil sticking to it. Flesh white, yellow under cuticle, soft. With sulphuric acid turns light brown. *Gills;* white or tinged cream, free, broad, edges minutely toothed, crowded. *Stipe;* slightly tapering upwards from the bulbous base, 15–27cm long, 3–4cm thick. White, lined above the prominent, soft, torn membranous ring. The basal bulb with several concentric warty rings. Flesh white, webby in the centre or hollow. *Spores:* white in mass, ovoid, smooth with a distinct projection at one end, in iodine they turn blue-black, very variable, average size 10.3×8.0 microns.

Habitat and distribution

Grows gregariously, sometimes in rings, under birch, less frequently under conifers. Widespread and common in Europe, North America, South Africa, Australia and New Zealand.

Occurrence

August to November in Europe, June to October in North America.

Culinary properties

Smells of earth or of rape-cole seed. Poisonous, but is fatal only when a large quantity is eaten. It contains much less muscarine than the poisonous *Clitocybe* and *Inocybe* species. Its principal toxins are ibotenic acid and muscimol which are intoxicants, causing nausea, followed by sleepiness, and a feeling of elation on waking. The recommended antidote is drinks of tea or coffee, never alcohol.

Amanita ovoidea

Fruiting body *Cap:* white, 10–30cm across, margin not striate, surface without warts. *Stipe:* white, cylindrical, powdery surface.

Ecology In groups in conifer and deciduous woods. Southern Europe. Edible, with the gills being more tasty than the flesh.

Amanita pantherina
THE PANTHER

Many deaths in Europe have been caused by this dangerous fungus. In North America it is the most common poisonous species west of the Rocky Mountains. It may be picked in error for the edible *Amanita rubescens*, but it can be distinguished by the larger white warts on its cap, and the lack of red stains where bruised.

Fruiting body

Cap: smoky-brown, darker in the centre, with an olive tinge in young specimens, decorated with white or cream patches. 5–8cm in diameter. Convex, soon becoming flat. Margin curved at first, striate. Cuticle slimy at first, then dry, with the warty remains of the veil sticking to it, especially in the centre. Flesh white, with potassium hydroxide it turns dark brown. *Gills:* shining white, free, curved, blunt at margin, narrowed next to the stipe, crowded. *Stipe:* tapers upwards from swollen base, 6–10cm long, 1–2cm thick. White, smooth, with a white, thick-edged ring, which soon becomes free. Base bulbous, with the remains of the volva in the form of 2–3 concentric hoops. Flesh white, firm, solid. *Spores:* white in mass, ovoid, smooth, with a small projection at one end, average size 11.0×9.5 microns.

Habitat and distribution

Found in deciduous woods, especially under birch, in coniferous woods in mountainous areas, in glades, on heaths. Widespread and frequent in Europe and North America, frequent in South Africa under trees imported from Europe.

Occurrence

August to October.

Culinary properties

Poisonous, often deadly. It contains muscarine in a much higher concentration than *Amanita muscaria*. Symptoms start after about three

Top, left: Amanita muscaria
Below: Amanita pantherina
Bottom: Amanita ovoidea

hours and include vomiting, diarrhoea, hallucinations, finally coma and sometimes death. One or two grains of atropine, given orally in a tincture, or, in extreme cases, an injection of atropine sulphate is the prescribed treatment.

Amanita phalloides
DEATH CAP

This is the most poisonous fungus known to man. All parts of the fruit body, even the spores, are poisonous, and its virulence is little affected by time. Specimens several years old have been found to be actively poisonous. If even one specimen becomes mixed with other toadstools gathered for food, they should all be discarded. Hands must always be washed after handling it. The common poisonous North American *Amanita* is the species *brunnescens*, which is very similar to the Death Cap, but has a more fragile volva and a sharply rimmed bulbous base to its stipe, which stains brown when handled. The Death Cap can also be confused with two other poisonous Amanitas, the *virosa* and *bisporigera* species. In South Africa, the Cape Death Cap (*A. capensis*) which is also deadly, is similar, but is never green; the cap is always whitish-buff to creamy, and it grows under oaks from August to October. Death Caps can easily be picked in mistake for the edible *A. citrina* species which grows in the same places.

Fruiting body

Cap: colour varies from light yellow to greenish-brown, with faint black radiating streaks. 7–12cm in diameter. At first ovoid or bell-shaped, becoming flattened. Cuticle slightly slimy when wet, smooth, rarely with a few remnants of the veil sticking to it. Flesh white, greenish beneath the cuticle. With sulphuric acid flesh and gills turn pinkish-lilac. *Gills:* white, may be tinged with green. Free or joined to the stipe by a line, crowded. *Stipe:* tapers slightly, upwards from the large basal bulb, 8–12cm long. Light greenish-yellow to pure white, smooth or minutely scaly, with a large white or pale green pendulous ring at the apex. The bulbous base is enclosed in a white, torn, bag-like volva *Spores:* white in mass, ovoid, smooth, with a short, stout projection at one end, in iodine they turn blue-black, average size 9.5 × 8.0 microns.

Habitat and distribution

Grows singly or gregariously, occasionally in rings, in deciduous woods, especially under beech and oak, in coniferous woods in moun-

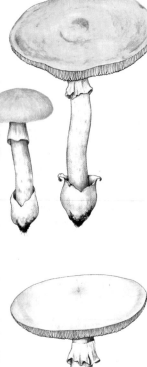

Above: different stages of growth of the extremely toxic Amanita phalloides
Far right: Amanita rubescens
Centre: Amanita porphyria

tainous areas, in pastures bordering on woods. Variable in Europe, becoming more common towards the south, locally abundant in North America and South Africa where it grows under oaks imported from Europe. It occurs in New Zealand.

Occurrence

July to October in Europe and North America, March to July in South Africa.

Culinary properties

Smells faint, nauseous in old specimens. Deadly poisonous, containing at least two groups of toxins, phallotoxins and amanitins. Phallotoxins react quickly, after six or twelve hours, causing stomach cramps, excessive vomiting and dehydration. They are destroyed partly by cooking and by the digestive juices. The amanitins react slowly, after 24 to 48 hours and usually after the victim has recovered from the initial symptoms, causing jaundice, coma, convulsions and finally death. In the past the chances of recovery from *Amanita phalloides* poisoning were slim, and depended mainly upon the general health and resistance of individual victims. Even now, there is no guaranteed antidote or method of treatment.

Amanita porphyria

Fruiting body *Cap:* smokey-brown tinged with violet, smooth. Convex. *Stipe:* base bulbous, surrounded by a loose, unequal volva. **Ecology** Coniferous woods, especially in mountainous areas. Frequent in Europe and North America. August to October.
Inedible.

Amanita rubescens
THE BLUSHER

The poisonous *Amanita pantherina* has often been picked in mistake for this species, with disastrous results. The Blusher can always be distinguished by its flesh which turns red when it is cut. It is highly recommended by some mushroom lovers, but it would seem wise not to gather it for food unless one is sure of its identification. In Europe and America it is particularly prone to attack by fly maggots and slugs, but in South Africa it does not become infested. This is probably

because it was introduced into that country in the roots of trees, but without the pests.

Fruiting body

Cap: colour varies from pale brownish-buff to dull reddish-brown, with off-white patches. 7–12cm in diameter. Long remaining convex, finally becoming flat. Margin slightly striate. Cuticle slightly slimy at first or when wet, with the remains of the veil, as soft, easily separable, mealy patches when wet, but smaller, harder, more closely adhering warts when dry. Flesh white, reddens when cut, thin, soft, with sulphuric acid there is no change. *Gills:* white, becoming spotted with red in old specimens. Narrowing towards the stipe, attached to it by a tooth, crowded. *Stipe:* tapers upwards from the swollen base, 6.5–10cm long, 12–25mm thick. White, becoming flushed with red from the base up. Slightly striate above the white, membranous ring. The volva in the form of warty scales at the base. Flesh white, red where cut or damaged by insects. *Spores:* white in mass, ovoid, smooth, with a distinct projection at one end, in iodine they turn blue-black, average size 9.6 × 6.6 microns.

Habitat and distribution

Grows singly, or scattered, sometimes in large groups. In deciduous and coniferous woods, in hedges, on heaths, in pastures. Common in Europe, North America east of the Mississippi and South Africa. It is found in Australia.

Occurrence
July to October, sometimes November in Europe, July to September in North America, April to October in South Africa.

Culinary properties
Tastes sweet at first, then astringent. Indigestible when raw, harmless when cooked. Caps are best fried in hot butter and then sprinkled with salt and pepper. Adds flavour to a dish when a single cap is quartered and mixed with bland-tasting fungi. Only young specimens should be gathered for food. These must be cut to check the flesh reddens before cooking.

Amanita solitaria
Fruiting body *Cap:* whitish to greyish cap, numerous small conical warts, margin fringed with remains of veil, 7–16cm in diameter. *Gills:* greenish-yellow. *Stipe:* with striate membranous ring, base enlarged and covered with scales.
Ecology In woods on calcareous and neutral soils. Southern parts of Europe and south-eastern North

America. Warm, dry summers. Edible but cuticle has unpleasant flavour and should be removed.

Amanita vaginata
GRISETTE
In many ways, this species resembles the deadly poisonous *Amanita phalloides*, the only marked difference being its lack of a ring. Therefore, great care must be taken to identify it correctly when gathering it for food. Close inspection is also recommended to ensure that each specimen is free from slugs. A white variety with exquisite flesh, var. *nivea*, grows in the Alps

and other mountainous regions. This toadstool is sometimes attacked by the parasitic fungus, *Volvariella surrecta*.

Fruiting body
Cap: pale ash-grey, sometimes darker and decorated with white patches in the centre. 4–8cm in diameter. At first ovoid or bell-shaped, soon becomes flattened with a central hump. Margin grooved, finely toothed. Cuticle at first slimy, sometimes with fragments of veil adhering at the centre. Flesh white, thin, fragile. *Gills:* white, free, broad, crowded. *Stipe:* rather slender, cylindrical, or narrowing towards the top, 12–15 cm long, 1–2cm thick. White to pale grey, almost smooth, minutely mealy, scaly. Base inserted deep into the ground, surrounded by a grey, bag-like, sheathing volva. *Spores:* white in mass, almost spherical, smooth, in iodine they turn blue-black, average size 11.3 × 10.3 microns.

Habitat and distribution
Grows singly or is scattered in deciduous woods, especially beech, under conifers in mountainous areas, on heaths, shady lawns. Common in Northern Europe, becoming rare towards the south. Widespread and common in North America, it also occurs in New Zealand.

Occurrence
July to October.

Culinary properties
It is said by some to be superior in flavour to *Agaricus campestris*, but others describe it as mediocre and fit only for cows. It should not be eaten raw. The flesh is very fragile

and collections of this species should be kept separate from larger fungi.

Amanita verna
Fruiting body *Cap:* rounded then flat, pure white, viscid, margin not striate. *Gills:* free, white. *Stipe:* tall, slender, striate above ring, powdery below ring, base bulbous.

Ecology In both conifer and deciduous woods. Europe and North America. Found in spring, hence its common name of the Spring Amanita, and also in autumn. Poisonous.

Amanita virosa
DESTROYING ANGEL
This wholly white, poisonous, toadstool, is much less common in Europe than *Amanita phalloides*. The deadly poisonous North American species *Amanita bisporigera*, is very similar, differing only in having two spores on each basidium instead of four. Young specimens could be gathered in mistake for *Agaricus campestris* and *A. arvensis*, with which it grows, but it can be distinguished by its persistently white gills, its bulbous base and volva.

Fruiting body
Cap: white, 5–9cm in diameter. Convex, often with a slight central hump. Margin ragged. Cuticle slimy, shining, smooth. Flesh white, with potassium hydroxide it turns yellow, with sulphuric acid it turns light pink. *Gills:* white, free, narrow, edges ragged, crowded. *Stipe:* may be slightly eccentric, slender, cylindrical upwards from a basal bulb, 10–15cm long. White, with a white frayed ring near the apex. Surface

Left : Amanita vaginata
Far left: Amanita solitaria
Below: Amanita verna
Bottom: Amanita virosa

split longitudinally forming scales. The base surrounded by a white, bag-like volva. *Spores:* white in mass, almost spherical, average size 11.3 × 10.3 microns, in iodine they turn blue-black.

Habitat and distribution
Grows singly or is scattered, on poor soil in deciduous woods, in coniferous woods in mountainous areas. Uncommon in northern Europe and northern North America.

Occurrence
August to October.

Culinary properties
Smells sweetly musty. Deadly poisonous, causing symptoms similar to those caused by *Amanita phalloides.*

Armillaria mellea
HONEY FUNGUS
This most destructive of all tree parasites is said to be most virulent in badly drained soils where tree roots are poorly developed. In North America, it causes widespread damage to oak trees. It also attacks gooseberry, red and blackcurrant bushes, vines, privet hedges, tea plants, hops, tomato plants, carrots, parsnips and rhubarb. A common cause of decay in mines, it can be found attacking pit props far below ground level, and also invades and blocks water pipes, often growing in running water, but always originating from rotten timber.

The spores of this species germinate on damp rotten wood, usually old stumps. Living trees are attacked by long, black, cord-like rhizomorphs, which spread from host to host. These rhizomorphs,

Below: Armillaria mellea
Below, right: Armillaria ponderosa

which inspired the name Bootlace Fungus, can apparently penetrate sound bark, or enter through cracks at wounds of the main roots, or where the roots join the trunk. In the tree a root rot develops which may lead to the premature death due to wind blow. The fungus can eventually spread to the trunk causing a soggy yellow or brown butt rot, which finally becomes white and fibrous. Only the base of the tree is affected in this way, and the sound timber higher up the trunk can be salvaged when it is felled. Rhizomorphs are often found in the absence of fruiting bodies, and until the connection between them was recognized they were given separate names.

Decayed wood permeated by the living mycelium of this fungus emits a glow which is known as bio-luminescence. In olden days when trees were worshipped by man, the possession of a luminous root was thought to increase the owners creativity, even to the extent of enabling him to produce gold by magic. This belief may have given rise to the idea of magic wands.

Armillaria mellea can be mistaken for *Collybia illudens,* a similar bio-luminescent species which is poisonous when raw. The Honey Tuft, as this species is sometimes called, has a strong, spicy flavour which upsets some people, so it would seem wise to try small amounts when eating it for the first time. Experts recognize at least two different varieties of this very variable species. *Armillaria tabescens,* which is superficially similar except that it lacks a ring, was once thought to be a variety, but is now regarded as a separate species.

Fruiting body
Cap: yellow to brown, covered with small, brown flecks when young. 5–15cm in diameter. At first convex, then flattened and eventually depressed in the centre. Margin at first with tufts of brown or black hairs, becoming smooth, striate when old. Cuticle at first velvety due to small curved scales which soon disappear, except in the centre. Flesh whitish, spongy. *Gills:* white at first, finally flesh colour. Adnate, but arched and can be slightly decurrent, rather distant. *Stipe:* parallel-sided or swollen at the base, 7.5–15cm long, 1–1.2cm thick. Whitish above the thick, yellow ring, below, yellow darkening downwards. Flesh firm and fibrous outside, soft or hollow in the middle. *Spores:* cream in mass, ellipsoid, smooth, average size 8.5 × 5.5 microns.

Habitat and distribution
Grows in tufts or large clusters, occasionally singly, on old deciduous or coniferous stumps, on the roots of living trees, shrubs and root vegetables, and on structural timber. Common in all temperate and tropical countries.

Occurrence
July to December.

Culinary properties
Has a rather strong taste and a bitter smell which disappears when cooked. It is rather tough and coarse, so only the caps from succulent young specimens should be used. Gentle cooking in an open pan is recommended to allow the smell to dissipate. It is also very good chopped and used in patties and croquettes. It dries well but in Italy the caps are preserved in vinegar, salt and oil. The Swiss use it as a condiment because of its strong taste.

Armillaria ponderosa
AMERICAN PINE MUSHROOM
The American Pine Mushroom is closely related to *Matsu-take,* the famous Japanese pine mushroom. Matsu-take hunting is one of the most remarkable customs of Japan, being cited in Japanese art and poetry. *Armillaria ponderosa* is gathered on a commercial scale by the Japanese residents of the northwestern United States. It is a very large fungus, often camouflaged by the pine-needles and sand grains which stick to its slimy cap.

Fruiting body
Cap: at first white or pinkish-buff, finally becoming tawny. 8–20cm broad. Uneven, convex, becoming flat. Margin with persistent remains of veil. Cuticle smooth, fibrillose, slimy when wet, shiny when dry. Flesh white, thick, firm. *Gills:* white

to buff, liver-brown where bruised. Cut away next to the stipe, becoming free, 8–12mm broad, crowded. *Stipe:* parallel-sided or tapering towards the base, 10–15cm long, 2–4cm thick. Coated by veil, buff to tawny below the ample, membranous, fluted ring. White and mealy above. Liver-brown where bruised. *Spores:* white in mass, broadly ellipsoid, smooth, with a central oil drop, average size 5.5 × 4.0 microns.

Habitat and distribution
Grows singly or gregariously, sometimes in tufts, on sandy soil in open coniferous woods. Locally abundant in North America, west of the Rocky Mountains.

Occurrence
October to December.

Culinary properties
Tastes agreeably spicy. It is recommended when roasted or boiled, but it tends to loose its flavour when dried or stored in salt.

Left: Bolbitius vitellinus
Below, left: Armillaria tabescens
Bottom: Boletinus cavipes

Armillaria tabescens
Fruiting body *Cap:* convex then expanded, 3–10cm in diameter, with dense, erect hairs in the centre, dry, yellow to reddish-brown. *Gills:* somewhat decurrent, pinkish to brownish, broad. *Stipe:* tall up to 20cm long, joined at base to other stipes, white near apex darkening to brown at base.
Ecology Forms dense clusters at the base of deciduous trees and around stumps. Parasitic on oaks in North America. Common in Europe and North America. Summer and autumn.
Edible provided it is cooked.

Bolbitius vitellinus
YELLOW COW-PAT MUSHROOM
This is a delicate species with a distinctive yellow cap, found on horse and cow dung.

Fruiting body
Cap: bright yellow, becoming paler with age, especially on the margin. 1–5cm in diameter. At first bell-shaped, then expanded and flat, sometimes slightly umbonate. Slimy and striate at first, drying, leaving cap margin radially grooved and often split. Flesh yellowish and very thin. *Gills:* ochreous-clay colour, with white edge when young, becoming rusty-cinnamon with age. Narrowly adnate, broad compared with thickness of flesh. Crowded, spreading as cap expands. *Stipe:* slender, tapering upwards, 6–12cm long, 2–4mm thick. Straw-yellow to whitish, sometimes with a powdery down, often translucent shining. Flesh pale-yellow, very fragile, finally hollow and collapsing. *Spores:* rust-colour in mass, smooth, ellipsoid with distinct germ-pore, 13.3 × 8.0 microns.

Habitat and distribution
Found on manured grass, sand dunes, in parks, on lawns, compost and rotting wood. Uncommon in Europe, North America, South Africa and Venezuela.

Occurrence
August to November in Europe, May to July in North America.

Culinary properties
No distinctive taste or smell, not recommended.

Boletinus cavipes
Fruiting body *Cap:* convex to umbonate, felty-scaly or fibrillose-scaly, yellow-brown to tawny-brown, margin shaggy. *Pores:* honeycomb-like, lemon-yellow becoming greenish, somewhat decurrent. *Stipe:* lemon-yellow and with a network above the ring, darker below, hollow, with thick, white floccose ring.
Ecology In groups under larch. Common in North America and southern Europe. Autumn.
Edible.

Boletus appendiculatus
Fruiting body *Cap:* red to brown, slightly downy, then smooth. *Pores:* lemon-yellow becoming greenish-yellow, blueing where touched. *Stipe:* barrel-shaped, lemon-yellow with bright yellow network, no ring. *Flesh:* pale lemon-yellow with sometimes a slight flush of blue.
Ecology Under oak and other deciduous trees. Southern Europe and North America. Edible.

Boletus aerus
Fruiting body *Cap:* date-brown to almost black when mature, minutely downy, dry. *Pores:* almost free, finally dark sulphur-yellow, vinaceous when bruised. *Stipe:*

Top: Boletus appendiculatus
Centre: Boletus calopus
Far right: Boletus aerus
Bottom: Boletus chrysenteron
Below: Boletus edulis

whitish, with brown network above and rusty network below, widest at the midpoint and tapering above.
Ecology Under deciduous trees especially oak, beech and chestnut. Uncommon in California and southern Europe, rare in the south of England. Autumn. Edible (good).

Boletus calopus
Fruiting body *Cap:* whitish-grey, finally olive. Minutely downy, becoming cracked when old. *Stipe:* swollen, red with conspicuous network. *Taste:* bitter. Similar to the poisonous *B. satanas.*

Ecology In deciduous and coniferous woods, especially under beech and oak. Widespread, locally frequent in Europe and north-eastern North America. August to November.
Inedible.

Boletus chrysenteron
RED-CRACKED BOLETUS
This common, very variable fungus is usually distinguishable by the red cracks on its cap. It is sometimes made unrecognizable by an attack of the parasitic fungus *Hypomyces.* This is not one of the better edible Boletes.
Fruiting body
Cap: reddish-brown, tinted olive, often cracking to show reddish

flesh. Less frequently paler and distinctly ochreous, flushing red or red-coral. 4–12cm in diameter. Convex then flattened. Cuticle downy at first, then smooth and breaking up into irregular patches resulting in a giraffe skin pattern. Flesh yellowish, red below cuticle, turning light blue when cut, finally fading to reddish-buff. With ammonia, potassium hydroxide or ferrous sulphate flesh turns grey-olivaceous. *Tubes:* sulphur-yellow finally tinted greenish. Up to 8mm long, depressed around top of stipe. *Pores:* yellow, finally dirty olive, slowly turn green where bruised. Large angular and unequal. *Stipe:* slender, swollen in middle, often curved, 4–8cm long, 10–15mm thick. Yellow at the top, flushed reddish below with more or less conspicuous, red, woolly granules. Flesh reddish-buff to yellow, turns light blue in base when cut. *Spores:* dark-olive, snuff-brown in mass, smooth, ellipsoid to spindle-shaped, average size 13.5 × 5.5 microns.
Habitat and distribution
Common in deciduous woods, especially oak, on mossy banks, in hedges and by sides of roads. In Europe, North America, Australia and South Africa.
Occurrence
August to November in Europe, July to September in North America.
Culinary properties
Slight taste and smell, tubes and stipe must be removed before cooking.

Boletus edulis
THE PENNY BUN or CEP
This is perhaps the most frequently eaten of all fungi in Europe. It has been appreciated since Roman times when, as a dish, it was chosen to conceal the poison which murdered many prominent Romans. When dried, it was thought to have many medicinal uses, such as the removal of freckles and blemishes.

Soaked in water, it produced a salve for dog bites. Dried fungi are used commercially to make packet mushroom soups. Attempts have been made to cultivate it, but no satisfactory techniques have yet been evolved for commercial production. Dried, it is richer in protein than any other dried vegetable except nuts. Bohemian lumberjacks have great faith in its capacity to prevent cancer.

Fruiting body

Cap: very variable, brownish to dark brick-colour, whitish at first, 6–20cm in diameter. Hemispherical, convex, then nearly flat. Cuticle at first hoary but this is gradually lost, becoming smooth as cap expands, remaining as a white line on the margin. Flesh at first compact, then soft, white, reddish under cuticle, unchanging. Very slight reaction with ammonia, potassium hydroxide or ferrous sulphate. *Tubes:* white becoming greyish-yellow. Up to 2cm long, depressed around stipe and nearly free. *Pores:* white to pale yellowish-green, when mature sometimes flushed dirty rust colour on margin, not bruising bluish. Small and round. *Stipe:* stout, may be bulbous, club-shaped or cylindrical, 3–23cm high, 3–7cm thick, 11cm thick at base. Pale-brown to white, minutely downy at base. Top half with network of slightly raised (white) veins. Flesh solid, firm, white or yellowish. *Spores:* deep olive-snuff-brown in mass, smooth, ellipsoid to spindle-shaped, average size 15.5 × 5.0 microns.

Habitat and distribution

Common in coniferous and deciduous woodlands, hedges, clearings, on sandy soil or on ground in mountainous forests. Many varieties are recognized, usually associated with different trees. Europe, North America especially the Rockies, Australia and South Africa.

Occurrence

August to November in Europe, July and August in North America.

Culinary properties

Tastes sweet and nutty, smells pleasant. The tubes may be removed before cooking. Sliced and dried it is available throughout the year.

Boletus erythropus

Fruiting body *Cap:* dark-brown, with a yellowish margin, blue-black where bruised. *Pores:* orange-red, small, blue when touched. *Stipe:* densely dotted with orange-red.
Ecology In deciduous or coniferous woods, along woodland paths and nearby pastures. Frequent to common in Europe and N. America. August to November
Edible.

Boletus fragrans

Fruiting body *Cap:* pale umber to purplish-chestnut, velvety, uneven shape. *Pores:* lemon-yellow, faintly blue when bruised. *Stipe:* apex yellow, central area reddish and base white, fusiform, with buried base, 7–9cm tall. *Flesh:* lemon-yellow except for reddish tinge immediately beneath cap surface, on exposure to air turning blue very slowly, taste mild.
Ecology In deciduous woods, especially in mountain areas. Rare, in continental Europe.
Edible.

Boletus impolitus

Fruiting body *Cap:* cinnamon or pale brown, at first with greyish down, becoming smooth, dry. Flesh unchanging when cut or bruised. *Stipe:* stout, yellow-ochre, dotted red at apex, streaked dark rusty-brown at base, which smells of iodoform when cut.
Ecology On clay soils, on sides of tracks, in deciduous woods, especially under oak. Variable in Europe, becoming more common towards the south. Rare in north-eastern North America. June to October.
Edible (excellent).

Boletus lupinus

Fruiting body *Cap:* at first pale brown becoming grey-olivaceous with a flush of red at maturity, turning blue when bruised, up to 20cm diameter. *Pores:* lemon coloured, red at maturity, small. *Flesh:* white to pale lemon colour, turning blue when cut. *Stipe:* cylindrical or somewhat bulbous, orange above with red central zone and coral or lemon-yellow below. Similar to the poisonous *B. satanas.*
Ecology Under oak and other deciduous trees. Europe.
Inedible.

Top: Boletus erythropus
Above: Boletus fragrans
Below, left: Boletus impolitus
Below, right: Boletus lupinus

Top: Boletus luridus
Far right: Boletus piperatus
Centre: Boletus parasiticus
Bottom: Boletus pinicola

Boletus luridus

This is a puzzling species because, although it can be poisonous, it is eaten in parts of France. This variability may be a product of local soil and climatic conditions. It would seem prudent not to eat it.

Fruiting body

Cap: olive-brown varying to almost reddish. 8.5–12cm in diameter, convex, narrow margin, free and incurved when young. Cuticle at first minutely-downy, becoming smooth and polished. Flesh thick yellowish, purple-red above tubes, turns blue when cut. With ammonia, turns buff or ochre with potassium hydroxide turns yellow or brick-red, with ferrous sulphate turns yellow then greenish-yellow and with Meltzer's reagent turns blue-black. *Tubes:* yellowish-green, becoming blue when cut. Up to 1.5cm long in large specimens. Free and barely reaching the stipe. *Pores:* orange-red, bruising dark blue, small. *Stipe:* usually stout, cylindrical, 8–14cm long, 1–3cm thick. Yellowish, often flushed orange at the top, becoming more red and darker downwards, covered by a red network. Base black, with yellow, root-like mycelium. Flesh reddish, turns blue on exposure to air. *Spores:* olive to brownish-olive in mass, smooth, ellipsoid to spindle-shaped, average size 13.0 × 5.5 microns.

Habitat and distribution

Found in deciduous woods and parks, especially under beech and oak, on calcareous soils. Can be found in coniferous woods in mountainous areas. Common in parts of Europe, widespread in North America and Australia.

Occurrence

August to November.

Culinary properties

Tastes and smells pleasant. Opinions vary as to the toxicity of this species. It contains muscarine, but the amount present varies greatly with environment. Unpleasant and sometimes dangerous symptoms are produced if alcohol is taken within twenty-four hours after eating this mushroom.

Boletus parasiticus

Fruiting body *Cap:* olive to yellowish-brown, minutely downy, becoming cracked. Irregularly convex. *Stipe:* slender, curved, grows around and beneath host.

Ecology Grows parasitically on the fungus *Scleroderma aurantium* which occurs on peaty soil, under birch. Uncommon in Europe, very rare in north-eastern North America. September to October.
Inedible.

Boletus pinicola

Fruiting body *Cap:* brown, date or chestnut coloured but almost black in centre, greasy at first then dry and downy, margin undulate. *Pores:* small, white and then green or olivaceous, with rusty spots at mouths. *Stipe:* red or buff at apex, chestnut to cinnamon below, covered in a white or dark cinnamon network. *Flesh:* whitish, becoming deep vinaceous in cap and stem cortex.

Ecology Under pines and other conifers and some deciduous trees. Rare in Europe. June to October. Edible.

Boletus piperatus
PEPPERY BOLETUS

This common species is remarkable in that it grows in both coniferous and broad-leaved woods. It has an unpleasant smell and can be distinguished by its brilliant yellow stipe base and strong peppery taste.

Fruiting body

Cap: yellowish-brown to cinnamon. 2–6cm in diameter. Initially convex then expanding and flattened. Cuticle slightly greasy or slimy, but soon dry, then becoming smooth and shining. Flesh yellow to cinnamon-brown, flushed red under cuticle and above tubes. With either ammonia, potassium hydroxide or ferrous sulphate flesh turns leaf-green. *Tubes:* cinnamon then rust, sometimes darkening when handled, slightly decurrent. *Pores:* coppery-reddish when mature. Angular, rapidly widening with age. *Stipe:* slender spindle-shaped, tapered downwards to almost pointed base, 4–7.5cm long, 2–20 mm thick. Cinnamon or pale-rust except for bright-yellow base and mycelial tuft. Smooth, silky shiny, but dotted at very top when fresh. Flesh solid, yellow, tinted reddish at the top. *Spores:* snuff-brown in mass, smooth, ellipsoid to spindle-shaped, average size 9.5 × 3.5 microns.

Habitat and distribution

Grows in sandy coniferous woods, birch scrub, mixed birch and pine woods and under beeches. Frequent to common in Europe, very common in North America. Has been recorded in South Africa.

Occurrence

August to November.

Culinary properties
Inedible due to its peppery taste.

Boletus pulverulentus
Fruiting body All parts turn blue when handled. *Cap:* colour variable, dark dull brown to milky-coffee, flushed red, olive or purplish. *Pores:* lemon-yellow. *Stipe:* tapers towards the base, yellow at apex shading to reddish-brown at the base.
Ecology Deciduous woods, especially under oak, chestnut, in glades, along paths, in gardens. Sometimes under exotic conifers. Variable in Europe, becoming more common towards the south. August to November.
Edible.

Boletus queletii
Fruiting body *Cap:* colour variable, reddish-brown to brick-red, dry, at first minutely downy. Flesh immediately turns greenish-blue when cut. *Pores:* rusty-brown, turn blue-black when bruised.
Ecology In deciduous woods, especially under beech, oak, lime. Rare in Europe, becoming locally common towards the south. August to October.
Inedible.

Boletus satanas
DEVIL'S BOLETUS
This is a rather rare, poisonous species, very similar to the more common *Boletus calopus*, *B. erythropos*, *B. lupinus* and *B. luridus*, but found under beeches and oaks on limestone and chalk. When mature it quickly decomposes to a putrescent mass.
Fruiting body
Cap: pale, almost white with an olivaceous buff or pale hazel flush, margin frequently very faintly flushed red. Finally flushed with ochre when old. 8–12.6cm in diameter. Convex, margin free, broad and strongly incurved. Cuticle at first minutely downy then smooth and leathery, except for minute cracks which may form at centre. Flesh pale straw or saffron turns dirty ochraceous with ammonia or potassium hydroxide. *Tubes:* yellowish-green quickly turning dark olivaceous blue on cutting, fading to greenish-grey, up to 2cm long, free. *Pores:* red, then blood-red when mature, remaining orange towards cap margin. Turn greenish when touched, small and round. *Stipe:* very stout, sometimes bellied, 6–9cm long, 5–6cm thick. Yellow at apex, red with ochre flush at base, netted with red throughout or towards the top when the base is minutely flecked with red. Flesh persistently dirty buff in lower part of stipe. *Spores:* olivaceous snuff-brown in mass, ellipsoid-spindle shaped, smooth, average size 13·0 × 5.5 microns.
Habitat and distribution
Grows characteristically in calcareous, deciduous woodland in southern temperate regions of Europe and North America. Locally frequent, but rare in many regions.
Occurrence
July to October.
Culinary properties
Poisonous but not deadly. Early symptoms involve nausea, vomiting and diarrhoea, normal health is usually restored in one or two days. Muscarine has been isolated from the flesh of this fungus.

Far left: Boletus pulverulentus
Left: Boletus satanas
Below: Boletus subtomentosus

Boletus subtomentosus
Fruiting body *Cap:* hazel to olive-brown, dry, downy, cracking to expose yellowish flesh. With ammonia cap turns chestnut. *Stipe:* tapers towards the base, pale brick-colour, occasionally with faint longitudinal ribs.
Ecology In deciduous woods. Common in Europe and North America. August to November. Edible.

Boletus versicolor
Fruiting body *Cap:* red to vinaceous, wavy margin, 3–6cm diameter. *Pores:* angular, lemon-yellow becoming green with age, blue when bruised. *Stipe:* slender and very long, up to 7.5cm, red except for the apex which is yellow. *Flesh:* buff to straw-coloured in cap, lemon-yellow in stipe apex, red and brown below, slowly turning blue when exposed.
Ecology Among grass beneath deciduous trees. Frequent in Europe. Edible.

Calocybe gambosum
SAINT GEORGE'S MUSHROOM
This is one of the earliest mushrooms to appear in the spring. Hence in parts of France it is known as the Spring Mushroom. It can

Below, left: Boletus queletii
Below: Boletus versicolor

usually be found for the first time each season, on or around Saint George's Day (23 April). It is highly regarded by enthusiasts, and is gathered and eaten on a large scale in China. The poisonous *Inocybe patouillardii* which has a pungent fruity smell could be mistaken for this mushroom so care must be taken when collecting it.

Fruiting body

Cap: creamy to whitish-buff, finally becoming pale tan. 5–15cm in diameter. Convex at first, then flattened. Margin at first incurved and downy, finally wavy and bent back. Cuticle smooth, but with drop-like spots, finally widely cracked. Flesh white, thick, soft, fragile. *Gills:* white to pale buff, rounded behind or with a decurrent tooth, finally wavy. Up to 5mm broad, crowded. *Stipe:* stout, curved, more than 5cm long, 1.3–2.5cm thick. Creamy to whitish-buff, smooth, downy at the apex. Flesh solid and firm. *Spores:* white in mass, ellipsoid, smooth, with a central oil drop, average size 6.3 × 3.8 microns.

Habitat and distribution

Grows singly, in clusters, or in large rings, in open grassland, pastures, beside hedges and in woodland clearings, especially on calcareous soil. Occasional to frequent in Europe, rare in north-east North America.

Occurrence

April to June in Europe, June to July in North America.

Culinary properties

Tastes and smells of newly-ground meal, some say it should not be stewed, but all enthusiasts agree that it is delicious when first sautéed and then cooked in a wine sauce.

Top, right:
Catathelasma imperialis
Centre: Cantharellula
umbonata
Far right: Clitocybe
cerrussata
Below: Calocybe
gambosum

Cantharellula umbonata

There is a great deal of resemblance between this species and the true Chantarelle with which it used to be classified. The moss among which it grows is usually closely covered with white mycelium, making it difficult to pick, without also removing a clump of moss.

Fruiting body

Cap: grey to black, paler on the margin. 3–4cm in diameter. At first convex, becoming shallowly funnel-shaped, with a central nipple. Cuticle hairy to cottony, shining (seen through a lens). Flesh soft, white, bruising red. *Gills:* shining white at first, finally with reddish spots. Decurrent, blunt-edged, repeatedly branching in pairs. *Stipe:* parallel-sided, sometimes wavy, 2.5–12.5cm long. Pale grey, hairy at the base. Flesh elastic. *Spores:* white in mass, ellipsoid to spindle-shaped, smooth, in iodine turn blue-black, average size 9.0 × 3.0 microns.

Habitat and distribution

Grows gregariously, in coniferous woods, among moss and heather, especially on gravelly acid soils. Occasional in Europe and North America.

Occurrence

September to November in Europe, August to October, sometimes in spring in North America.

Culinary properties

Not recommended for any form of consumption.

Catathelasma imperialis

Fruiting body *Cap:* up to 40cm in diameter, viscid, cracking from the centre, olive-brown to chestnut colour. *Gills:* buff to olive-grey, decurrent, closely packed, frequently forked. *Stipe:* tapering to base, up to 8cm wide, yellowish, with double ring from partial and universal veils.

Ecology In groups under conifers. Europe and north-west North America. Summer and autumn.
Edible but generally considered rather indigestible.

Clitocybe cerussata

Fruiting body *Cap:* at first convex then somewhat infundibuliform, white as if whitewashed, becoming tinged with flesh colour, margin fissured. *Gills:* whitish, somewhat decurrent. *Stipe:* rooting, no ring.

Ecology In clusters on debris from deciduous trees. Europe. Poisonous.

Clitocybe clavipes

This species is superficially similar to *Clitocybe nebularis* but it differs in its darker colours, and its slender nature. The base of its stipe is swollen and is rather like the base of a young onion plant. It is highly regarded by enthusiasts, but old specimens are often spoilt by slugs.

Fruiting body

Cap: grey-brown, with a slight olive tinge, margin often white. 4–7cm in diameter. Slightly umbonate at first, finally depressed in the centre. Cuticle smooth. Flesh greyish-white, soft, thick in the centre. *Gills:* white at first, finally pale primrose. Deeply decurrent, rather broad, distant. *Stipe:* narrows upwards from the club-shaped base, 3–7cm long, 2cm thick at the base. Whitish-grey, smooth or slightly fibrillose, hairy at the base. Flesh soft, spongy in the middle, fragile. *Spores:* white in mass, ellipsoid, smooth, average size 6.0 × 3.5 microns.

Habitat and distribution

Grows singly or in groups, on sandy soil in beechwoods and in coniferous woods in mountainous areas. Common in Europe, locally common in northern North America.

Occurrence

September to November in Europe, July to October in North America.

Culinary properties

Tastes and smells pleasant, because of its spongy flesh it does not stew well, but it is excellent when cooked in any other way. This is a winter species usually found on rich loam soil along the margins of woodland rides and paths.

Clitocybe cyathiformis

Fruiting body *Cap:* becoming funnel-shaped with strongly in-

rolled margin, greyish-brown or slate-grey, darker in wet weather. *Gills:* decurrent, paler than the cap, not crowded. *Stipe:* paler than cap, slender, streaked with dark striae, base covered with white down. *Spores:* white.

Ecology Woods and fields among grass and on dead leaves. Common in Europe and North America. Autumn and early winter. Edible.

Clitocybe dealbata

This poisonous fungus grows in grassy places alongside *Marasmius oreades*, from which it can be distinguished by its small size and its persistently white cap and gills. It has been known to fruit in large clusters on mushroom beds after accidental introduction.

Fruiting body

Cap: white or whitish-tan. 2–4cm in diameter. Flattened convex, margin at first incurved, finally spreading, wavy. Cuticle dry, dull, with a persistent bloom. Flesh white, thin. *Gills:* white with a faint tinge of yellow. Slightly decurrent, crowded. *Stipe:* short, thin, sometimes narrowing downwards, 2–4cm long. Whitish-tan, smooth, slightly powdery at the apex. Flesh fibrous, finally hollow. *Spores:* white in mass, ellipsoid, smooth, average size 4.5 × 2.5 microns.

Habitat and distribution

In grassland, lawns, golf links, dunes, pastures, fields, and on heaths. Common in Europe, North America, and Trinidad.

Occurrence

July to November in Europe and North America, September in Trinidad.

Culinary properties

Smells pleasantly of new meal. Poisonous, contains muscarine, is sometimes deadly if eaten in large amounts and should not be eaten on any account.

Clitocybe flaccida
RED-BROWN FUNNEL FUNGUS

This common toadstool sometimes forms very large clusters and is

Far left: Clitocybe clavipes
Centre: Clitocybe cyathiformis
Bottom, left: Clitocybe dealbata
(This specimen not in its usual, grassland habitat)
Below: Clitocybe flaccida

easily gathered in large enough quantities to make a meal. The tawny colour of its wavy, funnel-shaped cap is a distinctive feature which makes identification easy.

Fruiting body

Cap: reddish-leather brown, paler when dry, darkening with age. 5–8cm in diameter. At first convex, becoming funnel-shaped. Margin expanded or turned down, often wavy. Cuticle smooth and shining. Flesh pale tan, thin, fragile, becoming leathery. *Gills:* white becoming yellow or reddish. Deeply decurrent, curved, narrow, crowded, with intermediates. *Stipe:* rigid, curved, becoming compressed, base somewhat rooting, 4–5cm long, 1cm thick. Reddish-leather brown, at first smooth with a woolly base, becoming ridged and bark-like.

Flesh tough, hollow. *Spores:* white in mass, subglobose, minutely prickly (this is best seen by staining the spores with cotton blue) average size 4.3 × 3.5 microns.

Habitat and distribution
Grows singly or in tufts, sometimes in rings, on decaying debris, mainly in coniferous woods but sometimes in deciduous woods. Variable in Europe, becoming more common northwards. Very common in northeast North America.

Occurrence
September to December in Europe, July to October in North America.

Culinary properties
Tastes and smells slightly acidic. Only the caps should be used, as they are tender. Very good when sliced, sautéed and incorporated into a sauce to be served with roast beef. They are also good for pickling and ketchup.

Above: Clitocybe fragrans
Top: Clitocybe geotropa
Bottom: Clitocybe infundibuliformis
Far right: Clitocybe nebularis

Clitocybe fragrans
Fruiting body *Cap:* yellowish-grey, striate margin when moist. Paler when dry. Flat or slightly depressed. *Stipe:* slender, wavy, whitish-yellow. Smells of aniseed.
Ecology Among grass in deciduous woods, especially under alder. In coniferous woods in mountainous areas. Frequent in Europe and north-eastern America. July to November. Edible.

Clitocybe geotropa
This large toadstool is recognized by its funnel-shaped cap which always has a central umbo.
Fruiting body
Cap: pale pinkish-tan, 10—15cm (sometimes up to 20cm) in diameter. At first convex to flat, becoming depressed around a

central umbo. Margin incurved, then finally scalloped. Cuticle smooth. Flesh white, thick and firm. *Gills:* white, becoming pale tan, decurrent, 5mm broad, crowded. *Stipe:* tapers upwards from the base, usually longer than the cap diameter, 5—15cm long, up to 3cm thick. Pale pinkish-tan, fibrillose, downy at the base. Flesh solid. *Spores:* white in mass, subglobose to comma-shaped, smooth, average size 7.0 × 5.6 microns.

Habitat and distribution
Grows singly, sometimes in rings, on damp soil, in clearings in woods and in pastures. Frequent to common in Europe.

Occurrence
September to November.

Culinary properties
Young specimens are improved considerably when sliced and cooked slowly.

Clitocybe infundibuliformis
SLENDER FUNNEL FUNGUS
This neat, pretty species may be

recognized by its pale red colour and by the shape of its cap, which has been likened to a wine glass. It appears soon after the late summer rains.
Fruiting body
Cap: colour varies, yellowish, pinkish-flesh to tan. 4—8cm in diameter. At first convex, becoming funnel-shaped. Margin at first incurved, then wavy. Cuticle usually faintly silky-scaly in the centre. Flesh white, thin except in the centre. *Gills:* white, deeply decurrent, thin, crowded, with intermediates. *Stipe:* tapers upwards from the slightly swollen base, 4—7cm long, 0.6—1.3cm thick. Pale tan, smooth, often with abundant cottony mycelium at the base. Flesh fibrous. *Spores:* white in mass, egg-shaped to comma-shaped, smooth, length variable, average size 6.0 × 4.0 microns.
Habitat and distribution
Grows gregariously, in clusters, sometimes in rings, among deep litter in woods generally, under hedges, in grass on heaths especially in hilly areas. Common in Europe and North America.
Occurrence
July to November.
Culinary properties
Pleasant almond smell. Young caps are tender when cooked well. It is tough and leathery when old.

Clitocybe nebularis
CLOUDED AGARIC
This fungus was popularly known as the New Cheese Agaric because the smell of fresh specimens was reputed to be like cottage cheese. Today it takes its common name from the cloud-grey appearance of its cap and is often called the

Mist Fungus. It is said to be poisonous as its rich, spicy flavour upsets some people. In Europe, however, it is popular as a flavouring to improve mushroom dishes prepared with bland-tasting species. The caps of old specimens are sometimes attacked by the parasitic fungus *Volvariella surrecta*.

Fruiting body

Cap: pale greyish, darker in the centre. 6–15cm in diameter. At first broadly umbonate, finally flattened and slightly depressed in the centre. Margin pliant, soft, often wavy. Cuticle smooth, often minutely powdery. Flesh white, soft, thin at the margin. *Gills:* whitish, then pale yellowish-grey, slightly decurrent, thin, crowded. *Stipe:* stout, tapering upwards from the slightly club-shaped base, 7–15cm long, 2–3cm thick. Very pale grey, striate. Flesh solid, becoming spongy in the centre. *Spores:* white to cream in mass, ellipsoid, smooth, average size 6.0 × 3.8 microns.

Habitat and distribution

Grows gregariously, sometimes forming large tufts or clusters, in woods generally, especially under conifers, on heaths, or in gardens. Common in Europe, locally common in north-east North America, becoming more rare towards western North America.

Occurrence

August to November, sometimes to December.

Culinary properties

Has a strong aromatic flavour when cooked. It can be difficult to digest, and has been known to cause illness. Highly regarded by enthusiasts, it is excellent stewed and served in a white sauce made from the stock, or fried in egg and breadcrumbs. Some say it should be blanched in water for two minutes before cooking.

Clitocybe odora
FRAGRANT AGARIC

Two or three caps of this delicious toadstool are all that are needed to flavour an uninteresting dish. It has a distinctive colour and an attractive spicy smell, resembling that of aniseed.

Fruiting body

Cap: pale blue-green, fading with age or when dry. 4–8cm in diameter. Flattened, umbonate, irregularly lobed. Cuticle moist in wet weather, silky when dry. Flesh greenish, rather thick, soft. *Gills:* pale greenish, adnate, broad, rather crowded. *Stipe:* swollen at the base, 2.5–4cm long. Flushed blue-green. Flesh elastic, rather tough. *Spores:* white in mass, ellipsoid, smooth, average size 6.8 × 3.6 microns.

Habitat and distribution

Grows in clusters or solitary in the litter of deciduous woods, and among the needles of coniferous woods in the north and in mountainous areas. Common in Europe and North America.

Occurrence

August to November in Europe, August to September in North America.

Culinary properties

Smells strongly of aniseed. It is used mainly as a flavouring for less highly flavoured species. Its smell is preserved by drying. Dried specimens can be chopped or ground up for use in soups and stews.

Clitocybe rivulosa

It is possible to gather this dangerously poisonous species in mistake for *Marasmius oreades* which grows in similar places. *C. rivulosa* can be distinguished by its white cap and decurrent gills. In the past cases of poisoning used sometimes to be treated, in spite of strong opposition, with oral doses of atropine which is an alkaloid extracted from *Atropa belladonna* (Deadly Nightshade). Extreme cases would be given injections of atropine sulphate.

Fruiting body

Cap: dull white to pale pinkish-tan, concentrically zoned. 2–4cm (sometimes 5cm) in diameter. Flat to slightly depressed in the centre.

Margin incurved at first, then spreading and becoming wavy. Cuticle at first with a powdery bloom then becoming smooth. Flesh white, thin, firm. *Gills:* white, finally very pale flesh colour. Slightly decurrent, broad, very crowded. *Stipe:* short, thickish, often twisted, 5cm long, 2–5cm thick. Whitish to pale tan, fibrillose, downy at the apex. Flesh tough, elastic. *Spores:* white in mass, ellipsoid, smooth, average size 4.5 × 2.5 microns.

Habitat and distribution

Grows in troops or in rings, in short grass, on lawns, in pastures, on heaths, by roadsides and in clearings in woods. Common in

Above, left: Clitocybe odora
Below: Clitocybe rivulosa

Europe, uncommon in North America.

Occurrence

August to November.

Culinary properties

Poisonous, sometimes deadly. Contains considerable concentrations of muscarine, which has a pronounced effect on the sympathetic nervous system, causing, copious sweating, asthmatic breathing, double vision, slowing of the heart beat, low blood pressure and cold hands and feet. It also causes stomach cramps, vomiting and diarrhoea. In mild cases the symptoms subside quite quickly, but in an extreme case the victim may lapse into a coma and die from respiratory collapse.

markings, size 12.0 × 5.5 microns.

Habitat and distribution

Grows singly, scattered, sometimes in rings, on the ground in woods, pastures, mature sand dunes. Common in Europe, locally common in north-east North America.

Occurrence

July to November in Europe, June to October in North America.

Culinary properties

Tastes and smells of new meal. The flesh is always tender, very good in stews, patties and croquettes, and raw in salads with mayonnaise or French dressing. A popular Victorian way of serving this species was with minced beef, and it was also used to improve the flavour of vol-au-vents.

Above: Clitopilus prunulus
Top, right: Collybia confluens
Right: Collybia butyracea

Clitopilus prunulus
SWEET-BREAD MUSHROOM

Young specimens of this fungus can easily be mistaken for the poisonous species *Clitocybe rivulosa*. It is variable in appearance, but can be recognized by its strong mealy smell. It is a favourite with enthusiasts, French peasants call it *mousseron* meaning mushroom.

Fruiting body

Cap: white or greyish-white. 3–8cm in diameter. At first convex, finally depressed, irregular. Margin mealy, incurved, finally lobed. Cuticle dry, smooth, slimy when wet. Flesh white, soft. *Gills:* pale cream at first, then dirty pink. Deeply decurrent, narrow, crowded. *Stipe:* usually eccentric, short, narrowing downwards, 2.5–5cm long, up to 1cm thick. Greyish-white, striate, somewhat downy. Flesh solid. *Spores:* salmon-pink in mass, spindle-shaped with very fine longitudinal

Collybia butyracea

Fruiting body *Cap:* reddish-brown when moist, greyish-brown when dry. Drying from margin inwards. Convex with slight central hump. *Stipe:* tapers upwards from downy, white, swollen base. Cartilaginous.

Ecology In deciduous and coniferous woods, especially in mountainous areas. Common in Europe, north-eastern North America and south-eastern Australia. Reported from S. Africa. January to December. Edible (caps only).

Collybia confluens

Fruiting body *Cap:* convex or bell-shaped, then flattened, reddish-brown to flesh coloured, thin, tough, up to 5cm diameter. *Gills:* free, crowded, narrow, whitish or flesh coloured. *Stipe:* pinkish to reddish, 5–10cm tall, with dense covering of hairs.

Ecology In dense clusters among fallen leaves and other debris in both deciduous and conifer woods. Common in Europe and North America. Summer and autumn. Edible but not recommended.

Collybia dryophila

This common species grows under oak trees in Europe and under pines in the southern United States. Deformed fruiting bodies, with supernumerary caps growing on the gills, are sometimes produced when it forms very dense tufts.

Fruiting body

Cap: yellowish, with a brown centre. 2–5cm in diameter. Convex, then flat, sometimes depressed in the centre. Margin at first incurved, then flat. Cuticle smooth, with a buttery feel when wet. Flesh white, thin, rough. *Gills:* white, finally tinged yellow. Rounded behind, sometimes free, narrow, crowded. *Stipe:* hollow, parallel-sided above the slightly swollen, rooting base, 2.5–7cm long. Yellow or reddish-brown, smooth, downy towards the base. Flesh cartilaginous. *Spores:* white in mass, ellipsoid, smooth, average size 5.5 × 3.0 microns.

Habitat and distribution

Grows gregariously, sometimes in large dense tufts, in deciduous woods especially under oaks, and amongst heather in mountainous areas. Common in Europe and in

especially spruce. Common in Europe. September through to May. Edible.

Collybia fusipes
SPOOL FOOT
The fruiting bodies grow to form tufts from variously-shaped black structures, which in turn are attached to tree roots. These black structures are amalgamated stipe bases which have become enlarged and covered with a thick, black rind. This species causes a white rot in infected trees. In the past old specimens were used as a laxative.
Fruiting body
Cap: dark red, becoming reddish-brown to liver-coloured, sometimes with black spots when old. 3—8cm in diameter. Convex then umbonate, often deformed and irregular. Cuticle smooth, dry, sometimes splitting. Flesh pale reddish-brown, firm. *Gills:* white, finally pale reddish-brown. At first joined into a ring around the stipe, soon becoming free. Tough, pliant, broad,

connected by veins, distant. *Stipe:* hollow, spindle-shaped, longitudinally grooved and twisted, with several joined at the base, 7.5cm or more long, 1.3—2.5cm thick. Red-brown often purplish-brown at the base. Flesh fibrous, cartilaginous. *Spores:* white in mass, ellipsoid to pip-shaped, smooth, average size 5.0×2.8 microns.
Habitat and distribution
Grows singly, usually in tufts, at the base of oak and beech trees. Common in Europe, locally frequent in north-east North America.
Occurrence
April usually May to December in Europe, August to after frosts in North America.
Culinary properties
Use young caps only, they can be

cooked by any method, and are especially good in gravy, soups and chutney. They dry well.

Collybia maculata
SPOTTED TOUGH SHANK
The fruiting body of this toadstool quickly becomes covered in red-brown spots and streaks. It has been known to produce several layers of gills in tiers surrounding the stipe.
Fruiting body
Cap: white at first, but soon becoming spotted reddish-brown, finally cream with red blotches. 8—13cm in diameter, convex, then flat. Margin strongly incurved at first. Flesh white, firm, tough. *Gills:* cream, becoming spotted with red.

Top, left: Collybia dryophila
Bottom, left: Collybia esculenta
Centre: Collybia fusipes
Below: Collybia maculata

Rounded behind, sometimes free, narrow often with toothed edges, very crowded. *Stipe:* long, slightly swollen in the middle, narrowed downwards to the rooting base, 5—16cm long, 0.5—2cm thick. White, becoming streaked red-brown, striate or longitudinally furrowed. Flesh fibrous. *Spores:* pink in mass, subglobose, smooth, average size 5.0×4.0 microns.
Habitat and distribution
Grows in troops, sometimes in clusters, in forests, especially under beech, sometimes under conifers and on heaths. Frequent to common in Europe, locally frequent in North America.
Occurrence
July to November in Europe, September to after frosts in North America.
Culinary properties
Tastes slightly bitter, smells pleasant, the caps are good when stewed.

Collybia peronata
WOOD WOOLLY-FOOT
The prominent woolly outgrowths at the base of the stipe give this fungus its specific name, *peronata*,

mountainous areas in North America, where it grows abundantly in southern pine forests in rainy weather during the winter.
Occurrence
May to November in Europe, June to December in North America, October to November in Trinidad.
Culinary properties
It is delicious when fried in egg and breadcrumbs.

Collybia esculenta
Fruiting body *Cap:* convex then flat, ochre coloured or pale yellow, margin striate, moist to touch. *Gills:* white becoming pale yellowish, adnexed, crowded. *Stipe:* 2—7cm tall and up to 0.5cm wide, white then same as cap, base long rooting.
Ecology On cones of conifers,

which means 'booted'. It is a litter decomposer and when specimens are picked they are usually found to be attached by mycelium to several dead leaves.

Fruiting body

Cap: yellowish to reddish-brown. 2–5cm in diameter. Convex, then flat. Margin striate. Cuticle often wrinkled, finally pitted. Flesh yellowish, at first pliant, then leathery to membranous. *Gills:* yellow at first, then reddish-brown. Rounded next to the stipe, finally free. At first crowded, distant in old specimens. *Stipe:* tapers slightly upwards, finally compressed, curved at the base, 5–7cm long. Yellowish to brownish-yellow, woolly-hairy at the base. Flesh fibrous, finally hollow. *Spores:* white in mass, ellipsoid to pip-shaped, smooth, average size 8.0 × 3.5 microns.

Top: Conocybe tenera
Below: Collybia peronata
Bottom: Coprinus atramentarius

Habitat and distribution

Grows singly, sometimes in clusters, troops or arcs, on leaf litter, in both deciduous and coniferous woods. Common in Europe and North America.

Occurrence

August to November in Europe, August to September in northern North America, June to December in the south.

Culinary properties

The acrid taste is removed by cooking, it makes a highly flavoured and delicious dish. In parts of Europe, it is dried, crushed and used as a flavouring.

Conocybe tenera
BROWN CONE CAP

This small, fragile species has a world-wide distribution and is common on manured grass.

Fruiting body

Cap: dull ochre-brown when wet, paler when dry. 1–3cm in diameter. Conical, usually not striate, or only when wet. Smooth, when dry. Flesh yellowish, thin and fragile. *Gills:* cinnamon, curving upwards, adnate, rather narrow, crowded. *Stipe:* tense and straight, narrowing

upwards from a small basal bulb, 8–10cm long, 1–1.5cm wide. Honey-colour, finally tinged rusty from spores. Powdered at apex, faintly striate. Flesh slightly reddish, hollow and fragile. *Spores:* dark rust-colour in mass, smooth, ovoid with a distinct germ-pore, variable, average size 11.0 × 6.5 microns.

Habitat and distribution

Grows scattered or in groups among grass in pastures, woods, gardens or by roadsides. Sometimes on dung heaps. Common in Australia, South Africa, Europe and North America.

Occurrence

May to December in Europe, May to September in North America.

Culinary properties

Old specimens have a hot spicy smell, not recommended.

Coprinus atramentarius

This edible species grows in dense clusters in grass always near trees. If alcohol is taken at the meal where this mushroom is eaten a series of unpleasant symptoms will result. The poison causing this is identical to antabuse, a drug which is used in the treatment of alcoholism.

Fruiting body

Cap: dirty pale-brownish, with a greyish bloom which readily rubs off. 3–7cm high, 5–8cm in diameter when expanded. Oval then bell-shaped or conical. Radially grooved almost to disc, scaly towards the centre. Margin irregularly notched and lobed, splitting when the cap expands. Flesh thin, greyish. *Gills:* at first white then black and dissolving. Free, up to 1cm broad, cottony on the edge, crowded. Cap remains conical throughout spore discharge, gills are kept apart by long sterile outgrowths projecting from hymenium ends attached to opposite gill. *Stipe:* elongating, tapering upwards, leaving a ring-like zone at the slightly swollen base. 10–15cm long, 1–2cm thick. Silky white to very light brown, with small upward pointing scales below the ring. Readily separates from cap. *Spores:* black in mass, smooth, ellipsoid, average size 9.0 × 5.5 microns.

Habitat and distribution

Grows in clusters or gregariously in fields and gardens, in rich soil in waste places, often by the sides of ponds, has even been found bursting through asphalt, also in old stumps. Probably always originating from rotten wood. Common in

Europe and North America, especially after rain. It has also been recorded in Cape Province, South Africa and occurs in New Zealand.

Occurrence
August to December.

Culinary properties
Tastes delicate, best cooked slowly in a covered dish or it will loose flavour. They can also be sliced raw and served with salad. Must be eaten when young, before auto-digestion starts. If eaten with wine or other alcoholic drink, in a short time the face and sometimes other parts of the body become flushed purplish-red, this may recur to a lesser degree at the next meal if alcohol is drunk again.

Coprinus cinereus
Fruiting body
Cap: at first whitish-brown, becoming greyish-brown with whitish scales at the centre, finally slimy, margin striate, conical. *Stipe:* slender with a swollen, deeply rooting, base.
Ecology Produces successive crops on dung, manure heaps, rotting straw. Common in Europe and North America. January to December.
Edible, but must be cooked at once.

Coprinus comatus
SHAGGY INK CAP
This tall, shaggy fungus of open grassland and disturbed ground is found frequently in urban areas and is sometimes commonly called Lawyer's Wig. The *Fungi Candidi* of Roman literature, it was described by Pliny as closely resembling the apex of a 'Flamen's cap' (soldier's helmet). The black fluid produced by autodigestion can be boiled and strained and used as ink. It is an officially recognized species offered for sale in French markets,

where it is regarded as one of the most savoury of all the fungi.

Fruiting body
Cap: at first white, becoming ochraceous and even darker with age. 5–12cm high, at first cylindrical then expanding below, becoming bell-shaped, margin splits as cap expands. Cuticle with overlapping large shaggy woolly scales. Flesh white, thin except at centre. *Gills:* progressively white, pink, black and autodigesting producing a black liquid. Free, up to 12mm broad, very crowded. Flanges on the edge of each gill, keep them apart and allow effective spore discharge. *Stipe:* erect, slender, slightly narrowing upwards from a bulbous base, 10–15cm high, 12–17mm thick. It elongates as the spores mature. White and slightly fibrous with a conspicuous although soon disappearing white ring quite low down. *Spores:* black in mass, smooth, ellipsoid, very variable in size, average 12 × 8 microns.

Habitat and distribution
The typical gregarious species of waste land, rubbish-tips and road-sides, it is common throughout Australia, New Zealand, South

Africa, Europe, North America and Venezuela. Specimens have been known to force a way through the surface of hard tennis courts constructed on old rubbish tips.

Occurrence
April to November.

Culinary properties
A delicately flavoured fungus, it must be eaten before the cap expands and while the gills are still white. It is good raw in salads, stewed slowly in a covered dish or baked in a hot oven.

Coprinus disseminatus
TROOPING CRUMBLE CAPS
When found in large numbers, often more than a thousand may be on and around a single stump. It has been compared to a crowd of elfin children with identically-cut hair. A very short-lived species, lasting only 24 hours and fruiting after rain, it spreads from rotten stumps to surrounding soil or even nearby walls or pavements by means of a network of brownish-red mycelium, the tough strands of which can grow to a great length.

Fruiting body
Cap: yellowish or whitish, becoming grey or greyish-brown. 1cm in diameter, 5–10mm high. At first ovoid then becoming hemispherical and grooved almost to the centre. Flesh very thin and membranous. *Gills:* white, then grey, finally black. Adnate, rather broad and distant. *Stipe:* short, slender, often curved, 2–3cm long, 0.5–1mm thick. White, at first minutely hairy (seen through a lens). Flesh fragile, hollow. *Spores:* black in mass, ellipsoid, smooth, with a germ-pore, average size 9.5 × 4.5 microns.

Habitat and distribution
Grows in large, dense tufts, on and around the rotten stumps of deciduous trees, especially willows. Common in Europe, North America and Australia and New Zealand.

Top: Coprinus comatus
Far left: Coprinus cinereus
Below: Coprinus disseminatus

Occurrence
May to November in Europe, May to October in North America.
Culinary properties
Tastes mild, no distinctive smell, it cooks away almost to nothing, producing a delicious stock.

Coprinus lagopus
BONFIRE INK CAP
This extremely delicate and attractive edible species is difficult to gather in sufficient quantities to be worth cooking.
Fruiting body
Cap: white, then grey with apex

Right: Coprinus lagopus
Far right: Coprinus picaceus
Below: Coprinus micaceus

becoming date-brown or buff. 0.5–2cm high, 1–3.5cm in diameter. At first cylindrical bell-shaped or rarely conical, then expanding and becoming split, torn and revolute at the margin. Cuticle conspicuously hairy, the hairs soon partly greyish and falling off. Flesh white or greyish, rather thin. *Gills:* white then brown to violaceous black, hardly autodigesting finally withering, looking like low ridges as the cap margin turns back. Free, crowded, finally remote from the stipe. *Stipe:* straight and rather slender, greatly elongating, finally 10–15cm long, white, fibrillosely scaly, hollow, very hairy below. *Spores:* black in mass, subglobose, denticular, size 11.5 × 7.5 microns.
Habitat and distribution
Common, usually solitary or sometimes growing in small groups on the ground in deciduous woods. Europe, North East America and temperate areas of South Africa and Trinidad. It also grows on burnt ground, charred wood or plaster ceilings. Sometimes occurs in the open, but then often smaller.
Occurrence
July to November.

Culinary properties
Flavour attractive but not strong, eaten with enjoyment.

Coprinus micaceus
GLISTENING INK CAP
This common species has a glinting cap and grows in large crowded groups on or near rotten stumps. It is small and thin-fleshed, but is so plentiful that a basket can soon be filled. Its continuous growth on the same spot makes it a reliable source of food.
Fruiting body
Cap: ochre-brown to date-brown, 2–4cm high, 4–6cm in diameter. At first ovate, then bell-shaped, finally expanded. Deeply grooved margin finally almost turned back, wavy. Cuticle at first sprinkled with mica-like particles which quickly disappear. Flesh thin, fragile, pale yellowish. *Gills:* at first white, then pinkish, finally dark brown and dissolving. Adnexed and rather narrow. *Stipe:* slender, hollow, often twisted, 5–7cm long, 4–6mm thick. White, densely covered with short, stiff hairs, at least when young (seen with a lens), then slightly silky. Flesh white, easily splitting. *Spores:* blackish-brown in mass, bluntly lemon-shaped with large germ pore, average size 10.5 × 8.5 microns.
Habitat and distribution
Common in dense clusters on and around stumps of deciduous trees,

in streets, yards, gardens and fields. In Europe, North America, South Africa and Australia.
Occurrence
May to December in Europe, May to September in North America.
Culinary properties
Tastes and smells slight. Is good sliced raw in salads. A very delicate species easily spoiled by over cooking.

Coprinus picaceus
THE MAGPIE FUNGUS
This striking woodland fungus is easily recognized by conspicuous white patches on the dark cap.
Fruiting body
Cap: brown-black, striate up to the disc, with large irregular superficial white patches. 5–8cm high, 5–6cm in diameter. Narrowly oval, expanding to conical, breaks out of white veil leaving it as felty patches on membranous cuticle. Flesh thin and brownish. *Gills:* white, pale brown, finally black, free, up to 10mm broad, inflated, crowded. *Stipe:* finally tall, straight, rather slender

and smooth, tapering upwards from bulbous base, 12–15cm long, 8–16mm thick. White, scaly at the base. Flesh pale or white. *Spores:* black in mass, broadly ellipsoid, apiculate, size 16 × 11 microns.
Habitat and distribution
Found only occasionally, growing singly on rich soil in woods or on decaying trunks and branches. Europe, America and Australia.
Occurrence
September to November (June to August in North America).
Culinary properties
Inedible, tastes strong, acidic unpleasant.

Coprinus plicatilis
Fruiting body *Cap:* membranes, thin and almost translucent, pleated when young, pale margin darkening to brownish centre when mature becoming flattened with outrolled margin. *Gills:* joined to collar around stipe apex, scarcely auto-digesting. *Stipe:* very slender, whitish, brittle. Spores ellipsoid to broad ovoid, average size 11–13 × 6.5–10.5 microns.
Ecology Open grassland and grassy places in woods, roadsides,

on old cow and horse dung and richly manured soil. Common in Europe and eastern North America, reported from Australia. May to November. Edible, although it would probably be difficult to pick sufficient specimens to make a worthwhile meal.

Coprinus radiatus
Fruiting body Small. *Cap:* Grey, with pointed curved scales. At first ovoid, finally with curved back margin. *Stipe:* slender, white, hairy towards the base.
Ecology On recently deposited horse dung. Common in Europe. May to November.
Inedible.

Coprinus sterquilinus
Fruiting body *Cap:* at first white, becoming silvery-grey, with shaggy curved scales. Ovoid becoming flat, margin splitting as cap expands. *Stipe:* slender, with conspicuous ring towards the base.
Ecology On dung or manured ground. Occasional in Europe and north-eastern North America. June to October.
Edible.

Cortinarius albo-violaceus
Fruiting body *Cap:* whitish-lilac, at first bell-shaped, becoming flat with a central hump. *Stipe:* whitish-lilac, sheathed in a white coating from base to cortina.
Ecology On poor soil in deciduous woods. Frequent to common in Europe and north-eastern North America.
Edible.

Cortinarius anomalus
Fruiting body *Cap:* colour variable, brownish or greyish-violet, margin paler. *Gills:* at first deep violet. *Stipe:* club-shaped, apex violet, paler below a ring-like zone.
Ecology Deciduous woods, especially beech, oak or birch. Coniferous woods in mountainous areas. Widespread and frequent in Europe. August to November.
Inedible.

Cortinarius armillatus
This very large, striking species is instantly recognized by the red belts on the stipe. It grows singly, tufted or in rings, in the heaths and forests of more mountainous districts.
Fruiting body
Cap: brick-red when young, later tan-brown. 5–10cm in diameter. Bell-shaped to convex at first, soon becoming flat. Margin at first incurved often with reddish fragments of universal veil clinging to it. Cuticle dry, at first smooth soon fibrillose or scaly. Pale flesh, not very thick and rather spongy. *Gills:* at first pale cinnamon, then deep tan or even bay-brown. Adnate, sometimes with a decurrent tooth, very broad and distant. *Stipe:* tall, slender and slightly club-shaped, 7.5–15cm high, 1–2cm thick at apex up to 3.5cm at base. Pale brown, striate when old. Lower half encircled by 2 to 4 distinct cinnamon-red belts. Flesh dirty yellow. *Spores:* rusty-brown in mass, warty, ellipsoid or lemon-shaped, average size 9.5 × 6.5 microns.
Habitat and distribution
Found among heath vegetation under birches, also in the debris of coniferous forests, especially in the mountains. Is common in Europe, rare in North America but becoming more common northwards.
Occurrence
August to October.
Culinary properties
Tastes and smells mildly of radishes. The flesh is excellent and closely resembles that of *Pholiota squarrosa*.

Top, left: Coprinus plicatilis
Top, centre: Coprinus sterquilinus
Far left: Coprinus radiatus
Centre: Cortinarius albo-violaceus
Bottom, centre: Cortinarius anomalus
Bottom, right: Cortinarius armillatus

Above: Cortinarius balteatus
Above, centre: Cortinarius caerulescens
Above, far right: Cortinarius cinnabarinus
Centre: Cortinarius caesiocyaneus
Below, right: Cortinarius bolaris
Below, far right: Cortinarius cinnamomeus

Cortinarius balteatus

Fruiting body *Cap:* date colour in centre and violet or lilac near margin, floccose, flattened, shining when dry. *Gills:* pallid, then becoming tan, slightly decurrent, crowded. *Stipe:* up to 6cm tall, 3cm wide, whitish, minutely velvety. *Veil:* fibrillose, rust coloured.
Ecology In mixed woods and conifer plantations. Uncommon in Europe. September to October. Edible.

Cortinarius bolaris

Fruiting body *Cap:* cream, densely covered in cinnamon-red, hairy scales. *Stipe:* short, with cinnamon-red streaks.
Ecology Deciduous woods, especially under beech or birch, under conifers in mountainous areas. Occasional in Europe and north-eastern North America. August to November.
Inedible.

Cortinarius caerulescens

Fruiting body *Cap:* blue or violet becoming ochre from the centre, convex, then expanded to flat, 5–10cm diameter. *Gills:* amethyst blue becoming rust coloured, edges

somewhat toothed, *Stipe:* blue then brownish, up to 7cm tall, basal bulb somewhat heart-shaped. *Veil:* filamentous, violet.
Ecology In both deciduous and conifer woods, and on heaths. Europe. Autumn.
Edible but not recommended.

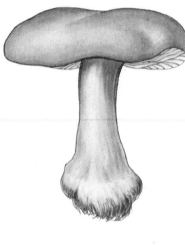

Cortinarius caesiocyaneus

Fruiting body Young specimens wholly pale blue, except white basal bulb at the base.
Ecology On ground in deciduous woods, especially beech, under conifers in mountainous areas. Frequent in Europe and north-eastern North America. August to September.
Inedible.

Cortinarius cinnabarinus

Fruiting body Wholly scarlet-red. *Cap:* at first silky, becoming shiny. Convex, with a slight central hump. *Stipe:* tapers towards the top, with fine longitudinal streaks.
Ecology Singly or in groups on sandy soil in beech woods. Occasional in Europe, frequent in north-eastern N. America, reported from Australia. August to November.
Edible.

Cortinarius cinnamomeus

A very juicy, edible toadstool with a decided but pleasant flavour, great care must be taken to identify it correctly as it is very variable. Characteristically it has a silky yellow-brown cap and yellow, never red, gills.
Fruiting body
Cap: yellowish olive-brown, tinged reddish at centre. 2–5cm in diameter. Convex then expanded and umbonate. Margin at first incurved and joined to top of stipe by yellow web-like cortina; then wavy. Cuticle dry silky scaly with yellowish radiating fibrils, becoming almost smooth. Flesh dirty olive-yellow, thin and fragile. *Gills:* shining yellow, sometimes tinged saffron, then flushing tawny-brown as spores mature. Adnate, rather broad and distant. *Stipe:* slender, tapering upwards, sometimes wavy, finally becoming tubular. 5–10cm long, 4–7cm thick. *Spores:* rusty-brown

in mass, smooth ovoid, average size 6.5 × 4.0 microns.
Habitat and distribution
Common in mossy peaty places in pine or birch woods, or among moss in *Sphagnum* swamps. A frequent species on high mountains. Found in Europe, North America and South Africa.
Occurrence
August to December.
Culinary properties
Tastes and smells mildly of radishes. It is popular in Germany served with sauces as a vegetable. Can also be used sliced in salads.

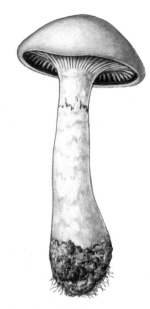

Cortinarius fulgens

Fruiting body *Cap:* orange to rusty-brown, slimy, smooth. Convex, becoming flat. *Gills:* at first yellow. *Stipe:* yellow with dark rusty streaks, towards the depressed basal bulb.

Ecology Deciduous woods, especially beech, under conifers in mountainous areas. Occasional to frequent in Europe, rather rare in north-eastern North America. September to November.
Inedible.

Far left: Cortinarius collinitus
Top, centre: Cortinarius delibutus
Left: Cortinarius fulgens
Below: Cortinarius fulmineus
Bottom: Cotinarius elatior

Cortinarius delibutus

Fruiting body *Cap:* golden yellow to yellowish-brown, slimy. *Gills:* at first bluish-lilac. *Stipe:* club-shaped, slimy, yellowish below faint reddish-violet, ring-like zone.

Ecology In deciduous woods, especially under birch, aspen or beech. In coniferous woods in mountainous areas. Occasional in Europe.
Inedible.

Cortinarius elatior

Fruiting body *Cap:* olive-brown, slimy, margin furrowed up to halfway to the centre. *Gills:* rather thick, transversely veined. *Stipe:* spindle-shaped, whitish, tinged violet or blue, with darker bands towards the base.

Ecology On the ground in deciduous woods. Common in Europe. August to October.
Inedible.

Cortinarius fulmineus

Fruiting body *Cap:* tawny to rusty-tawny, central part of cap with rusty scales, margin golden and incurved at first. *Gills:* golden-yellow to rusty. *Stipe:* golden to tawny-yellow, basal bulb which is sometimes rooting, cortina white or pale yellow. *Flesh:* white becoming yellow.

Ecology In deciduous woods and occasionally under conifers. Uncommon in Europe.
Edible.

Cortinarius collinitus

This very glutinous woodland species usually has dirt and leaf litter sticking to the cap, and therefore has to be peeled before being cooked. It is recognized by this and by the bands of blue scales on the stipe.

Fruiting body

Cap: yellowish-brown, chestnut in the centre. 5–10cm in diameter. Convex, umbonate, shiny when wet, shining when dry. Flesh firm, pale brown. *Gills:* pale then finally misty brown, dusted with spores when mature. Adnate, rather broad. *Stipe:* tall, straight tapering downwards and rooting. 5–10cm long, 6–13mm thick. Yellow-brown with slimy, pale bluish belt-like scales. It is solid, and cracks transversely when dry. *Spores:* rust-brown in mass, ellipsoid, stippled, average size 15.5 × 8.0 microns, length very variable.

Habitat and distribution

Found frequently in coniferous woods, more rarely in deciduous woodland, growing gregariously or in tufts. Widespread throughout Europe and North America.

Occurrence

August to October.

Culinary properties

Strong wood taste and smell, which is subdued by cooking. Do not be put off by its unappealing appearance.

Above: Cortinarius
glandicolor
Right: Cortinarius
largus
Far right: Cortinarius
pholideus
Centre: Cortinarius
orellanus
Bottom, right:
Cortinarius praestans
Bottom, left:
Cortinarius hinnuleus

Cortinarius glandicolor
Fruiting body   *Cap:* dark brown, dry. Convex with a pronounced central hump. *Stipe:* slender, wavy, brown with white, ring-like belt.
Ecology   In bogs, on heaths, especially under birch, alder, sometimes under conifers. Frequent in Europe. September to November. Inedible.

Cortinarius hinnuleus
This very variable species is always recognizable by the white band around the stipe and the strong smell of gas tar.
Fruiting body
Cap: tawny- or yellow-brown when wet, drying paler especially on the edge, variegated with rusty stains when old. 3–7cm in diameter. Broadly bell-shaped at first then expanding to become recurved and umbonate. Margin at length often splitting. Flesh ochre-brown, thin, watery, soft and very fragile. *Gills:* ochre at first then cinnamon, flushing rusty-brown with spores. Adnate, thin with minutely lacerated edges. Distant and often connected by veins. *Stipe:* tall and rather slender, unequal, sometimes curved, 5–7cm long, 4–7mm thick. Slightly paler than cap with a distinct white belt-like zone just above the middle. Flesh soft and very fragile, easily splitting longitudinally. *Spores:* rusty-brown in mass, ovoid, scarcely rough, size 7.8 × 4.5 microns.
Habitat and distribution
Locally common in deciduous, coniferous or mixed woods. Under willows on open dunes, in clearings and in the shade. Europe and northern North America.
Occurrence
August to November.
Culinary properties
Unpleasant smell. Not recommended.

Cortinarius largus
Fruiting body   *Cap:* convex, becoming flat, with slight umbo, date-brown with violet tinge around margin, slightly viscid. *Gills:* blue-grey becoming hazel brown, adnate. *Stipe:* white with violet tints, fibrillose, 6–13cm tall. *Veil:* filamentous, white.
Ecology   In deciduous and pine woods. Europe. Autumn. Edible.

Cortinarius orellanus
Fruiting body *Cap:* orange-tawny, umbonate, dry, with deeper coloured fibrillose scales, margin undulate. *Gills:* tawny and then rust colour, broad, rather sparse. *Stipe:* somewhat wider in the middle, slightly paler than cap, with fibrillar striae. *Veil:* tawny, fibrillose.
Ecology   Under both deciduous and conifer trees. Uncommon in continental Europe and the west coast of North America. August to October.
Deadly poisonous. Very slow-acting toxin affects the kidneys long after the mushroom is eaten.

Cortinarius pholideus
This delicate species can be recognized by the black scales on its cap

and the brown, downy bands on its stipe.
Fruiting body
Cap: hazel-brown with black scales. 3–7cm in diameter. Convex then expanded and umbonate. Cuticle with pointed downy scales from remains of veil. Flesh thin, whitish-brown. *Gills:* at first dirty-lilac, later dark-cinnamon, almost free, broad. *Stipe:* tall, slender, slightly narrowed upwards, 4–10cm long, 5–12mm thick. Faintly lilac at apex, hazel-brownish with concentric brown scales below. Flesh spongy pale brown-white, usually infested with larvae. *Spores:* rust-brown in mass, ovoid, average size 7.8 × 5.5 microns.
Habitat and distribution
Found in groups or tufts under birches, in wet peaty soil, on decaying debris, on very rotten wood, on sandy heaths or moorland. Common in Europe. Locally frequent in northern North America.
Occurrence
August to October in Europe, August to September in North America.
Culinary properties
Tastes and smells mild but not recommended.

Cortinarius praestans
Fruiting body *Cap:* globose when young, becoming convex,

viscid in wet weather, brown with tinge of violet at margin, remains of white universal veil often present on cap. *Gills:* becoming brown, adnate to slightly decurrent. *Stipe:* covered with the remains of the universal veil, becoming ochre colour when mature, base bulbous. *Veil:* at first violet or pale violet, remains adhering to cap margin; striated radially, then deeply grooved.

Ecology Forming rings in birch and oak woods. Not generally found in Europe. September to October. Edible.

Cortinarius semisanguineus

This common, more northerly species is found singly or in clusters on acid soils and identified by the blood-red gills and silky cap and stipe.

Fruiting body

Cap: tawny to cinnamon-yellow, often rich tawny-brown. 2—5cm in diameter. Convex then expanded and umbonate; margin thin often split. Cuticle dry with silky fibrillose remains of cortina sticking to it. Flesh dingy yellowish-brown, thin except in the umbo. *Gills:* at first blood-red, finally tinged rusty-brown. Adnate, broad, often with a wavy edge, crowded. *Stipe:* slender, slightly thickened towards the base, wavy, 3—6cm long or longer if growing in *Sphagnum*. 2—6mm thick. Yellowish-brown with olive brown silky fibrils. Fibrous and solid. *Spores:* rust-brown in mass, smooth ellipsoid, average size 7.8 × 5.0 microns.

Habitat and distribution

Commonly found in coniferous and birch woods, on heaths on sandy soils, and in swamps among *Sphagnum*. Europe and northern North America.

Occurrence

August to November.

Culinary properties

Tastes and smells mild, edible but of little culinary value.

Cortinarius torvus

Fruiting body *Cap:* purple-brown, convex then flattened, with fibrils. *Gills:* very broad, violet then cinnamon brown, thick. *Stipe:* enlarging towards the base, violet at apex, surrounded below with sheath which terminates in a ring just above the middle. *Veil:* white, fibrillose. *Smell:* of fruit or camphor.

Ecology Under beech, or sometimes mixed woods. Infrequent in North America but more common in Europe. Late summer and autumn. Edible but of poor quality.

Cortinarius violaceus

One of the most beautiful autumnal fungi, it is plentiful among moss and ground litter of woods especially in hilly and mountainous districts. Some say it is as crisp and juicy as an apple and one of the best edible Cortinarii.

Fruiting body

Cap: dark violet, 5—10cm in diameter, at first convex with an incurved margin and enclosed in a web-like veil, then expanding to nearly flat. Cuticle covered in a dark woolly down which cracks into scales, at length becoming metallic shining. Flesh rather thick, tinged violet. *Gills:* cap colour when young, turning to brownish-cinnamon when mature. Rounded or deeply notched against the stem, rather thick and broad. Distant and connected by veins. *Stipe:* long, stout and club shaped, 7.5—12.5cm long, 1—3cm thick. Violet with darker fibrillose scales. Flesh solid, violaceous, spongy in the base. *Spores:* rusty-brown in mass, broadly ellipsoid, rough, average size 12.5 × 8.0 microns.

Habitat and distribution

On the ground among pine needles or fallen leaves in coniferous or birch woods, occasionally in beech woods. Locally common throughout Europe, North America and Australia.

Occurrence

August to October.

Culinary properties

Taste and smell similar to the cultivated mushroom; it is eaten everywhere. When cooked, colour becomes quite dark.

Crepidotus mollis

Easily recognized by its soft, pliant horizontal cap with brown gills and spores, this woodland species grows in overlapping tiers on dead trees.

Fruiting body

Cap: cream colour, drying whitish at first, finally pale yellowish-brown. 1—5cm in diameter. Shell or kidney shaped, often with a wavy margin. Cuticle thick and gelatinous. Whitish flesh soft and watery. *Gills:* pale at first then watery-cinnamon, sometimes spotted. Thin, narrow, crowded, often banded. *Stipe:* rudimentary, eccentric lateral and thickly downy, or fruiting body can be without any stalk. *Spores:* snuff-brown, ellipsoid, smooth, average size 8.3 × 5.5 microns.

Left: Cortinarius torvus
Far left: Cortinarius semisanguineus
Below, right: Crepidotus mollis
Bottom: Cortinarius violaceus

Habitat and distribution
Common on the stumps and decaying branches of deciduous trees. Found in south-eastern Australia, South Africa and Europe, rare in North America.

Occurrence
July to November.

Culinary properties
No noticeable taste or smell.

Above: Crepidotus variabilis
Right: Cystoderma granulosum
Top, right: Entoloma clypeata
Bottom, right: Entoloma nidorosum
Below, right: Cystoderma amianthinum
Below: Cystoderma caracharias

Crepidotus variabilis
Fruiting body Small. *Cap:* lies flat on substrate with gills facing upwards. Silky white, minutely downy, fan- or kidney-shaped. *Gills:* at first white, finally pale cinnamon, radiating from a point at one side. *Stipe:* lateral, very short, or absent.
Ecology On twigs, fallen branches of deciduous trees. Common in Europe. January to December. Inedible.

Cystoderma amianthinum
Fruiting body *Cap:* bright yellow to yellow-ochre, radially wrinkled, margin toothed. Finally flat. *Stipe:* slender, ochre, scaly up to inconspicuous ring. *Spores:* turn blue-black in Melzer's iodine.
Ecology On ground in coniferous woods, on heaths, under gorse. Common throughout Europe. August to November.

Cystoderma caracharias
Fruiting body *Cap:* pinkish-beige to flesh colour. Margin finely toothed. Bell-shaped, then flat with small central hump. *Stipe:* pinkish-grey, warty up to the prominent, membranous ring.
Ecology On the ground in coniferous woods. Frequent in Europe. August to November.
Edible.

Cystoderma granulosum
This species can be recognized by the hoary sheen on its granular cap and stipe. It is similar to, and grows in the same places as *Cystoderma amianthinum*, but the latter is smaller and much more common.

Fruiting body
Cap: reddish-brown, fading with age to rusty-yellow or reddish-yellow. 3—6cm in diameter. Convex

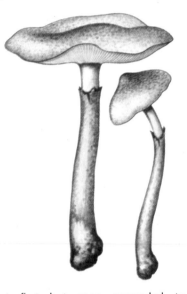

at first but soon expanded to almost flat. Cuticle rough with granular or rough scales giving it a hoary lustre, often radially wrinkled. Flesh thin tinged reddish. Cuticle turns rusty-brown with potassium hydroxide. *Gills:* white to cream-coloured. Rounded behind and usually slightly adnexed. *Stipe:* short and stout, slightly thickened at base, 2—5cm long, 4—8mm thick. Pale red, rather coarsely hairy-granular up to slight, finally disappearing ring, paler and smooth above. *Spores:* white in mass, smooth, ovoid, turn red-brown in iodine, average size 4.3 × 2.8 microns.

Habitat and distribution
Grows gregariously, sometimes in loose tufts, among leaf mould and mosses in coniferous or deciduous woods, and in bogs. Occasional to frequent in Europe, locally common in North America.

Occurrence
August to October.

Culinary properties
Tastes and smells slight. Is fleshy for its size, and of pleasing quality. Stipes must be removed before cooking.

Entoloma clypeata
Experts disagree about the edibility of this fungus and it would not be wise to gather it for food. A stocky toadstool growing in clusters, it is recognized by its streaky, spotted cap.

Fruiting body
Cap: greyish to yellowish-brown, variegated with darker lines and spots. 5—10cm in diameter. At first bell-shaped, becoming flattened and umbonate. Margin wavy, cuticle smooth. Flesh thick and fragile, whitish when dry, dark and translucent when wet. *Gills:* at first pale grey, finally powdered with pink spores, rounded behind, becoming free. Broad with toothed edges, somewhat distant. *Stipe:* rather thick, short, often curved, up to 7cm long, 1—2cm thick. Off-white, becoming ash-grey, fibrillose with a powdery apex. Flesh fibrous, hollow, fragile. *Spores:* salmon-pink in mass, broadly ellipsoid, angular, average size 9.8 × 8.5 microns.

Habitat and distribution
Grows singly or in small clusters, sometimes in rings, on rich soil in gardens and pastures, under briar hedges, in deciduous woods, along footpaths and roadsides. Widespread and frequent in Europe and North America.

Occurrence
April to June in Europe, May to August in North America.

Culinary properties
Tastes indistinct, smells faintly of meal. Said by some to be poisonous, although it is eaten in Europe.

Entoloma nidorosum

Fruiting body Closely resembles *Entoloma rhodopolium*, but differs from that species in having a distinct smell which has been described as of burnt flesh, nitric acid or even ammonia. It can also appear more faded in dry weather.
Ecology On ground under bushes. Widespread in Europe. Poisonous.

Entoloma prunuloides

Fruiting body *Cap:* at first creamy-white, becoming yellow, slightly slimy. Bell-shaped, finally flat with a central hump. *Gills:* at first cream. *Stipe:* short, sometimes curved, white, smooth.
Ecology Grassland, gardens, open woodland. Rare to occasional in Europe and North America. June to October.
Inedible.

Entoloma rhodopolium

Fruiting body *Cap:* bell-shaped then flattened, margin incurved then wavy, hyaline-greyish fading to whitish-brown, streaked with darker spots. *Gills:* white and then pink, sparse. *Stipe:* up to 10cm, white, somewhat striate, apex powdery. *Spores:* yellowish pink.
Ecology Gregarious in deciduous woods, especially beech. Widespread in Europe.
Poisonous.

Entoloma sinuata

Some specimens of this poisonous fungus can be mistaken for *Agaricus campestris*, from which it differs in lacking a ring on its stipe and having pink, wavy gills. It has been responsible for a large number of poisoning accidents in France. The symptoms are unpleasant but healthy adults rarely die as a result of eating this fungus.
Fruiting body
Cap: greyish-tan, often with white areas. 7–12cm in diameter. At first bell-shaped, finally umbonate. Margin inrolled, later becoming wavy and split. Cuticle slightly sticky and shiny in wet weather. Flesh thick, white, firm, brownish under cuticle. *Gills:* at first yellowish, finally pink with yellow edges. Abruptly rounded behind, broad, rather distant. *Stipe:* usually short, stout and curved, 7–15cm long, 2–3cm thick. Silky-white, powdery at the apex. Flesh solid and firm. *Spores:* bright flesh-pink in mass, subglobose, angular, average size 9.5 × 7.5 microns.
Habitat and distribution
Grows gregariously or in small

clusters, in open deciduous woods, especially beech and oak, on field dykes and on cultivated or cleared land. Occasional to frequent in Europe, uncommon in North America.
Occurrence
July to October.
Culinary properties
Tastes indistinct, smells faintly mealy. Poisonous but not deadly, causing headaches, stomach pains, violent sickness and diarrhoea.

Flammulina velutipes
WINTER MUSHROOM

Also known as the Velvet Foot, the bright-yellow cap and dark-brown

Left: Flammulina velutipes
Far left: Entoloma prunuloides
Centre: Entoloma sinuata
Bottom, left: Entoloma rhodopolium

velvety stipe of this fungus makes it easy to recognize. It is a weak parasite, entering the host tree through cracks or injuries. Its mycelium forms a layer under the bark where it does considerable damage, loosening the bark and causing a sapwood rot. It also grows on dead stumps and structural timbers. Capless forms have been found almost a mile below ground level growing on pit-props. It fruits in the winter and although it often becomes frozen, normal growth seems to continue after it thaws out. An Arctic variety, *spongiosa*, has been described from Alaska. The American form of this species is slightly smaller than that found in Europe. In Japan this species is called *Yenoki-take* as it fruits on Yenoki or elm trees. It is highly prized by the Japanese because it appears early in the spring when other fungi are absent.
Fruiting body
Cap: yellow-ochre, with a brownish centre. 2–6cm in diameter, convex, then flattened, often irregular. Margin thin, spreading, often bent back, finally striate. Cuticle powdery when young, becoming smooth and slimy in old specimens. Flesh yellowish, soft, thick in the centre. *Gills:* at first pale cream, finally brownish. Broad, rounded next to the stipe, distant. *Stipe:* tapers downwards from apex, curved, often twisted, 2–6cm long, 0.5–1cm thick. Dark brown, with a yellow, powdery apex, densely velvety. Flesh fibrous, finally hollow. *Spores:* white in mass, cylindric to ellipsoid, smooth, average size 8.5 × 3.5 microns.
Habitat and distribution
Grows in tufts, on stumps, trunks and branches of deciduous trees, on gorse and gooseberry bushes, and on coniferous wood in moun-

tainous areas. Common in Europe and North America, reported from Venezuela and Argentina.

Occurrence
September to March in Europe, January to December, especially after severe frosts in North America.

Culinary properties
Has a strong taste, is best used as a flavouring. It should be peeled before cooking as dirt sticks to the cuticle. Chopped and dried, it makes a good addition to the normal range of kitchen herbs and spices. It is recommended as a base for creamed soups.

Right: Galerina hypnorum
Top: Galerina unicolor
Bottom, right: Gomphidius glutinosus
Below: Galerina paludosa

Galerina hypnorum
Fruiting body Small. *Cap:* yellow, striate almost to centre when wet, brownish-ochre when dry. Almost bell-shaped. *Stipe:* very slender, often wavy. Yellow, flushed rusty-brown towards the base, smooth.
Ecology Woods, heaths, moors, bogs, among moss. Widespread and common in Europe. Occasional in northern North America. July to November.
Inedible.

Galerina paludosa
Fruiting body *Cap:* honey-yellow to reddish-ochre. Bell to cone-shaped, smooth, striate halfway to centre. *Stipe:* slender, wavy. Flaky, rough up to cobwebby ring, which becomes detached early.
Ecology On *Sphagnum*. Occasional to frequent in Europe. May to October.
Edibility unknown.

Galerina unicolor
This is a rather rare species found in conifer woods. It can be recognized by the persistently dark chestnut margin of its cap and by its silky stipe.

Fruiting body
Cap: date-brown with darker striate margin when moist, drying dull ochre-brown from centre outwards. 3–4cm in diameter. At first convex, soon flattened. Margin extending beyond the gills. Cuticle smooth, slimy, shining. Flesh brownish, thin. *Gills:* pale, then brownish-cinnamon, adnate, narrow, crowded. *Stipe:* slender, equal, can be rather tall, up to 7cm long, 2–3mm thick. Pale above thin membranous ring, dark brown with covering of silky fibrils below. Base with white cottony mycelium. *Spores:* brown in mass, smooth, ellipsoid, average size 7.0×5.8 microns.

Habitat and distribution
Often forms tufts on decaying conifer twigs, stumps, or logs. Locally frequent in Europe, Australia and northern North America.

Occurrence
September to November in Europe, spring and autumn in North America.

Culinary properties
No taste or smell recorded.

Gomphidius glutinosus
This fungus forms a mycorrhizal association with conifers especially spruce. It is recognized by the glutinous cap, the blackening bands around the apex of the stipe and yellow flesh in base of stipe.

Fruiting body
Cap: greyish-violet, turning purple-brown, often mottled with black spots, 5–12cm in diameter. Convex and then slightly depressed with age. Very glutinous, strongly streaked towards the pale ochreous undulate margin. Flesh thick, very pale grey, flushing clay-pink especially below cuticle. With ammonia or potassium hydroxide flesh turns a wine-brick colour, and with ferrous sulphate it turns dark green. *Gills:* pale grey at first finally blackish grey. Decurrent, narrow, distant, mucilaginous and easily separable from cap. *Stipe:* short, stout, tapering downwards. 5–10cm long, 1–2cm thick. Apex pale grey with slimy remains of veil which blackens as it dries, grey-brown downwards. Flesh light yellow in the base. *Spores:* sepia in mass, ellipsoid-spindle shaped, average size 18.5×5.8 microns.

Habitat and distribution
Widespread, found under various types of conifers, particularly spruce, but apparently not in native Scots Pine woodland or near larch. Common in Europe and northern North America.

Occurrence
July to November in Europe, June to November in North America.

Culinary properties
No distinct taste or smell, edible, chiefly used for making ketchup.

Gomphidius rutilus
This is a characteristic species of Scots Pine woods. It can be recognized by its dark, waxy gills and by the distinctive shape of its cap. It is not highly regarded as a source of food and is gathered only when there is nothing better available.

Fruiting body
Cap: brown with reddish tinge, Margin yellowish. 3–15cm in diameter. At first bell-shaped, then expanded with a rather pronounced umbo. Margin sticky when moist,

paler and shining when dry. Cuticle at first sticky, soon dry and minutely scaly. Flesh reddish-yellow to pale tan, with ammonia it turns violet, with ferrous sulphate turns dark green, with Meltzer's reagent turns dark violet, with ethanol turns red. *Gills:* at first dull olivaceous, finally sombre black, deeply decurrent, broad, distant, branched. *Stipe:* straight, sometimes narrowed downwards, 6–12cm long, 1–8mm thick. Yellow, streaked purplish, with sticky, cottony remnants of veil forming a ring-like zone at the apex. Flesh yellow, rhubarb-yellow in the base. *Spores:* sombre black to sepia in mass, smooth, ellipsoid to spindle-shaped, average size 18.5 × 6.3 microns.

Habitat and distribution
Grows singly, among moss always under pines, after wet weather. Frequent and widespread in Europe and North America.

Occurrence
July to November, sometimes December.

Culinary properties
Tastes and smells slightly astringent but not unpleasant. Some people find it difficult to digest, it is used mainly in ketchup.

Gymnopilus junonius
This is a very imposing and elegant fungus found in deciduous woods. It is easily recognized by the rich-tawny colour of its cap.

Fruiting body
Cap: golden-brown. 6–12cm in diameter, convex. Margin at first incurved and woolly, sometimes wavy later. Cuticle breaking up into minute, radiating fibrils. Yellowish flesh, firm, thick in centre, thin on margin. *Gills:* at first yellow, then rusty-brown. Adnate with decurrent tooth, narrow, crowded *Stipe:* stout, swollen in middle, tapering into short root at base, 4–12cm long, 7–15mm thick. Slightly paler than cap, with a thin membranous ring close to apex. *Spores:* rusty in mass, rough, broadly ellipsoid, average size 8.5 × 6.3 microns.

Habitat and distribution
Grows in tufts at the base of deciduous trees, and on stumps especially oak. Variable in Europe, becoming more common towards the south-west. Infrequent in North America and Australia.

Occurrence
September to November in Europe,

August to September in North America.

Culinary properties
Inedible, due to the remarkably bitter taste.

Gyroporus castaneus
This is a very neat-looking fungus of deciduous woodland. It is easily recognized by the rough texture of its stipe, by its unchanging flesh, and by its yellow spore print.

Fruiting body
Cap: cinnamon or reddish-brown, darkening with age. 3–10cm in diameter. At first convex, then flat or depressed. Cuticle dry, at first minutely-velvety, becoming smooth. White flesh, firm, brittle up to 1cm thick. Shows no colour change with chemicals. *Tubes:* white becoming creamy-yellow, up to 7mm long, free, depressed around stipe. *Pores:* white, then yellowish, small and rounded. Never bruising blue. *Stipe:* equal or tapering upwards, sometimes slightly swollen midway, 3.7–9.5cm long, 11–30 mm thick. Cap colour, minutely velvety, sometimes irregularly grooved at the top. Flesh sometimes flushed clay-pink. *Spores:* Lemon-yellow in mass, smooth, ellipsoid, average size 9.5 × 5·0 microns.

Habitat and distribution
In glades in deciduous woods, on soil or in moss, especially under oaks. Can be found under conifers in mountainous areas. Occurs frequently in Europe, becoming less common northwards. Widespread and common in North America.

Occurrence
September to November in Europe, June to September in North America.

Culinary properties
Sweetish, nutty taste, pleasant smell. It is delicious raw or cooked.

Left: Gyroporus castaneus
Far left: Gomphidius rutilus
Centre: Gymnopilus junonius
Below: Gyroporus cyanescens

Gyroporus cyanescens
INDIGO BOLETUS

Fruiting body *Cap:* pale ochre with brown velvety down, dry. Flesh turns bright blue when cut. *Pores:* lemon-yellow. *Stipe:* slightly swollen towards the base, tough, finally hollow. *Spores:* lemon-yellow in mass.

Ecology On poor soils, in woods, on heaths, often under birch or spruce, especially in mountainous areas. Uncommon in Europe and eastern N. America. July to Nov. Edible (excellent).

Hebeloma crustuliniforme
FAIRY CAKE MUSHROOM

This is a very variable fungus, which is said by some to be poisonous and is sometimes commonly referred to as 'poison pie'. A very small form, only 1.5–2.5cm in diameter, with broad and crowded gills and a hollow stipe, is found at high altitudes in the Alps.

Fruiting body

Cap: pale watery-tan, sometimes darker in the centre. 3–7cm in diameter. Convex then expanded. Margin inrolled and downy. Cuticle smooth, slightly slimy when moist. Firm whitish flesh, translucent when moist. *Gills:* at first watery-greyish, finally date-brown. Rounded behind, narrow, edges beaded with drops of moisture in wet weather. *Stipe:* short, rather thick, somewhat bulbous, 3–7cm long, 1cm thick. Whitish, coarsely powdered above, sometimes almost down to base. *Spores:* pale brown in mass, rough, ellipsoid to almond-shaped, average size 12.0 × 7.0 microns.

Habitat and distribution

Top, right: Hebeloma mesophaeum
Centre: Hebeloma longicaudum
Bottom, right: Hebeloma radicosum
Below: Hebeloma crustuliniforme

Grows singly or in groups or sometimes in rings, prefers damp soil in woods, gardens, pastures and hedges. Associated with an alpine flora on mountains. Common in Europe, infrequent in North America.

Occurrence

August to November.

Culinary properties

Tastes bitter, smells strongly of radish, may be poisonous.

Hebeloma longicaudum

Fruiting body *Cap:* pale yellowish-beige, darker in the centre, smooth, slimy. Convex. *Stipe:* tall, with basal bulb, whitish-beige, almost smooth.

Ecology Boggy woods, upland moors. Occasional in Europe and northern North America. August to November.
Inedible.

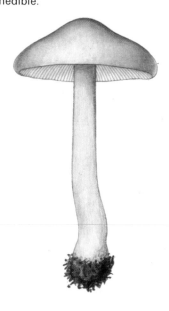

Hebeloma mesophaeum

This fungus is a common species of hilly and mountainous areas which grows in very dense groups. It is suspected of being poisonous.

Fruiting body

Cap: date-brown with paler margin. 2–4cm in diameter. Convex then flattened, margin with dingy-white remnants of veil. Cuticle smooth, silky, shining. Flesh pale brown, thin. *Gills:* whitish at first then dingy brown. Adnate, cut away next to stipe. Rather broad with white fringed edge, crowded. *Stipe:* slender, sometimes twisted, 4–6cm long, 3–5mm thick. At first whitish with remains of veil, then pale brownish sometimes with a ring-like zone near the top. Flesh dark brown in the base. *Spores:* brown in mass, almost smooth, ovate, average size 9.5 × 5.5 microns.

Habitat and distribution

A gregarious species growing in woods and on heaths especially under pine or birch, in shrubberies, flats between sand-dunes, marshes and under willows in the Alps.

Locally common in Europe, North America and Australia.

Occurrence

August to December.

Culinary properties

Inedible, due to strong taste and smell of radish, is said by some to be poisonous.

Hebeloma radicosum

Fruiting body *Cap:* convex or umbonate with festooned margin, ochraceous or brownish, with large darker scales adhering to the cuticle, slightly viscid or dry. *Gills:* whitish then greyish-brown, with paler edges. *Stipe:* fusiform, whitish above ring, covered with brownish-grey scales below ring, base with long root-like extension.

Ecology Solitary in beech and oak woods, especially around old stumps. Widespread and common in Europe.

Edible but not recommended.

Hebeloma sinapizans

Fruiting body *Cap:* convex to obtuse, cream colour to reddish-brown. *Gills:* pallid at first, not visibly beaded. *Stipe:* becoming hollow with a projection down into the cavity from the cap, sometimes rooting, pallid clay-brown with paler apex.

Ecology In boggy ground under spruce, and in other moist mixed and deciduous woods. Rare in Europe and North America. Poisonous.

Hygrocybe coccinea

This is a brightly coloured grassland species, with a cap which changes from red to yellow as it expands, and a red stipe with a yellow base.

Fruiting body

Cap: at first bright scarlet, changing to golden yellow from centre outwards. 2.5–5cm in diameter. Convex, then flat and often unequal. Cuticle slimy at first, smooth. Flesh red to yellowish. *Gills:* at first yellow and purplish next to the

stipe, flushing red. Adnate with a decurrent tooth, watery-soft, distant and connected by veins. *Stipe:* narrowing downwards, compressed, hollow 5cm long, 3–9mm thick. Scarlet upwards from yellow base, often furrowed. Flesh continuous with that of cap, red to yellowish. *Spores:* white in mass, smooth, broadly ellipsoid, average size 8.3 × 4.6 microns.

Habitat and distribution

Grows in troops, among short grass in pastures and lawns, in clearings in woods, and among willows in mountainous regions. Common in Europe, North America and Australia.

Occurrence

June to December in Europe, July to October in North America.

Culinary properties

Tastes and smells slight, adds a touch of colour when cooked and added to rice dishes.

Hygrocybe conica

This small species has a pointed cap and a tendency to blacken when bruised, or as it ages. Experts differ as to the edibility of this fungus, but most agree that it is too small to be of much interest as food. It was used as an old-time cure-all, whose medicinal virtues were proportional to its offensiveness.

Fruiting body

Cap: yellow, orange or scarlet, blackening with age or when handled. 1–5cm in diameter. Sharply conical, often lobed. Margin splitting and turning back. Cuticle slimy when wet, shining when dry. Thin flesh, yellowish, becoming black when cut. *Gills:* white to pale yellow, blackening when bruised. Narrow towards the stipe and free, ending in an abrupt tooth at the margin. Rather crowded. *Stipe:* straight stiff, 7–15cm long, 6mm thick. Yellow or flushed reddish, blackening when bruised, striate. Flesh fibrous, hollow. *Spores:* white in mass, smooth, broadly ellipsoid, size 11.5 × 6.0 microns.

Habitat and distribution

Grows singly or in groups, in grassy places in woods and copses, in pastures, meadows, lawns, old sand-dunes and by roadsides. Common in Europe, North America and Australia, also found in Trinidad and New Zealand.

Occurrence

July to November in Europe, August to October in North America, where it sometimes appears in spring.

Culinary properties

No distinctive taste or smell. There is a doubtful report that this species caused the deaths of four individuals in China.

Left: Hygrocybe conica
Far left: Hebeloma sinapizans
Bottom, left: Hygrocybe coccinea
Below: Hygrocybe laeta

Hygrocybe laeta

Fruiting body *Cap:* orange or flesh-brown, slimy, striate. Convex then flat. *Gills:* decurrent. *Stipe:* slender, orange-brown, tinged with blue at the apex, smooth.

Ecology Grassland, heaths, bogs. Frequent in Europe and North America. August to December. Inedible.

Hygrocybe miniata

Fruiting body Small, colours soon fade. *Cap:* red-lead colour, smooth or minutely scaly. Finally

flat, often depressed. *Gills:* yellow often tinged red. *Stipe:* slender, orange-red, smooth.

Ecology Grassland, open woodland, bonfire sites. Widespread and frequent in Europe, North America and Australia. June to October. Edible (excellent).

Hygrocybe nivea

This fungus is found in grassy places everywhere in Europe, but infrequently in North America. It is wholly ivory white and, although it is quite small, it can be easily gathered in sufficient quantities to make it worthwhile as a source of food.

Fruiting body

Cap: white, sometimes faintly greyish in the centre. 1–5cm in diameter. At first convex, then expanded and more or less lopsided. Margin striate. Cuticle slimy when moist,

smooth when dry. Thin flesh, white, translucent when wet. *Gills:* white, arched and decurrent, rather broad, distant. *Stipe:* slender, straight, tapering downwards, 5cm long, 2–5mm thick. White, dry and firm. *Spores:* white in mass, smooth, broadly ellipsoid or pip-shaped, average size 8.5 × 5.0 microns.

Habitat and distribution

Grows gregariously in damp places among short grass in pastures, meadows, heaths, under willows and pines in Alpine regions. Common in Europe, infrequent in North America.

Occurrence

September to December in Europe, August to September in North America.

Culinary properties

Tastes and smells pleasant. Delicate flavour but is highly recommended, especially as volume decreases very little when cooked.

Hygrocybe pratensis
BUFF CAPS

This is a common species of grassy places, and is called the Meadow Hygrophorus in France. Its variable shape seems to be connected with changes in the weather. The colours are also variable, and tend to fade. Some forms are almost white. It is a very good edible fungus.

Fruiting body

Cap: pale tan-yellowish to buff. 2–7cm in diameter. Convex, then umbonate, finally top-shaped. Margin often cracked when dry. Cuticle smooth and moist in rainy weather. Flesh buff, compact in centre, thin towards margin. *Gills:* pale buff, decurrent, at first arched, then extended to form an inverted cone. Very broad in the middle, thick, firm, brittle, distant often connected by veins at the base. *Stipe:* stout, gradually thickened upwards into cap, 4–5cm long, often more than 1.5cm thick. Paler than cap, finely striate. Flesh spongy. *Spores:* white in mass, broadly ellipsoid or egg-shaped, average size 7.0 × 4.8 microns.

Habitat and distribution

Grows gregariously, often in tufts, sometimes forming arcs, in pastures, meadows, lawns, in gardens, on heaths and under willows in mountainous areas. Common in Europe and North America.

Occurrence

August to December in Europe, July to September in North America.

Culinary properties

Smells and tastes very slight and delicate. Requires careful cooking, is liable to be tough unless cooked slowly. It is particularly good in croquettes and pâté.

Hygrocybe psitticina
PARROT FUNGUS

This attractive fungus grows in grass in open places. It is small but plentiful, and can often be gathered in large enough quantities to make it worth eating.

Fruiting body

Cap: deep bluish-green fading to yellowish, finally varying deep reddish-purple, pinkish-flesh or dingy citron-yellow. 1–3cm, sometimes 5cm, in diameter. At first bell-shaped then expanded and umbonate. Margin slightly striate. Cuticle glutinous. Thin flesh, greenish, translucent when moist. *Gills:* yellow, green next to stipe, adnate, broad, not distant. *Stipe:* parallel sides, sometimes wavy, 4–7cm long, 2–5 mm thick. At first green, flushing yellowish from the base. Apex remaining green. Slimy, smooth. Flesh tough, hollow. *Spores:* white in mass, smooth, broadly ellipsoid, average size 8.8 × 4.9 microns.

Habitat and distribution

Grows gregariously, sometimes in tufts in meadows, pastures, lawns, and among ferns and moss in

Top: Hygrocybe miniata
Top, right: Hygrocybe pratensis
Right, centre: Hygrocybe psitticina
Below: Hygrocybe nivea

clearings in woods. Frequent to common in Europe and North America.

Occurrence

July to December in Europe, July to October in North America.

Culinary properties

Tastes and smells slight. Decreases little in volume when cooked.

Hygrocybe punicea
SCARLET WAX GILL

This is one of the largest and most beautiful species of *Hygrophorus*. It is recognized by its slimy, blood-red cap and by the white base of its stipe. It is not as common as the similar, but smaller, *Hygrocybe coccinea*, with which it often grows in grassy places.

Fruiting body

Cap: scarlet or blood-red when fresh, soon fading. 4–8cm sometimes 10cm in diameter. Bell-

shaped, usually irregular and lobed. Cuticle slimy. Flesh yellow, thin and fragile. *Gills:* at first yellow, becoming flushed with red. Notched near the stipe and almost free, broad, distant. *Stipe:* inflated in the middle, 4–10cm long, 1–2cm thick. Scarlet with a white base. Covered with coarse, dark fibrils. Flesh whitish, hollow. *Spores:* white in mass, smooth, broadly ellipsoid, average size 9.8 × 5.3 microns.

Habitat and distribution

Found in pastures, fields, on heaths and commons, by roadsides and along the edges of woods. Common in Europe and North America.

Occurrence

August to December in Europe, July to September in North America.

Culinary properties

Tastes and smells slight, decreases very little in volume when cooked.

Hygrophoropsis aurantiaca
FALSE CHANTARELLE

Called the False Chantarelle because of its close resemblance to *Cantharellus cibarius*, it can be distinguished, by its plate-like gills. It can also be confused with the poisonous species *Clitocybe olearia*.

Fruiting body

Cap: orange-yellow. 3–7cm in diameter. Soon flattened, then funnel-shaped. Margin finally turned up, sometimes wavy. Cuticle dry, smooth to minutely downy. Flesh yellowish, tough, pliant. *Gills:* orange-red, decurrent, narrow, crowded and forked. *Stipe:* short, curved, slightly tapering upwards from the base. 2.5 to 5cm long, 0.5cm thick. Orange-yellow, smooth, flesh tough, finally hollow. *Spores:* white in mass, ellipsoid, smooth, in iodine they turn red-brown, average size 6.3 × 4.4 microns.

Habitat and distribution

Grows gregariously, in coniferous woods, or under conifers on heaths.

Common in Europe, and in the northern hills and mountains of North America.

Occurrence

August to November in Europe, July to October in North America.

Culinary properties

Tastes mild, is very tough and uninteresting, not recommended.

Hygrophorus agathosmus

Fruiting body   *Cap:* olive or yellowish-grey, margin paler, slimy With a central hump. *Gills:* white. *Stipe:* stout, dotted with pale brownish-yellow granules. Smells of bitter almonds.

Ecology   Coniferous woods, especially in mountainous areas. Occasional to frequent in Europe. August to November.
Edible.

Above: Hygrophorus agathosmus
Centre: Hygrophoropsis aurantiaca
Bottom, left: Hygrocybe punicea
Left: Hygrophorus chrysaspis

Hygrophorus chrysaspis

Fruiting body   *Cap:* convex then flattened, very viscid in wet weather, pure white becoming cream and then rusty-brown, *Gills:* decurrent, pale cream becoming pale orange when mature, *Stipe:* up to 6cm tall, base narrow, cream becoming brown below and spotted ochre above. Fruiting body has strong smell of ants, similar to that of the related species *Hygrophorus eburneus*.

Ecology   Under beech, on calcareous soils. Europe. Autumn. Edible.

Right: Hygrophorus
chrysodon
Far right: Hygrophorus
hypothejus
Bottom: Hygrophorus
eburneus

change with potassium hydroxide. *Gills:* white, strongly decurrent, thick, distant, sometimes veined at base. *Stipe:* slender, tapering downwards, often wavy, 6–15cm long, 3–8mm thick. White, glutinous, mealy granular at the top. Flesh white, firm. *Spores:* white in mass, smooth, broadly ellipsoid to egg-shaped, average size 9.0 × 4.5 microns.

Habitat and distribution
Grows gregariously, sometimes forming tufts, in deciduous or coniferous woods, under oaks and, more rarely, beech, on heaths and in pastures. Frequent and widespread in Europe and North America.

Occurrence
August to November in Europe, September to October in North America.

Culinary properties
Tastes mild, smells faint and mild, of good flavour, but poor texture.

Hygrophorus chrysodon
Fruiting body *Cap:* convex then flattened, with golden-yellow scales which are more common at the margin, 3–8cm diameter. *Gills:* white to cream, somewhat decurrent, waxy. *Stipe:* viscid, white except at top which is covered with tiny yellow scales, fleshy, 3–8cm tall.
Ecology In deciduous and conifer woods, especially in mountainous areas. Common in Europe and North America. Summer to winter. Edible but not highly recommended.

Hygrophorus eburneus
This wholly white, woodland fungus is easily confused with the common beech wood species, *Hygrophorus chrysaspis*. The latter is identified by its brownish reaction with potassium hydroxide.
Fruiting body
Cap: white, 2–6cm in diameter. At first convex then expanding and slightly umbonate. Margin at first incurved and hairy, soon becoming smooth. Cuticle smooth, very glutinous when wet. White flesh, compact and thick in centre, no colour

Hygrophorus hypothejus
This species is resistant to frost and can be found in late autumn or at the beginning of winter. Young specimens are easily recognized by their very slimy, olive-brown caps and yellow gills. Mature specimens can be very variable in size. It is considered to be useful as a snack, for which purpose it can be carried around in the dried state.
Fruiting body
Cap: at first olivaceous-brown, darker in centre, fading to yellowish, sometimes orange when rotten. 2–6cm in diameter. Convex then flattened and slightly depressed. Smeared with gluten when young, becomes streaky and shiny when dry. Flesh thin, white, becoming

pale yellow. *Gills:* yellow, finally almost saffron, decurrent, thick, distant. *Stipe:* tapers downwards, 5–10cm long, 6–8mm thick. White to yellowish, apex paler, slime-coated upwards to woolly ring. *Spores:* white in mass, smooth, ovoid, size 8.0 × 4.5 microns.

Habitat and distribution
Found among grass and moss in pine woods, under pines on heaths, and on sandy soil. Frequent to common in Europe, frequent in North America, very common in Australia.

Occurrence
After the first frosts, October to November.

Culinary properties
Tastes and smells mild, is crisp and nutty when dried, but not good for cooking.

Hygrophorus marzuolus
Fruiting body *Cap:* flattened or depressed, brown becoming black-ish, dry. *Gills:* decurrent, connected by small veins, white becoming grey or blackish with lighter col-

coloured edges. *Stipe:* squat, grey at base, lighter above.
Ecology In groups in mountain-ous woods such as oak, chestnut, beech and various conifers. Often hidden under dead leaves. In con-tinental Europe. Winter through to spring.
Edible and highly regarded.

Hygrophorus olivaceo-albus
Fruiting body *Cap:* whitish-olive with dark olive-brown slimy centre. Finally flat. *Gills:* white. *Stipe:* slender, slimy, white, spotted with brown up to ring-like zone.
Ecology Coniferous and deci-duous woods. Occasional in Europe. August to November.
Inedible.

Hygrophorus penarius
Fruiting body *Cap:* convex and somewhat humped, almost dry, whitish with tinge of straw colour in centre, 6–10cm diameter. *Gills:* slightly decurrent, similar colour as cap. *Stipe:* stout, dry, with minute granules, colour as cap, 3–6cm tall.
Ecology In beech woods. North America and continental Europe. Edible.

Hygrophorus russula
Fruiting body *Cap:* nearly flat when mature, pinkish or violet, streaked with reddish-purple hairs, viscid in wet weather, margin in-rolled. *Gills:* adnate or slightly de-current, pale pink with purple-red spots when old. *Stipe:* cylindrical, dry, white at first, with purple-pink spots usually quite visible in upper part.
Ecology Scattered or in groups in deciduous and mixed woods. Com-mon in Europe and North America. Appears late summer and into the autumn.
Edible.

Hypholoma capnoides
This tufted species grows only on conifer stumps. In North America

Above: Hygrophorus russula
Top: Hygrophorus olivaceo-albus
Above, left: Hygrophorus marzuolus
Bottom: Hygrophorus penarius

Above: Hypholoma
capnoides
Centre: Hypholoma
dispersum
Bottom: Hypholoma
fasciculare

there is an intermediate form between *H. capnoides* and the closely related species, *H. sublateritium.*

Fruiting body

Cap: ochre-yellow, often brownish in the centre, paler towards the margin. 2–6cm in diameter. Convex, then flat, with a slight umbo. Slightly slimy when wet, smooth when dry. Flesh pale yellow, thin. *Gills:* whitish at first, turning slowly greyish-lilac to chocolate-brown. Adnate, separate easily from the stipe, rather broad, crowded. *Stipe:* parallel-sided, slender, wavy, 5–7.5cm long. Yellow, becoming tinged brown from the base up, with silky remains of veil in young specimens. *Spores:* purplish-brown in the mass, ellipsoid, smooth, with a conspicuous germ-pore, average size 7.5 × 4.5 microns.

Habitat and distribution

Grows in crowded tufts, occasionally in rows, on old conifer stumps, especially in mountainous areas. Frequent in Europe, common throughout the coniferous forest zone of North America, also found in Venezuela.

Occurrence

April to November in Europe, September to first frosts in North America.

Culinary properties

Mild taste and smell, it can easily be gathered in sufficient quantities to be worth cooking.

Hypholoma dispersum

This small species is found among litter and on old stumps in coniferous woods. It is recognized by its solitary habit, its bell-shaped, pale tawny cap, and its slender, silky, zoned stipe.

Fruiting body

Cap: tawny-honey coloured, yellowish on the edge. 2–6cm in diameter. At first bell-shaped, soon expanded and slightly umbonate. Margin with silky veil fragments in young specimens. Cuticle smooth or slightly scaly. Flesh thin, pale brown. *Gills:* at first pale yellow, becoming darker. Adnate, broad, crowded. *Stipe:* slender, tense, straight, 4–7cm long. Greyish-brownish, silky-striate with silky, whitish, zone-like markings. Flesh rusty-brown, tough. *Spores:* purplish-brown in mass, ellipsoid, smooth, with a distinct germ-pore, average size 8.3 × 4.5 microns.

Habitat and distribution

Grows singly or in small groups on conifer stumps, wet conifer humus, twigs and chips, and at saw-mills. Locally frequent in Europe, North America and Australia, especially in mountainous areas.

Occurrence

August to November in Europe, April to November in North America.

Culinary properties

Has a very bitter taste, which is almost removed by cooking.

Hypholoma fasciculare
SULPHUR TUFT

Old tree stumps covered in bright yellow clumps of this fungus are among the most beautiful sights to be seen on a woodland walk in late autumn. It is distinguished from several similar species by the greenish tints on its mature gills. The gills of decayed specimens are sometimes attacked by the parasitic fungus *Collybia cirrata.* The fact that this bitter-tasting toadstool upsets some people, has led to the mistaken belief that it is poisonous. It can be eaten, but is only gathered when there is nothing else available.

Fruiting body

Cap: sulphur-yellow, with reddish-brown centre. 3–7cm in diameter. Convex, then expanded and umbonate. Margin incurved and with cobweb-like remnants of yellow-olive veil when young. Cuticle smooth and dry. Flesh yellow and thin. *Gills:* at first yellowish-green, turning olive-green to chocolate brown. Adnate, very crowded. *Stipe:* slender, wavy, often joined with several others at the base, 5–10cm long 1–1.3cm thick. Sulphur-yellow and dirty brownish towards the base. Streaky and with some cottony veil fragments in young specimens. *Spores:* purplish-brown in mass, ellipsoid, smooth, average size 6.6 × 4.3 microns.

Habitat and distribution

Grows in very large, dense tufts, usually on the stumps of deciduous trees, but can occasionally be found on conifers, fence posts and sometimes in greenhouses. Widespread and common in Europe and North America, it also grows in Australia and South Africa.

Occurrence

January to December in Europe, October until after the first frosts in North America.

Culinary properties

The bitter, soapy taste disappears on cooking, and the flavour can be improved by the addition of a little lemon juice or sherry. It is recommended for making mushroom chutney.

Hypholoma sublateritium
BRICK CAPS
There is a certain amount of disagreement as to the edibility of this fungus. It is eaten in North America, but European authors say it is poisonous. At one time it was used as an emetic or purgative. This is one of the largest of the *Hypholoma* species and is recognized by its brick-red cap.
Fruiting body
Cap: brick-red in the centre, yellow towards the edge, 5–7.5cm in diameter. At first convex, becoming flat. Margin incurved with whitish veil fragments in young specimens. Cuticle smooth, dry. Flesh compact, yellowish. *Gills:* at first dingy-yellow, finally greyish-violet to chocolate-brown. Adnate, narrow, crowded. *Stipe:* stout, usually narrowed towards the base, 7.5–10cm long, 5–12mm thick. Yellow at the top, becoming red down-

wards, base soon turns rusty-brown. Slightly scaly, with a ring-like zone near the apex. Flesh reddish-brown towards the base. *Spores:* purplish-brown in mass, ellipsoid, smooth, average size 6.5 × 3.8 microns.
Habitat and distribution
Grows in dense tufts on old stumps of deciduous trees. Common in Europe and North America.
Occurrence
August to November in Europe, October to after frosts in North America.
Culinary properties
No distinctive taste when fresh, becoming bitter when old, or infested by maggots.

Inocybe asterospora
Fruiting body
Fairly large, graceful. *Cap:* with reddish-brown radial streaks on a pale background. Flat, with a pronounced central hump. *Stipe:* slender, base sharply bulbous.

Yellow-ochre with reddish-brown longitudinal streaks.
Ecology Singly, in rich damp soils, along woodland paths, especially under beech, in parks, on sand dunes under *Salix repens*. Variable in Europe, becoming more common towards the south. August to November.
Poisonous.

Inocybe casmiri
This small species is distinguished by its dark brown cap covered with tiny, erect scales, by the absence of a bulb at the base of the stipe, and by its preference for conifer woods.
Fruiting body
Cap: dark snuff-brown. 2–3cm in diameter. Convex then flat, densely velvety with minute pointed scales, erect in the centre and recurved towards the margin. *Gills:* at first cream then clay to yellowish-brown with white, minutely fringed edges. Adnate, slightly cut out near stipe, crowded. *Stipe:*

slender, cylindrical and wavy, length about twice that of cap diameter. Flushed cap colour from base upwards, lower half covered with dark, rather shaggy, fibrillose scales. *Spores:* snuff-brown in mass, globose with numerous conical warts and one rather large wart at the apex. Average size 19.0 microns in diameter, but very variable.
Habitat and distribution
In sandy soil in coniferous woods especially under larch, also in moist alder groves. Occasional throughout Europe and West Australia.
Occurrence
August to November.
Culinary properties
Tastes mild, with a slightly earthy smell. Too small to be worth collecting for food.

Top: Inocybe asterospora
Far left: Hypholoma sublateritium
Centre: Inocybe casmiri
Left: Inocybe dulcamara

Inocybe dulcamara
Fruiting body Very variable in size. *Cap:* pale brownish-yellow, tawny in the centre, minutely scaly. Finally flat. *Stipe:* pale at first, becoming dirty yellowish-brown.
Ecology Coniferous woods, under dwarf willow up to 2,600 metres, on sand dunes under *Salix repens*. Frequent in Europe. July to November.
Edibility unknown.

Inocybe fastigiata
This striking fungus is variable in colour and size. It has a streaky, yellow-brown, sharply-pointed cap.
Fruiting body
Cap: yellow ochre to brownish. 2–5cm in diameter. At first conical then becoming slightly expanded and prominently umbonate. Margin at first turned inward, finally expanded and cracked. Cuticle minutely cracked and with distinct radiating fibrils. Flesh white, thin. *Gills:* yellowish, finally olive or grey. Rounded behind, becoming free,

Right: Inocybe
fastigiata
Far right: Inocybe
lacera
Bottom: Inocybe
geophylla

narrow, crowded. *Stipe:* cylindrical or slightly narrowing upwards, sometimes wavy or twisted, 4–8cm long, 4–5mm thick. White or pale yellow, becoming darker with age. *Spores:* snuff-brown in mass, smooth, ellipsoid to bean-shaped, very variable, average size 12.0 × 6.5 microns.

Habitat and distribution
Grows gregariously on the ground in deciduous woods, or under conifers in coniferous areas, and in the mountains. Common in Europe, frequent in North America.

Occurrence
June to November in Europe, July to September in North America.

Culinary properties
Smells strong and rather unpleasant. It is said by some to be dangerously poisonous.

Inocybe geophylla
This is one of the most common *Inocybe* species of Europe where it grows in troops, and North America where it grows singly. The American plants are only half the size of European specimens. There is some disagreement as to whether or not this species is poisonous, so it should not be collected for food. The variety *lilacina* is sometimes described as a separate species as it is never found in mixed groups with *Inocybe geophylla* and is therefore assumed to grow from different mycelium.

Fruiting body
Cap: white with yellowish centre (or lilac in var. *lilacina*) 4–7cm in diameter. At first conical with incurved margin, then expanded and strongly umbonate. Smooth, silky, shining, often cracking at the edge. Flesh thin and white. *Gills:* white at

first finally dirty greyish-brown, adnexed or free, narrow, thin and crowded. *Stipe:* slender, with a small swelling at the base, often wavy. Up to 5cm long. White, smooth, silky, shining with a powdered apex. Flesh solid and firm. *Spores:* snuff-brown in mass, smooth, obliquely ovoid, average size 9.3 × 5.5 microns.

Habitat and distribution
Found on damp soil or litter in deciduous or coniferous woods, also among grass, along woodland paths and under hedges. It is recorded as growing in association with larches. Common throughout Europe and North America.

Occurrence
June to November.

Culinary properties
Smells more or less spermatic, nauseous to some people. Is said by some to be poisonous.

Inocybe lacera
This is a variable species with several varieties occurring in different habitats: var. *holophila* on sand-dunes, var. *heterocystis* on mountains and var. *pruinosa* on alluvial sands and river-banks. It is distinguished from other *Inocybe* species by the smooth stipe apex, and the very elongate spores.

Fruiting body
Cap: fawn-brown to mouse-grey, olive tinged on margin, 2–4cm in diameter. Convex then umbonate. Cuticle fibrillose or minutely scaly, finally becoming ragged with scales on umbo. Flesh white, thin on margin. *Gills:* at first pale olive-grey, finally dirty olive-brown. Rounded behind, broad distant. *Stipe:* short, tapering downwards, 3–4cm long, 4–5mm thick. Brown with red fibrils, smooth at apex, base with tuft of white mycelium. Flesh rusty-brown. *Spores:* snuff-brown in mass, smooth, narrowly ellipsoid, elongate, average size 12.3 × 5.0 microns.

Habitat and distribution
Grows on sand or gravelly soils, in coniferous woods, heaths, sand-dunes, and on mountains up to 2,600m. Widespread and common in Europe, apparently rare in North America.

Occurrence
June to November.

Culinary properties
Tastes and smells mild, poisonous.

Inocybe maculata
Fruiting body *Cap:* dark brown, with pale scales, remnants of veil, at the centre. Conical. *Stipe:* pale at apex and base, finely streaked red-brown elsewhere. *Smell:* slightly aromatic, nauseous.

Inocybe napipes
Fruiting body *Cap:* dark brown to hazel, almost smooth, conical then convex with a pointed central hump. *Stipe:* slender, bulbous at the base. Base and apex white, pale brown elsewhere.
Ecology Woodland, bogs, especially under *Betula*. Occasional to frequent in Europe. August to November.
Poisonous.

Inocybe patouillardii
This is a deadly poisonous species of chalk and limestone areas, which slightly resembles *Agaricus campestris* when young, but becomes wholly stained bright red in old age.
Fruiting body
Cap: whitish at first, later yellowish-brown, becoming bright pinkish-red where cracked or bruised.

Ecology Deciduous woods, along paths, tracks, associated with *Glechoma hederacea*, Ground Ivy. Common in Europe. August to November. Poisonous.

Culinary properties
Flesh has an offensive smell. It can cause serious poisoning, as it contains large quantities of muscarine. It is very dangerous in early stages of growth as it can be mistaken for *Agaricus campestris*, with fatal results.

Laccaria amethystina
AMETHYST FUNGUS
In dry weather this is an inconspicuous species which can be easily overlooked, but when it is wet it becomes a beautiful dark violet. It is one of the prettiest woodland fungi and is sometimes commonly known as the Red Cabbage Fungus.
Fruiting body
Cap: dark purple when moist, pale lilac when dry. 1—4cm in diameter. At first convex, then flat. Cuticle smooth, becoming scurfy towards the centre. Flesh purplish, thin.

Left: Inocybe patouillardii
Far left: Inocybe maculata
Bottom, left: Inocybe napipes
Bottom, right: Laccaria amethystina

4—7cm in diameter. Bell-shaped then expanded and umbonate. Margin at first incurved, later lobed and split. Cuticle minutely silky fibrillose. White flesh, thick in centre of cap. *Gills:* whitish then olive-yellowish with whitish edges, eventually stained vermillion. Adnate, adnexed or nearly free, thick and fairly crowded. *Stipe:* thickish, irregularly cylindrical, often with a bulbous base. Length very variable, 2—7cm sometimes longer, 1—2cm thick. Whitish at first then streaked with red. Flesh tinged reddish. *Spores:* snuff-brown in mass, smooth, ellipsoid or bean shaped, average size 11.3 × 6.5 microns.
Habitat and distribution
Found occasionally growing in groups in chalky woods or parkland, especially under beeches or limes. Throughout Europe.
Occurrence
May to November.

Gills: dark purple, decurrent, broad. *Stipe:* parallel-sided, sometimes wavy, 5–7cm long, up to 1cm thick. Purple, finely streaked with white, with a dense white down at the base. Flesh fibrous, elastic, finally hollow. *Spores:* white in mass, subglobose, with pointed spines, size 10.0 microns in diameter.

Habitat and distribution
Grows singly or in troops, in deciduous woods, or in coniferous woods in mountainous areas. Common in Europe and North America.

Occurrence
August to December in Europe, June to frosts in North America.

Culinary properties
Caps are tough and insubstantial, but are pleasing when cooked well.

Right: Laccaria laccata
Far right: Lacrymaria velutina

wet. *Gills:* flesh colour, finally white and powdery. Adnate, with a decurrent tooth, broad, rather thick and distant. *Stipe:* slender, often curved or twisted, 7–10cm long, up to 1cm thick. Dingy flesh colour, with a dense white down at the base. Flesh fibrous, elastic, tough. *Spores:* white in mass, spherical, spiny, average size 8.0 microns in diameter.

Habitat and distribution
Grows in troops, in woods, pastures, meadows, on heaths, in bogs and along roadsides. Very common in Europe, North America and South Africa.

Occurrence
July to December in Europe, June to October in North America.

and firm, thin on margin. *Gills:* dark brown tinged purplish, soon becoming mottled as spores ripen. Edges white cottony, 'weeping' bead-like drops in damp weather. Adnate, narrow, crowded. *Stipe:* stoutish or slender, somewhat thickened at base which usually has a tuft of white mycelium. 6–12cm long, 5–10mm thick. Slightly paler than cap, striate and whitish at the top, brownish and scaly with fibrils from remains of veil lower down. The base sometimes stains yellowish when bruised. *Spores:* black in mass, lemon shaped, coarsely warty, average size 10.3 × 6.0 microns.

Habitat and distribution
Common in deciduous woods, it is also found in coniferous woodland. Grows solitary or in clusters usually on trunks and decaying stumps, along woodland roads and paths, more seldom on the ground. Found in Europe, North America and South Africa.

Occurrence
July to October in Europe, May to November in North America.

Culinary properties
Flavour delicate, a favourite edible species, often used in ketchup.

Laccaria laccata
THE DECEIVER
This nondescript toadstool sometimes known as the Hoax Fungus has few features to aid identification. Enthusiasts disagree about its gastronomic value, but as it grows profusely and is available for many months of the year, it could be a valuable source of food.

Fruiting body
Cap: red-brown when moist, yellow ochre when dry. 1–6cm in diameter. Convex, sometimes flattened. Margin sometimes wavy or scalloped, striate when moist. Cuticle smooth when moist, minutely rough when dry. Flesh red-brown, thin, translucent when

Culinary properties
Has little flavour and tends to be tough, but it can be good if cooked well. Dries well.

Lacrymaria velutina
WEEPING WIDOW
This very variable species is known by its conspicuous streaky veil which remains on the cap and stipe. It is edible and can be found in woods everywhere.

Fruiting body
Cap: whitish at first then dull yellowish brown. 1–8cm in diameter. Steeply convex with a slight umbo at centre. Margin and cuticle with remains of a conspicuous fibrillose veil. Flesh white, thick

Lactarius blennius
This is a distinctive toadstool which is recognized by the rings of dark-brown, droplike, spots on its cap. It is found in beech woods, and is said to be the most common *Lactarius* species in central France.

Fruiting body
Cap: olive-brown to greenish, with concentric zones of darker spots. 4–10cm in diameter. At first convex, soon becoming depressed in the centre. Cuticle slimy, margin incurved and downy at first. Flesh white, thick, firm. 'Milk' is white, turns grey on exposure to air. *Gills:* white, bruising dirty grey, slightly decurrent, narrow, crowded. *Stipe:* stout, narrowing sharply at

the base, 2.5–5cm long, 2.5cm thick at the apex. Pale olive-brown, slimy. *Spores:* pale cream in mass, broadly ellipsoid, banded with a distinct projection at one end, average size 7.5 × 6 microns.

Habitat and distribution
Found in deciduous woods, always under beech. Common in Europe and in appropriate areas in North America.

Occurrence
August to November.

Culinary properties
Inedible, even when well cooked, due to the very bitter taste.

Lactarius camphoratus
Fruiting body Fairly small. *Cap:* rusty-brown, somewhat zoned, finally depressed with a small central umbo. *Gills:* finally tinged purple. *Stipe:* dark rusty-brown. *Milk:* watery, slightly sweet. Dry specimens have characteristic smell of curry.
Ecology Coniferous woods, on damp ground. Widespread and common in Europe and North America. July to November.
Edible.

Lactarius chrysorrheus
Fruiting body *Cap:* becoming depressed and funnel-shaped, orange to yellowish with darker spots in concentric circles or zones, 4–10cm diameter. *Gills:* slightly decurrent, cream to pale ochre, often with reddish-brown stains when mature. *Stipe:* squat, 4–7cm tall, up to 2.5cm wide, dry, reddish, often spotted with darker patches. *Milk:* white rapidly turning yellow, acrid taste, hence its common name—the Sulphur Milk Cap.
Ecology Under oak, chestnut, pine and spruce. Common in Europe and North America. Summer and autumn.
Poisonous.

Lactarius controversus
Fruiting body *Cap:* 6–30cm diameter, becoming funnel-shaped, margin inrolled and slightly tormentose, white with indistinct flesh-coloured zones. *Gills:* decurrent, white becoming pale pink, very crowded. *Stipe:* short, stout, white. *Milk:* white, acrid.
Ecology Grows in large rings especially under poplars and creeping willow. Rare in northern Europe, more frequent in south. September to October.
Edible but only after prolonged cooking.

Lactarius deliciosus
SAFFRON MILK CAP
Some of the earliest known illustrations of fungi are the representations of *Lactarius deliciosus* in the frescoes of Herculaneum and Pompeii. In Germany it is regarded by some as the best of all edible fungi. In China it is gathered and eaten on a large scale, and it is one of the officially recognized edible species sold in French markets. Always found growing under conifers, it is often buried by pine needles. In favourable seasons a giant form, 10–30cm broad, can often be found.
Fruiting body
Cap: reddish-orange with darker concentric zones, finally staining green in the centre. 4–10cm in diameter. Convex, soon becoming centrally depressed. Margin smooth, at first incurved. Cuticle slightly sticky or dry. Flesh soft, pale in the centre, stained reddish by milk around the edge, milk rapidly turns carrot coloured when exposed to the air. *Gills:* reddish, becoming flushed or spotted with green. Somewhat decurrent and arched, narrow crowded, often branched. *Stipe:* hollow, narrows towards the base, 2.5–5cm long, 2.5cm thick. Reddish-orange, becoming green where bruised, spotted or pitted, dry, sometimes with a faint bloom when young. Flesh fragile. *Spores:* cream in mass, broadly ellipsoid, decoration variable warted or netted, average size 8.5 × 6.5 microns.

Above: Lactarius controversus
Above, left: Lactarius blennius
Centre: Lactarius chrysorrheus
Bottom: Lactarius camphoratus

Right: Lactarius
deliciosus
Centre: Lactarius
fuliginosus (*var.*
albipes)
Bottom: Lactarius
glyciosmus

Lactarius glyciosmus
COCONUT-SCENTED MILK CAP

This small species is distinguished from the similar *Lactarius vietus*, which is also found under birches, by its distinct smell of coconuts.

Fruiting body
Cap: greyish-lilac. 2–6cm in diameter. At first convex, soon slightly depressed with a central nipple. Margin sometimes striate. Cuticle dull, minutely rough or velvety. Flesh pale-yellow with a pinkish flush. Milk is white, does not alter colour when exposed to the air. *Gills:* yellowish at first, finally greyish-lilac. More or less decurrent, narrow and crowded. *Stipe:* slender, 3–5cm long, 5–8mm thick. Whitish grey, sometimes yellowish, becoming tawny where handled. Downy at first, then smooth. *Spores:* cream in mass, subglobose with a network of ridges and a distinct projection at one end, size 8.0 × 5.8 microns.

Habitat and distribution
Grows in troops, in woods and on heaths, especially under birch, and conifers in the Alps. Variable in Europe, becoming more common towards the north, occasional in north-east North America.

Occurrence
August to November in Europe, September in North America.

Culinary properties
Tastes bitter, smells strongly of coconut. It is highly flavoured when cooked and an acquired taste.

Lactarius mitissimus

Fruiting body *Cap:* bright tawny-orange, dry. Margin wavy. Finally depressed with a central nipple. *Gills:* pale yellowish-pink, frequently with minute red spots. *Stipe:* slender bright orange. *Milk:* white, plentiful, mild or slightly bitter.

Habitat and distribution
Grows gregariously, sometimes in clusters, always under conifers, in woods and on heaths, on moist, but well drained, soils. Frequent in Europe, locally frequent in North America along the Pacific coast in the pine forests of the Rocky Mountains, and in the Great Lakes area. It is also found in South Africa.

Occurrence
August to November in Europe, July to September in North America.

Culinary properties
Tastes mild, with an aromatic smell, it is delicious when cooked slowly and well. Can be served in stews, casseroles, in a sauce on toast, or sliced in soups. It is especially recommended when cooked with *Fistulina hepatica* in butter and a little stock for at least 45 minutes, then flavoured with Worcestershire sauce or sherry. It should be washed before cooking to remove as much of the milk as possible.

Lactarius fuliginosus

Fruiting body *Cap:* at first pale tan, finally dark sooty-brown, dry, velvety. Margin finely wavy. Soon becoming depressed, sometimes with a central nipple. Flesh slowly turns rose-pink when cut. *Gills:* bruise salmon-pink. *Stipe:* at first white, soon becoming brown. *Milk:* tastes slightly acrid.

Ecology Deciduous woods, especially under oak. Frequent in Europe and north-eastern North America. July to November.
Inedible and possibly poisonous.

diameter. At first convex, finally funnel-shaped. Margin long remaining incurved, finally straight. Cuticle smooth. Flesh white, plentiful, firm, with formalin it very slowly turns violet-blue. *Gills:* white at first, becoming creamy yellow with age. More or less decurrent, arched, then straightening as the cap expands, narrow, very crowded, branched into pairs. *Stipe:* stout, narrowing downwards, 2.5–5cm long, it can be equal to the cap diameter, 1–2cm thick. White, at first powdery. Flesh firm and solid. *Spores:* white in mass, subglobose almost smooth, with a distinct projection at one end, average size 8.0×6.4 microns.

Habitat and distribution

Grows gregariously, sometimes in rings. In deciduous woods, and in new pine plantations behind dunes, especially after forest fires. Variable in Europe and North America, becoming more common towards the south. It is also found in Australia.

Ecology Coniferous and deciduous woods. Widespread and frequent in Europe and North America. August to November.
Edible.

Lactarius pallidus

Fruiting body *Cap:* pale tan or flesh coloured, slimy. Finally depressed. *Gills:* crowded, narrow. *Stipe:* stout, at first creamy-white, finally flesh coloured or pale tan. *Milk:* white, bitterish or slightly acrid.
Ecology In troops in deciduous woods, especially under beech, birch, under hedges. In mountainous areas. Frequent in Europe, widespread in North America. July to November.
Inedible.

Lactarius piperatus

North American red squirrels collect large quantities of this toadstool for winter food. They store it in mass in holes in trees and old birds nests, and separately on the branches of trees where it dries. In good seasons it has been used as a fertilizer on impoverished ground. It was said to be a cure for consumption and was used in the treatment of kidney stones. The milk was believed to be an effective antidote in the treatment of warts. When attacked by the parasitic fungus *Hypomyces lactifluorum* it becomes mutilated almost out of recognition.

Fruiting body

Cap: white, tinged cream, often with brown spots. 6–15cm in

Occurrence

August to November in Europe, July to October in North America.

Culinary properties

Tastes very acrid or peppery, no distinctive smell. It should never be eaten raw. When cooked it is meaty but coarse.

Lactarius porninsis

Fruiting body *Cap:* orange or yellowish, flat or slightly depressed, smooth, viscid when wet. *Gills:* pale orange. *Stipe:* same colour as cap, moist but not viscid. *Milk:* white, not changing on exposure to air. *Flesh:* bitter taste but not peppery.
Ecology In groups under conifers, especially larch. Frequent in North America and Europe. Autumn. Edible if blanched and cooked well.

Above: Lactarius piperatus
Top: Lactarius mitissimus
Bottom: Lactarius pallidus

Habitat and distribution
It is always found growing under oaks, on very poor soil. Common in the deciduous forest areas of Europe, infrequent and confined to the north-east in North America.
Occurrence
July to October in Europe, August to November in North America.
Culinary properties
Tastes mild, almost sweet, with a strong, rancid oily smell. It is highly esteemed in some parts of France.

Lactarius rufus
RED MILK CAP
The taste of this toadstool is so bitter that it is said that even maggots will not eat it and it is often called, as a result, the Pepper Fungus. A common species in conifer plantations, it is recognized by the colour of the cap.
Fruiting body
Cap: dull reddish-brown. 4–8cm in diameter. Convex, finally depressed, usually with a central nipple. Margin incurved when young. Cuticle at first minutely woolly, soon becoming smooth. Flesh, pale, milk, white. *Gills:* yellowish, finally flushed red, often spotted. Decurrent, crowded, sometimes forked. *Stipe:* parallel-sided, 5–10cm long, up to 1cm thick, red-brown, with a whitish base. Flesh firm. *Spores:* creamy in mass, broadly ellipsoid, finely netted, with a distinct projection at one end, average size 8.5 × 6.5 microns.
Habitat and distribution
Found under pines, and less commonly beeches, on sandy and calcareous soils, especially in mountainous areas. Common in Europe, locally common in North America.

Top: Lactarius
porninsis
Right: Lactarius
pyrogalus
Bottom: Lactarius
quietus

Fruiting body
Cap: dull reddish-brown with darker concentric zones, 4–8cm in diameter. Convex, becoming flattened, finally depressed in the centre. Turned downwards at the margin. Cuticle sticky at first, soon dry and smooth. Flesh pale sand-coloured, flushing red-brown. Milk is white, turns primrose-yellow on exposure to the air. *Gills:* whitish becoming pale brownish-red. Weakly decurrent, almost adnate, rather broad, crowded, forked next to the stipe. *Stipe:* longitudinally furrowed from apex to base, 4–8.5cm long, 10–15mm thick. Reddish-brown, flushing from base up. Flesh spongy, soon hollow. *Spores:* cream in mass, ovoid, decorated with spines and short bars, size 8.0 × 7.0 microns.

Lactarius pyrogalus
Fruiting body *Cap:* brownish-grey, darker in the centre, usually tinged violet. Finally depressed. *Gills:* at first pale yellow, finally deep ochre. *Stipe:* tapers towards the base, pale brownish-yellow. *Milk:* white, very acrid.
Ecology On ground in deciduous woods, especially under hazel and alder. Frequent in Europe, infrequent in northern North America. July to November.
Inedible and possibly poisonous.

Lactarius quietus
OAK MILK CAP
This mushroom is very similar to *Lactarius chrysorhaeus*, which, however, exudes bright yellow milk and grows in oak woods on good mull soils. It is easily recognized by its beautiful brown colour, its zoned cap and distinctive smell.

cream with yellow edges, staining dark yellow. *Stipe:* whitish tending to yellow, thick, soon hollow. *Milk:* white changing quickly to sulphur-yellow.

Ecology Under conifers in groups or scattered. Common in mountainous areas of Europe, and in Pacific north-west of North America. Late summer and autumn. Poisonous.

Lactarius serifluus

Fruiting body *Cap:* becoming deeply depressed, umber with darker centre, dull, smooth, margin incurved. *Gills:* yellowish flesh-colour to reddish, decurrent. *Stipe:* paler than cap. slender, up to 5cm tall, tapering below. *Milk:* watery.

Ecology On ground in deciduous woods, especially beech, and conifer plantations. Common in Europe. Late summer to autumn.
Edible but not recommended.

Occurrence
August to November.
Culinary properties
Inedible due to its very bitter taste which is not destroyed by boiling. It is said by some to be poisonous. Burning taste is a useful identification character.

Lactarius sanguifluus
Fruiting body *Cap:* carrot or reddish-brown with darker concentric zones, becoming funnel-shaped, margin inrolled, *Gills:* adnate to slightly decurrent, ochraceous becoming violet or purplish, thin. *Stipe:* squat, tapering towards base, becoming hollow, eventually the colour of the cap. *Milk:* dark red becoming purplish-brown when exposed to air. *Flesh:* when exposed the peripheral flesh becomes speckled with red dots.
Ecology Scattered or in groups under conifers, especially Douglas fir. Uncommon in Europe, common in N. America summer to autumn. Edible.

Lactarius scrobiculatus
Fruiting body *Cap:* yellow with poorly defined zones, viscid, smooth, deeply depressed in centre, margin inrolled with matted hairs. *Gills:* adnate to decurrent,

Left: Lactarius scrobiculatus
Top: Lactarius rufus
Bottom, left: Lactarius sanguifluus
Below: Lactarius serifluus

Lactarius subdulcis
This brightly coloured mushroom has an unpleasant but distinctive taste. It is found commonly throughout Europe and North America in association with beech, and with hornbeam in warmer areas.
Fruiting body
Cap: cinnamon-red. 3–6cm in dia-

meter. Convex, becoming flattened and depressed in the centre. Margin thin, incurved, sometimes wavy. Cuticle smooth. Flesh white to pink, deep red under the cuticle. Milk is white, not changing colour when exposed to the air. *Gills:* white, sometimes tinged with red. More or less decurrent, rather narrow, crowded. *Stipe:* slender, tapering slightly upwards, 2.5–6cm long. Pale pinkish-red at first, becoming darker from the base up. Smooth, sometimes hairy at the base. *Spores:* cream in mass, ellipsoid, warty, with a distinct projection at one end, average size 9.0×6.5 microns. Sometimes confused with *L. mittissimus* and *L. aurantacous.*

Habitat and distribution
Grows gregariously or scattered, in deciduous woods, copses, fields, on all types of soil, especially under beech and hornbeam. Found under conifers in mountainous areas. Common in Europe and America.

Occurrence
August to November in Europe, July to October in North America.

Culinary properties
Tastes bitter, reminiscent of ivy, no distinctive smell. It is said by some to be delicious after long, slow cooking.

Top: Lactarius tabidus
Below: Lactarius subdulcis
Below, right: Lactarius torminosus
Bottom: Lactarius trivialis

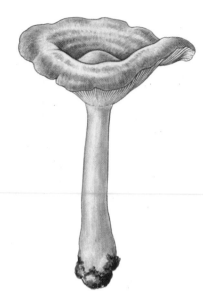

Lactarius torminosus
SHAGGY MILK CAP
This species is always found under birches with which it forms a mycorrhizal association. It is widely believed to be poisonous, but when boiled and rinsed it is perfectly safe and is highly regarded in Scandinavia and Russia.

Fruiting body
Cap: pink-flesh colour with whitish concentric zones. 5–10cm in diameter. Convex, then flattened be-

coming depressed in the centre. Margin incurved and very woolly, shaggy when young. Cuticle slimy at first or when moist. Flesh whitish-flesh colour. Milk is white, unchanging when exposed to the air. *Gills:* tinged flesh-colour, adnate or slightly decurrent, narrow, crowded. *Stipe:* more or less cylindrical 4–7cm long. Pale flesh-colour, delicately downy (seen with a lens). Flesh soft and pithy in the centre. *Spores:* pale cream in mass, sub-globose or broadly ellipsoid, faintly

netted with a distinct projection at one end, average size 7.5 × 5.2 microns.

Habitat and distribution
Usually grows singly, but sometimes forms rings, always under birches, in woods, on heaths, and in mountainous areas. Frequent to common in Europe and North America.

Occurrence
July to November in Europe, August in North America.

Culinary properties
Tastes very strong and peppery, no distinctive smell. It contains gastro-intestinal irritants which cause severe abdominal cramps, vomiting and diarrhoea if eaten raw. These toxins are destroyed by cooking. It is regarded as a delicacy in Eastern Russia, Finland and Sweden, where it is preserved in salt, and eaten with oil and vinegar. In Norway it is roasted and added to coffee.

Lactarius trivialis
Fruiting body *Cap:* glutinous, violet-grey when young, becoming dingy flesh colour with ill-defined zones, margin hairy. *Gills:* pale straw colour to pinkish-buff with rusty stains. *Stipe:* greasy, pinkish-buff above and straw-yellow below, pitted with darker spots, hollow.

Lactarius tabidus
Fruiting body Fairly small. *Cap:* pale rust, margin striate when moist. Almost always with central nipple. *Gills:* pale cinnamon-ochre, sometimes flecked with red. *Milk:* white, on handkerchief turns yellow in c. 60 seconds, mild.
Ecology Deciduous woods, under birch, willow, alder, on highland moors, often mountainous areas. Common in Europe. August to November.
Edibility unknown.

Latex: white becoming greenish, acrid taste after a few moments.

Ecology On wet mossy ground under spruce and fir. Europe and North America. Autumn. Not regarded as edible.

Lactarius turpis
UGLY MILK CAP

It is easy to overlook specimens of this dingy fungus, as they blend with the litter of fallen debris under

birch trees, and they become rather dark and unattractive in old age. A drop of ammonia or any other alkali turns the cap deep purple.

Fruiting body

Cap: dark olive-brown, at first with a yellowish-orange margin. 6–14cm in diameter. Convex, becoming depressed in the centre. Margin at first covered with woolly down which soon disappears. Cuticle becomes slimy and sometimes furrowed with age. Flesh firm, white or greyish-brown. Milk white, unchanged when exposed to the air. *Gills:* at first pale yellow, soon becoming mottled and with brown spots, especially where bruised. Decurrent, crowded and forked. *Stipe:* stout, tapering slightly downwards, 4–7.5cm long, 1–2.5cm thick. Pale olive-brown with a distinct yellow-brown apex, becoming slimy and pitted when old. Flesh hard and solid. *Spores:* very pale cream in mass, broadly ellipsoid, netted with a distinct projection at one end, average size 7.0 × 5.5 microns.

Habitat and distribution

Grows singly or in groups, in woods and copses, on heaths, especially in bogs and always under birch. Common in western Europe, rare or locally frequent in northern North America.

Occurrence

August to November in Europe, August to September in North America.

Culinary properties

Has a very bitter taste, although, it is said by some to be eaten in Europe when there is no alternative.

Lactarius uvidus

European examples of this toadstool are regarded with suspicion, and it would seem prudent not to gather them for food. The lilac bruises on its cap, gills and stipe distinguish it from other *Lactarius* species.

Fruiting body

Cap: brownish-grey with a faint lilac flush. 4–10cm in diameter. At first convex, finally saucer-shaped. Margin at first incurved, slightly powdery, thin, finally spreading. Cuticle slimy. Flesh turns lilac when cut or bruised. Milk white, turning lilac when exposed to the air. *Gills:* white, finally dirty pale yellow, bruising lilac, adnate or slightly decurrent, rather narrow, crowded. *Stipe:* uneven, wavy, 4–7cm long, 6–12mm thick. Pale, but soon flushed ochre from base up, bruising lilac, smooth. *Spores:* ochre in mass, broadly ellipsoid, spiny and irregularly netted, with a distinct projection at one end, average size 10.0 × 20.0 microns.

Habitat and distribution

Grows gregariously, in damp woods, thickets and swamps, especially under birch. A rather infrequent species in Europe and North America.

Occurrence

August to November in Europe, August to September in North America.

Left: Lactarius turpis
Bottom: Lactarius uvidus

Culinary properties

Tastes slightly bitter, no distinctive smell. It is considered poisonous in Europe.

Lactarius vellereus
WOOLLY FUNGUS

This conspicuous white toadstool is often abundant in more northerly deciduous woods where it can easily be mistaken for *Russula delica*. It is sometimes attacked and mutilated by the parasitic fungus *Hypomyces lactifluorum*. There is some disagreement as to the edibility of *L. vellereus*, but as it is known to upset some people it would seem prudent not to gather it for food.

Fruiting body

Cap: pure white becoming yellowish when old. 10–20cm in diameter. Convex then finally depressed in the centre. Margin persistently incurved. Cuticle velvety downy. Flesh white, firm. Milk white, sparse, does not change colour when exposed to the air. *Gills:* whitish becoming pale ochre, weakly decurrent, fairly broad, sometimes forked. *Stipe:* short and stout, sometimes tapering downwards. 1.3–2.5cm long, 1.5–3cm thick. White, finely downy. Flesh solid and firm. *Spores:* creamy-white in mass, subglobose, nearly smooth, with a distinct projection at one end, average size 10.6 × 8.8 microns.

Habitat and distribution

Grows in clusters often in large numbers, in deciduous woods, especially oak and aspen and along woodland roads. More common in northern Europe and eastern North America.

Occurrence

September to November in Europe, July to September in North America.

Culinary properties

Tastes very acrid, smells hot and peppery. It is said by some to be poisonous, and by others to be edible if it is first boiled and rinsed to remove the unpleasant taste.

Right: Lactarius vietus
Far right: Lactarius volemus
Bottom, right: Lactarius zonarius
Bottom, left: Lactarius vellereus

Lactarius vietus

Fruiting body *Cap:* purplish-grey-brown, slimy when moist, dull grey when dry. Flat or slightly depressed. *Gills:* at first white finally pale ochre, stained grey where bruised. *Stipe:* pale greyish-brown. *Milk:* white, turns grey on gills in 15–20 minutes, acrid.

Ecology Sometimes in troops, in woods, in bogs, on heaths, especially under birch. Europe. August to November. Inedible.

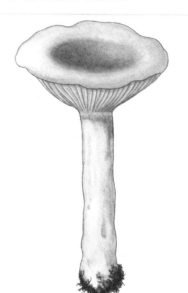

Lactarius volemus

When a large enough quantity of this toadstool is available, an excellent dish can be prepared if it is cooked skilfully. Recognized by its brilliant orange colour, it is closely related to *L. corrugis*.

Fruiting body

Cap: bright tawny-orange, paler towards the margin. 7–11cm in diameter. Convex at first, becoming flattened and eventually slightly depressed in the centre. Margin dry, usually somewhat cracked. Flesh firm, yellowish-white, milk-white, sticky and abundant. *Gills:*

cream bruising brownish, weakly decurrent, crowded. *Stipe:* slightly tapering upwards from rounded base, 2.5–10cm long. Whitish powdery at the apex, orange below. Flesh firm. *Spores:* white in mass, globose, ridged, average size 9.0 microns in diameter.

Habitat and distribution

Grows gregariously or is scattered, in mixed open woodland, especially under beech. Occasional to frequent in Europe, common up to the southern limits of the conifer belt in North America.

Occurrence

August and September in Europe.

Culinary properties

Tastes mild, smells of rotting fish when old. Delicious and crisp when raw, it becomes hard and unattractive if not cooked well. Long slow cooking is recommended, or it can be baked in butter and olive oil with strips of fat bacon.

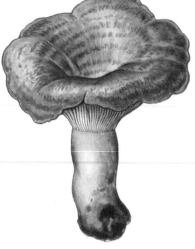

bruising red and then sepia or greenish.

Ecology Under aspens and pines. Common in northern North America and southern Europe. Autumn.

Edible, highly thought of in North America.

Leccinum carpini

Fruiting body *Cap:* ochre becoming buff, 3–16cm diameter. *Pores:* small, white and then yellowish-buff, becoming violet-black when bruised. *Stipe:* 8–9cm tall, almost equal but slightly swollen midway up, ochre to buff, covered below with scales which darken to almost black. *Flesh:* white to straw coloured in stipe, rose or grey in

cap, rapidly blackening when exposed to air.

Ecology Under hornbeam, oak and hazel. Widespread in Europe and North America.

Edible but it becomes black when cooked.

Leccinum crocipodium

Fruiting body *Cap:* hazel cinnamon or fulvous, finally olivaceous, or blackish in centre, soon cracking in centre, velvety, 3–12cm. *Pores:* lemon-yellow and darkening on touch. *Stipe:* swollen towards base, pale ochre to straw colour, with yellow scales which become darker at maturity. *Tubes:* lemon-yellow, becoming greyish-brown.

Lactarius zonarius

Fruiting body *Cap:* convex with a depressed centre and inrolled margin, sticky, alternating bands of pale orange and darker brownish-yellow. *Gills:* adnate or decurrent, tinged yellowish. *Stipe:* light orange to yellowish, smooth, 2–6cm tall, stout, narrowing at base. *Milk:* white, acrid taste.

Ecology In grassy places in woods, especially under conifers. Uncommon in North America and Europe.

Inedible.

Leccinum auriantiacum

Fruiting body *Cap:* orange to apricot, smooth or minutely downy, dry but sticky in wet weather. *Pores:* minute, white, becoming vinaceous where bruised. *Stipe:* cylindrical or narrowed near apex, scaly with scales at first white then orange brown, 8–14cm tall. *Flesh:* white,

Left: Leccinum carpini
Bottom, left: Leccinum auriantiacum
Below: Leccinum crocipodium

Ecology Under oaks, beech and other deciduous trees. Eastern and central North America and southern Europe. Summer and autumn. Edible but not highly recommended.

Leccinum scabrum
COW FUNGUS

One of the commonest edible mushrooms, it is highly prized and one of the officially recognized species sold in French markets. However, it has very soft and rather unpleasantly spongy flesh and should only be gathered when young. There are reports from Norway that cattle have become addicted to eating it.

Fruiting body

Cap: greyish to dark brown. 4.5–15cm in diameter. Convex, margin does not overhang the tubes. Cuticle soft, dry, but in wet weather becoming quite tacky, smooth or irregularly wrinkled. Flesh white, watery and very soft, usually unchanging or slightly pinkish when cut. With ferrous sulphate flesh turns greenish-grey, and with formaldehyde quickly pink. *Tubes:* white at first becoming dingy. Up to 18mm long, free, leaving a deep, broad depression around apex of stipe. *Pores:* white then dingy, becoming ochraceous or pale cinnamon flush in mass, smooth, round. *Stipe:* tall, narrowing upwards, solid, 7–20cm high, 2–3cm thick. White to greyish, roughened by brown to blackish scales which are paler and arranged in lines at the apex. *Spores:* snuff-brown with a cinnamon flush in mass, smooth, ellipsoid-spindle shaped, average size 5.5 × 17.0 microns. Pale straw colour in ammonia.

Habitat and distribution

A very common species, found throughout the northern and southern temperate zones, always under birches in sandy or low, wet places in woods and on heaths. Under poplars in North America.

Occurrence

July to November (occasionally in Spring in North America).

Culinary properties

Smells pleasant and is delicious, although not as good as *B. edulis*. The junction between cap and stipe is nearly always infested with larvae and the stem and tubes should be discarded before cooking.

Lentinellus cochleatus

This distinctive toadstool usually grows in dense clusters on decaying beech stumps. It can be recognized by its toothed gills and fragrant aniseed smell.

Fruiting body

Cap: buff to pale date-brown. 2–10cm in diameter. Irregular, funnel-shaped. Margin wavy. Cuticle smooth. Flesh pale pinkish-clay, rather tough, pliant. *Gills:* pale watery-brown, becoming tinged pink with age. Very decurrent, edges toothed. Crowded. *Stipe:* sometimes central or completely lateral, most frequently eccentric, always grooved up to 1cm long, 1cm thick. Flesh colour at the top, becoming reddish-brown towards the base, smooth. Flesh firm, solid. *Spores:* white in mass, sub-globose, prickly, in iodine they turn blue-black, average size 4.5 × 3.6 microns.

Habitat and distribution

Grows in compact tufts, sometimes singly, on old stumps of deciduous trees, especially beech. Frequent in Europe and North America.

Occurrence

August to November.

Culinary properties

Smells fragrantly of aniseed. Young specimens are tender, and have an excellent flavour when cooked well. Dried fruiting bodies can be grated and used as a flavouring.

Lentinus lepideus
SCALY LENTINUS

This is a saprophytic fungus which attacks coniferous wood. It tolerates coal-tar preservatives and will even grow on creosoted railway-sleepers and telegraph poles. The annual replacement cost of rotten railway

sleepers in Britain has run into millions of pounds, and, not surprisingly, this fungus used to be known as the 'train wrecker'. In mines and houses where there is little or no light the cap is replaced by long, antler-like growths.

Fruiting body

Cap: pale yellowish with brownish scales. 4–10cm in diameter. Irregularly convex, finally depressed. Cuticle cracking into scales. Flesh white, firm, tough and pliant. *Gills:* whitish, may become bright yellow, decurrent, wavy next to the stipe, broad with toothed edges, rather distant. *Stipe:* short, stout, very irregular, with a hard rooting base, sometimes eccentric, 2.5–6cm long, 1–2cm thick. White with brown fibrils or scales below ring-like zone on apex. Flesh whitish, almost woody, stains yellowish when hand-

Top, right: Lentinus lepideus
Right: Lentinellus cochleatus
Bottom: Leccinum scabrum

led. *Spores:* white in mass, smooth, ellipsoid, 13.0 × 4.5 microns.
Habitat and distribution
Grows singly or in groups, on coniferous wood in damp, dark places and light sunny spots, on railway sleepers, telegraph poles, woodpaving blocks, in houses, cellars and mineworkings. Less frequent in the British Isles than in Central Europe, very common in North America.
Occurrence
May to October.
Culinary properties
Tastes pleasant, finally becoming strong, smells slightly of liquorice. Is tender when young, only the tender parts of the cap of older specimens should be used. It should be cooked slowly or used in soups. A reliable species which dries well.

becoming dingy brown at the base. Apex with reflexed ring which soon falls off. Flesh very hard. *Spores:* white in mass, smooth, ellipsoid, average size 9.5 × 3.3 microns.
Habitat and distribution
Grows gregariously or in tufts, on old hardwood stumps, especially willow and poplar. Common in subtropical regions of Europe, North America, Australia and Venezuela.
Occurrence
Spring to autumn.
Culinary properties
Tastes and smells agreeable. It is eaten in Europe, but it is not particularly digestible.

Lepiota americana
A relative of *Lepiota badhami,* which has a smooth margin to its cap and a bulbous stipe base, this

species is found only in North America. It grows in grass around old willow stumps and is recognized by its reddish-brown umbo and the scales on its cap. When cooked it has a pleasant flavour which is reminiscent of that of *Lepiota procera.*
Fruiting body
Cap: at first wholly reddish-brown, later becoming white with reddish-brown patches 2.5—10cm in diameter. Ovoid when young, expanding to convex with a central umbo. Margin thin, generally with short, radiating lines. Cuticle at first smooth, breaking up as the cap expands into large scattered patches, except on the umbo. *Gills:* white, free, do not quite reach the stipe, broad at the margin, narrowed and more or less joined

Left: Lentinus tigrinus
Bottom: Lepiota americana

Lentinus tigrinus
Under abnormal conditions this species produces a monstrous form in which the gills are overgrown by mycelium, so that the underside of the cap is an even surface. This species is thinner and more leathery and regular than *Lentinus lepideus.*
Fruiting body
Cap: white, variegated with black scales. 2—5cm in diameter. At first convex, then flattened, finally funnel-shaped. Margin often split when dry. Cuticle of adpressed hairy scales. Flesh whitish, thin, fragile when fresh, leather when dry. *Gills:* white, decurrent, narrow with toothed edges, crowded, unequal. *Stipe:* slender, usually narrowing downwards, often curved, 5cm long. Whitish, minutely scaly,

behind, crowded. *Stipe:* tapers upwards from club-shaped base, or is sometimes spindle-shaped, 7—12.5 cm long, 4—6mm thick at the apex. Whitish, becoming reddish when handled, smooth with a small membranous, thick-edged ring. *Spores:* white in mass, ellipsoid, smooth, average size 9.0 × 6.0 microns.
Habitat and distribution
Grows singly or in clusters, in grass or around old stumps, especially willow. Common in the deciduous forest areas of North America.
Occurrence
July to October.
Culinary properties
Tastes and smells agreeable. Caps are meaty and delicious especially if grilled or fried. If cooked in liquid it turns the stock reddish-brown.

Lepiota bucknallii

Fruiting body Small. *Cap:* at first bluish-violet, finally whitish-grey. Margin minutely toothed. Bell-shaped, becoming convex with a slight central hump. *Stipe:* bluish-violet, becoming darker towards the base. Smells strongly of coal gas.
Ecology On damp soil in deciduous woods. Rare to occasional in Europe. August to October. Edibility unknown.

Lepiota clypeolaria
THE SHIELD FUNGUS

Specimens of this species vary greatly in colour and size, but they can always be recognized by the loose, velvety scales on their stipes, and, when mature, by the shield-shaped, concentrically decorated cap.
Fruiting body
Cap: at first yellowish-brown to pale reddish, finally with concentric pale brown zones. 3–7cm in diameter. Convex or bell-shaped at first, finally umbonate. Margin with

Top: Lepiota bucknallii
Far right: Lepiota echinata
Bottom, right: Lepiota cristata
Bottom, left: Lepiota clypeolaria

tooth-like veil fragments, finally curled back. Cuticle felty, breaks up into concentric rings of scales as cap expands. Thin flesh, white and soft. *Gills:* white to yellowish with a minutely woolly edge. Free, up to 5mm broad, narrow at the margin. Very soft, crowded. *Stipe:* slender, sometimes slightly tapering upward or with a pointed base, 4–7.5cm long, 1.5cm thick. Whitish-yellow, sheathed up to an inconspicuous ring by loose, woolly scales. Apex whitish. Flesh white, fragile, hollow. *Spores:* white in mass, smooth, spindle-shaped, average size 13.5×5.0 microns.
Habitat and distribution
Grows singly or scattered, on litter in coniferous or deciduous woods, under hedges and in hot houses. It is especially common in hilly or mountainous regions. Frequent to common in Europe and Australia, locally common in North America.
Occurrence
September to November in Europe, July to October in North America.
Culinary properties
Tastes agreeable, smells faintly, but pleasantly, of gas. Not recommended.

Lepiota cristata
Fruiting body *Cap:* umbo and scales reddish-brown on a white background. At first bell-shaped. *Stipe:* slender, pale brownish-pink below small membranous ring, smooth. Smells strong and unpleasant.

Ecology Sometimes in tufts, on lawns, in pastures, golf links, less often by woodland paths, occasionally in greenhouses. Frequent to common in Europe and North America. June to November. Inedible and possibly poisonous.

Lepiota echinata
Fruiting body Small. *Cap:* dark brownish-grey, remains of veil hang tooth-like on margin. Flesh red. *Gills:* bright wine-red, finally reddish-brown. *Stipe:* dark brownish-grey, mealy granular.
Ecology Sometimes in tufts, or in troops, in deciduous woods, especially along paths, on rich soil in gardens, on compost heaps, on

bonfire sites. Occasional to frequent in Europe. August to November.
Edibility unknown.

Lepiota excoriata

This is a large species which is found in pastures throughout the temperate zones. The variety *montanus*, which is very stout and short, with a spherical bulb to its ringless stipe, grows on lower alpine slopes in the Mediterranean region.

Fruiting body

Cap: dirty white, slightly brownish in centre. 6–10cm in diameter. At first ovoid, finally expanded and slightly umbonate. Cuticle breaks up into large scales and appears as if drawn upwards from the fringed margin. Flesh white unchanging. *Gills:* white, free, separated from stipe by collar. Soft, broad, crowded. *Stipe:* rooting, narrowing upwards from slightly bulbous base, 4–6cm high, up to 5mm thick. White or greyish with narrow flaring ring. Flesh spongy, separates easily from that of cap. *Spores:* white in mass, smooth, ellipsoid with germ pore, large, average size 18.0 × 9.5 microns.

Habitat and distribution

Found in pastures and lawns, ploughed soil, on heaths and in mountainous areas. Occasional to frequent in Europe, widespread in North America and Australia.

Occurrence

August to November in Europe, May to September in North America.

Culinary properties

Slight taste and smell but is highly recommended.

Lepiota felina

Fruiting body *Cap:* small, up to 2.5cm diameter, conical convex, covered with minute, erect, pointed dark scales, whitish background, *Gills:* white, free. *Stipe:* tall, fibrillose, base dirt-grey with dark squammules, membranous ring above middle.

Ecology On rich soil in conifer woods. Widespread but rare in Europe.
Not edible.

Lepiota friesii

This fungus is so variable in size that in the past mycologists divided it into two separate species: *Lepiota friesii* which is large and fruits late in the season, and *L. acutesquamosa* which is smaller and fruits earlier.

Fruiting body

Cap: pale brown with dark brown warts. 5–10cm in diameter. At first conical then expanded and umbonate. Cuticle broken up into conical warts which leave small scars when rubbed off. In American specimens warts are sometimes absent except at the centre. Thick flesh, white and soft. *Gills:* whitish often spotted brown. Free, narrow, crowded and usually forked. *Stipe:* narrows slightly upward from swollen base, 7–10cm long, 1–2cm thick. Off-white, belted with dark scales towards the base, white and

Top: Lepiota felina
Left: Lepiota excoriata
Below: Lepiota friesii

powdery above the lax, membranous ring. *Spores:* white in mass, smooth, ellipsoid, average size 6.0 × 2.5 microns.

Habitat and distribution

Grows gregariously, in grassy places and on bare soil, in woods, pastures, gardens, and roadsides. Occasional in Europe and Australia, rare in North America.

Occurrence

August to November in Europe, July to September in North America.

Culinary properties

Tastes bitter, smell can be slightly unpleasant when cut or bruised, even so it is highly recommended by some enthusiasts.

Above: Lepiota leucothites
Right: Lepiota mastoidea

Lepiota leucothites
THE MODEST LEPIOTA

At some stages of development this species resembles the deadly *Amanita phalloides* and *Amanita verna,* but it is distinguished from these by the lack of a volva at the base of its stipe. It can also be confused with the poisonous, green-spored *Lepiota* species.

Fruiting body

Cap: white, becoming dirty-pink or smoky-brown with age. 6–10cm in diameter. At first subglobose to ovoid, then flattened or bluntly umbonate. Cuticle thin, splitting into granules. Flesh white, soft, thick, abruptly becoming thin at the margin. *Gills:* at first white then tinged flesh-colour. Free, narrowed behind and not quite reaching the stipe, crowded. *Stipe:* narrows slightly upwards 5–10cm long, 6–12mm thick. White, smooth or silky up to narrow, fringed ring,

powdery above. Flesh rather firm, white. *Spores:* white in mass, smooth, ovoid, average size 8.4 × 5.3 microns.

Habitat and distribution

Grows gregariously or scattered, in pastures, gardens, fields after harvest, vineyards, parks, on lawns, golf courses and by roadsides. Occasional to common in Europe, common throughout the United States and southern Canada.

Occurrence

August to November in Europe and North America.

Culinary properties

Tastes mild and pleasant, smells faintly acidic. Considered by many to be as good as *Agaricus campestris* and is usually free from insects. Not recommended because of confusion with similar, poisonous species, and because some people are allergic to it.

Lepiota mastoidea

Fruiting body *Cap:* very like *Lepiota procera,* prominent umbo, pale ochre, minute granular squammules. *Gills:* white, free. *Stipe:* less scaly than *Lepiota procera,* with rather narrow membranous ring.
Ecology In grassy places in deciduous and conifer woods and in fields. In Europe. Autumn.
Edible.

Lepiota morgani
GREEN-LINED PARASOL

This is one of the largest North American meadow mushrooms, with a cap which can attain a diameter of up to 35cm. It is recognizable by its size, by its large, movable ring and by its green gills. Wholly green specimens of this species have been recorded. It is poisonous to most people, and can, unfortunately, be mistaken for some of the edible *Lepiota* species.

Fruiting body

Cap: creamy-buff to pale brown. 10–12cm, sometimes 20cm in diameter. Globose then convex and finally flat. Margin at first torn and woolly. Cuticle breaks up, except in centre, into irregular scales as cap expands. Flesh white, thick, firm. *Gills:* white at first, soon changing to dull green, finally dingy brown. Free, remote from stem, rather broad and crowded. *Stipe:* stout, tapers upwards from club-shaped base, 10–20cm long, 1–2cm thick above and 2–4cm thick at base. Whitish or greyish-white to pale brown, smooth, with a large, thick, movable ring. Flesh firm. *Spores:* bright to dull green, smooth, lemon-shaped, size 10.5 × 7.0 microns.

Habitat and distribution

Grows gregariously, often forming large rings, in meadows, pastures

and open woods, Especially common after rain. Frequent in North America, most abundant in the south and west, although locally frequent further north. Also found in South Africa.

Occurrence
May to October.

Culinary properties
No distinctive taste or smell. Poisonous, rarely fatal, causing vomiting, nausea and diarrhoea, these symptoms end rapidly and patients recover in one or two days.

Lepiota procera
PARASOL MUSHROOM

This is one of the largest and best known of the edible fungi. It can sometimes grow to a height of 40cm, with a cap diameter of over 18cm. Its scaly cap and stipe and its wide-flaring double ring make it easy to identify. It does not resemble any poisonous species and so it is completely safe to gather it for food. It is very popular in Italy as its soft flesh absorbs the olive oil and garlic which is much used in local cuisine. This species is officially recognized as edible in France and is sold in the local markets.

Fruiting body
Cap: at first uniformly brown, then becoming greyish-brown with dark brown patches. 10–20cm in diameter. At first ovoid, becoming flattened with a slight to prominent umbo. Margin thin, turned down and fringed. Cuticle smooth at first, breaking up into coarse scales as the cap expands. Flesh white, soft, not very thick when compared with the size of the cap. *Gills:* white, free, separated from the stipe by a collar of firm tissue, crowded. *Stipe:* tapers upwards from bulbous base, 12.5–30cm long, 1–2cm thick. Light brown, concentrically banded with darker brown scales, with a

large, double, movable ring near the apex. The stipe is readily removable from the cap leaving a deep cavity. *Spores:* white in mass, broadly ellipsoid, smooth with a distinct projection at one end, average size 18.0 × 9.5 microns.

Habitat and distribution
Grows singly or in small groups, sometimes in rings, in glades or along the edges of woods, in pastures, on heaths, on golf links above dunes, and along roadsides. Frequent to common in Europe, eastern North America and Australia.

Occurrence
July to November.

Culinary properties
Tastes and smells mild and agreeable, the gills have a pleasant nutty flavour. The stipe is tough and should be discarded together with the scales on the cap. It should be cooked quickly as it becomes tough and leathery if stewed or baked for too long. Delicious fried or grilled in butter, especially good when broiled on a stick over an open fire. It is used for stuffing game birds. It dries well when cut in pieces and strung on a string near the stove.

Lepiota rhacodes
SHAGGY PARASOL

This is a very good edible species and at the turn of the century it was sold in London markets. It grows well in laboratory culture. It is readily recognized by its shaggy, scaly cap and smooth stalk with a flared, double ring.

Fruiting body
Cap: at first completely bay-brown, becoming variegated as cap expands. 8–15cm in diameter. Ovoid, then expanded and umbonate. Cuticle at first smooth, soon becoming cracked and separating into persistant polygonal, concentric scales, which are curled upwards

and attached to the surface with beautiful radiating fibres. Flesh firm, pink, orange-yellow when cut. *Gills:* whitish sometimes reddening. Free, separated from stipe by a collar, tapering towards each end, crowded. *Stipe:* long, at first conical, tapering upwards from distinctly bulbous base, 10–20cm long, 2–5 cm thick, more at the base. Smooth, dirty white, bruising reddish with a prominent double movable ring near apex. Flesh whitish, reddening when cut, easily separates from

Top: Lepiota procera
Left: Lepiota morgani
Below: Lepiota rhacodes

that of the cap. *Spores:* white in mass, smooth, ovoid, sometimes with germ pore, average size 10.5 × 6.5 microns.

Habitat and distribution
Grows singly or in dense clusters, usually near human habitations, on rich soil or old compost heaps, in farmyards, on stable litter, even indoors in riding-stables, growing on spent tan-bark covering the floor. In light places in coniferous woods and on ant hills. Occasional to frequent in Europe, widespread, but not abundant, in North America where it is found mostly in the west, it is also found in Australia and New Zealand.

Occurrence

July to November in Europe, August to September in North America.

Culinary properties

Tastes and smells pleasant. Highly recommended, although it is only good when fresh. Can be cooked by any method, after removing the shaggy cuticle.

Lepista irina

Fruiting body *Cap:* whitish-beige to pale pinkish-flesh colour. Convex then flat. *Gills:* at first white, then brownish-flesh colour, almost decurrent. Stipe pale beige, white at the apex. Smell pleasant, sweet, reminiscent of iris or violets. **Ecology** In woods, pastures. Occasional to frequent in Europe. September to November. Edible.

Top, right: Lepista nuda
Far right: Lepista saevum
Below: Lepista irina

Lepista nuda
WOOD BLEWITS

The Wood Blewits or Great Violet Rider is a common woodland toadstool which fruits in late autumn and through the winter months if the weather is mild. It has been successfully cultivated on beds of beech leaves, but the resulting growth was too slow to be commercially viable. Highly regarded by enthusiasts, it is one of the few wild species sold in shops in England.

Fruiting body

Cap: lilac, dark violet in the centre, becoming reddish-brown when old. 6–10cm in diameter. Convex, then flat. Margin incurved and often wavy. Cuticle smooth, moist. Flesh pale violet, thick in the centre. *Gills:* pale lilac, finally reddish. Rounded behind, narrow, crowded. *Stipe:* parallel-sided, 5–10cm long, 1–2cm thick. Pale violet, fibrillose, mealy at the apex. Flesh solid. *Spores:* pale pink in mass, ellipsoid, smooth to minutely prickly, with a central oil drop, average size 7×4.5 microns.

Habitat and distribution

Grows singly, in clusters, sometimes in rings, in deciduous or coniferous woods, pastures, on garden compost heaps, and on old sand dunes. Commonly found in Europe and North America.

Occurrence

October to December in Europe, September to October in N. America.

Culinary properties

Flavour delicate, is good when sliced and cooked gently in its own juice, then simmered in butter and thin cream.

Lepista saevum
BLEWITS

This is a saprophytic, litter decomposing fungus, commonly found among decaying vegetation in late autumn, and even in the winter in mild weather. Recognized by its pale fawn cap and blue stipe, it is a favourite edible species. It is sold in shops in the English midlands.

Fruiting body

Cap: pale tan to greyish. 6–12cm in diameter. Rounded at first, then flattened. Margin incurved and frosted, projects slightly beyond the gills, finally becoming irregularly upturned. Cuticle dry. Thick flesh is grey when moist, white when dry, at first compact becoming spongy. *Gills:* white, then flesh-coloured. Rounded next to the stipe, broad, crowded. *Stipe:* stout, swollen at the base, approximately 7cm long,

2cm thick. Flushed blue, with lilac or violet fibrils. Flesh solid. *Spores:* pale pink in mass, ellipsoid, smooth to minutely rough, with a central oil drop, average size 7.5×4.5 microns.

Habitat and distribution

Grows singly, in rings, troops or occasionally in small clusters, mainly in open grassy places, less often in deciduous woods or under hedges. Frequent to common in Europe and North America.

Occurrence

September, usually October to December.

Culinary properties

It is substantial, has a good flavour and is especially good in patties, croquettes, stews, and when sliced raw in salads.

Leptonia sericellus

This delicate fungus is often found scattered among grass in open places. Its whitish colour distinguishes it from other *Leptonia* species.

Leptonia asprella
Fruiting body *Cap:* smut-brown or grey, blackish-blue in the centre, striate. At first convex, becoming flat, slightly depressed. *Gills:* at first grey. *Stipe:* slender, steel-blue, sometimes brownish-blue, smooth, shining.
Ecology Grassland, heaths, boggy meadows, lawns. Occasional in Europe and northern North America. August to November. Edibility unknown.

Leptonia lampropus
Fruiting body *Cap:* dark brownish-blue, minutely scaly. At first bell-shaped then convex. *Gills:* white at first. *Stipe:* slender, brownish-blue, whitish at the base.
Ecology Grassland, on heaths, grass verges, in meadows, under willows. Occasional to frequent in Europe and northern North America. August to November. Edibility unknown.

Lyophyllum connatum
Fruiting body Wholly white. *Cap:* smooth, margin wavy. Convex then flat. *Gills:* finally yellowish-grey. With ferrous sulphate gills turn violet in one minute. *Stipe:* tall, slender, cottony towards the apex.
Ecology Usually in tufts, on the ground in deciduous woods, along woodland paths, beside streams. Under conifers in mountainous areas. Rare to occasional in Europe. September to December.
Edible but can be mistaken for dangerously poisonous *Clitocybe* species.

Fruiting body
Cap: at first yellowish-white then very pale ochre, with a brownish centre. 0.5–2cm in diameter. Convex becoming flat and depressed in the middle. Margin incurved and downy at first. Cuticle smooth or minutely scaly. Flesh white, fragile and translucent when wet. *Gills:* white at first, then flesh-coloured. Adnate, often with a decurrent tooth, broad with wavy edges, distant. *Stipe:* short slender, up to 2–5cm long, 1–2mm thick. Whitish shining, powdery at the apex. Flesh soft or slightly tough and fibrous, hollow, translucent when moist. *Spores:* flesh-colour in mass, ellipsoid, size 11.0 × 7.0 microns.

Habitat and distribution
Found on poor soils, in pastures, on lawns, in glades in woods and in peat bogs. Occasional to frequent in Europe and North America.

Occurrence
July to October in Europe, August to September in North America.

Culinary properties
Tastes indistinct. Not recommended.

Lyophyllum decastes
Fruiting body *Cap:* grey-brown, streaked with radiating fibrils, moist feel but not viscid, margin incurved at first, lobed. *Gills:* adnate to slightly decurrent, white. *Stipe:* 3–6cm tall and up to 3.5cm thick, with minute fibrils, white with brown stains near base, no ring.

Above: Lyophyllum decastes
Top, left: Leptonia sericellus
Centre: Leptonia lampropus
Bottom, left: Leptonia asprella
Bottom, right: Lyophyllum connatum

Ecology Clusters on ground growing from stumps or buries roots, on compost and by roadsides. Frequent in Europe, uncommon in North America. Summer and autumn.
Edible.

Macrocystidia cucumis
CUCUMBER SLICE

This small, dark brown fungus is easily recognized by its strong fishy smell.

Fruiting body

Cap: dark brown to almost black, paler around the edge and when dry. 1–6cm in diameter. Conical to bell-shaped, with an incurved margin. Cuticle powdery. Flesh brown, thin, fragile. *Gills:* pale yellowish to flesh colour. Cut away next to the stipe, narrow, crowded. *Stipe:* slender, narrowing towards the base. 2–6cm long. Dark brown to black, paler at the apex, velvety. Flesh solid, finally hollow. *Spores:* reddish-ochre, brown in mass, ellipsoid, smooth, average size 8.8 × 4.5 microns.

Habitat and distribution

Grows in small groups or is scattered on damp rich soil, along woodland paths, banks of streams and in pastures. Fairly common and widespread in Europe.

Occurrence

September to November, occasionally also in May and June.

Culinary properties

Has a strong fishy or cucumber smell. Not recommended.

Top, right: Marasmius androsaceus
Centre: Marasmius alliaceus
Below: Macrocystidia cucumis

Marasmius alliaceus

Sometimes the odour of this insignificant toadstool is so strong that it is smelt before it is seen. *Marasmius scorodonius* is similar and also smells of garlic, but it grows in grass, and can be recognized by its shining, reddish-brown stipe.

Fruiting body

Cap: often milk-white when young, then becoming clay-brown. 1–4cm in diameter. Hemispherical, then convex, finally flattened. Margin striate. Cuticle smooth, dry. Flesh membranous, tough. *Gills:* white,

rounded behind, becoming free, rather distant. *Stipe:* tall, rigid, parallel-sided, rooting, up to 20cm long. Black, minutely velvety. Flesh horny. *Spores:* white in mass, ovoid, smooth, average size 9.9 × 6.4 microns.

Habitat and distribution

Grows on dead, sometimes buried wood and leaves of beech and oak trees, and of coniferous trees in mountainous areas. Frequent in Europe and North America.

Occurrence

August to November in Europe, August to October in North America.

Culinary properties

Smells strongly and persistently of garlic. During the Second World War it was chopped and used as a seasoning by the peasants of Eastern Europe.

Marasmius androsaceus
HORSEHAIR FUNGUS

Heather growing in boggy ground is frequently parasitized by the Horsehair fungus, which enters living stems through the dead ends of small branches. It is also a

decomposer breaking down conifer needles and other vegetable debris. Long lengths of horsehair-like mycelium wind around the stems of the infected plant. These twine-like strands resemble those of the tropical Horsehair Blight (*Marasmius crinis-equi*) which were used by American troops for sewing on buttons.

Fruiting body

Cap: pale reddish-brown, darker in the centre, finally black. Approximately 1cm in diameter. At first hemispherical, becoming flattened, finally umbilicate. Cuticle radially wrinkled. *Gills:* white to dirty-flesh colour, adnate, narrow, rather distant. *Stipe:* very slender, rigid, often bent and twisted, 3–6cm long. Shiny black. Flesh black, tough, wiry. *Spores:* white in mass, pip-shaped, smooth, average size 8.0 × 3.6 microns.

Habitat and distribution

Grows in troops in heather, among conifer needles, fallen leaves and twigs. Common in Europe and northern North America.

Occurrence

May to November in Europe, July to September in North America.

Culinary properties

Inedible.

Marasmius foetidus

This stumpy little fungus is rather rare. It can be recognized by its strong, unpleasant smell and its furrowed cap.

Fruiting body

Cap: date-brown when moist, greyish-buff when dry, with darker radiating lines. 1–3cm in diameter. At first convex, becoming flat and depressed in the centre, radially furrowed. Margin incurved at first. Cuticle slimy when wet. Flesh reddish-brown, thin, almost membranous. *Gills:* yellow to rust-coloured, joined to a collar around the stipe, distant. *Stipe:* stout, tapering towards the base, 2–3cm long, 1–2mm thick. Dark brown to almost black at the base, minutely

velvety. *Spores:* white in mass, pip-shaped, smooth, average size 9.0 × 3.8 microns.

Habitat and distribution
Grows in groups, on rotten branches, sometimes on stumps of deciduous trees, especially beech and hazel. Rare to occasional in Europe and North America.

Occurrence
August to December.

Culinary properties
Smells strong and foetid. Not recommended.

Marasmius lupeletorum
Fruiting body *Cap:* pale brown, slightly striate, convex. *Gills:* yellowish, broad, distant. *Stipe:* slender, fawn, becoming darker towards the densely woolly, hairy base.
Ecology Singly or in twos or threes, on leaf litter of deciduous

woods, especially beech. Under conifers in mountainous areas. Frequent to Europe. October to November.
Edibility unknown.

Marasmius oreades
FAIRY RING MUSHROOM
The well known Fairy Ring Mushroom or Scotch Bonnet grows in clearly demarcated rings, which increase in size year by year. Circles can be found which measure many metres in diameter and growth rates of 10–20cm a year are not uncommon. This mushroom can be confused with two poisonous grassland species, *Clitocybe rivulosa* and *C. dealbata.* It can be recognized by its tan cap and free gills. Highly recommended by enthusiasts, it is one of the officially recognized edible species sold in

French markets. Before the Second World War it could be bought in delicatessens in London.

Fruiting body
Cap: reddish-tan when wet, pale tan to buff coloured when dry. 2–6cm diameter. At first convex, then flat with a rounded boss in the centre. Margin striate, sometimes wavy in old specimens. Flesh pale tan, thick in the centre. *Gills:* pale tan, free, broad, distant, alternately long and short. *Stipe:* slender, straight, 5–7cm long, 6mm thick. Pale tan, smooth above, covered with a white down below. Base

Top: Marasmius foetidus
Left: Marasmius oreades
Bottom: Marasmius lupeletorum

with a blunt root. Flesh tough, pliable, solid. *Spores:* white in mass, pip-shaped, smooth, average size 9 × 5.5 microns.

Habitat and distribution
Grows gregariously, in complete or partial rings, in grass, on lawns, golf links, in meadows and on heaths. Common in Europe and North America.

Occurrence
July to November in Europe, June to October in North America.

Culinary properties
Tastes pleasant, smells faintly of almonds. A delicious species when cooked with care, the caps are best stewed or fried in hot butter or oil. Dries well and is readily reconstituted when soaked in water.

Marasmius ramealis
At first glance, twigs colonized by large numbers of this tiny toadstool, appear to be covered in delicate white blossom.

Fruiting body
Cap: off-white to pale flesh colour, especially in the middle. 1cm in diameter. Convex, then flattened or

depressed in the centre, wrinkled. Flesh thin, white to reddish. With ammonia cap turns yellow. *Gills:* white, adnate, narrow, crowded. *Stipe:* short, slender, usually curved upwards from the base, up to 1cm long. Pale flesh colour, mealy. *Spores:* white in mass, ellipsoid to pip-shaped, smooth, average size 9.5 × 3.4 microns.

Habitat and distribution
Grows gregariously on dead twigs and bramble stems, in woods and hedgerows. Common in Europe.

Occurrence
July to October.

Culinary properties
Too small to be worth eating.

Marasmius rotula
Fruiting body Very small. *Cap:* whitish, membranous, radially grooved. Convex. *Stipe:* thread-like, horny, shining black.

Ecology In groups, on decaying sticks, roots, in deciduous woods. Frequent in Europe, very common in North America. May to September.
Inedible.

Melanoleuca cognata
Fruiting body Almost completely dirty yellowish-tan. *Cap:* smooth, convex then flat. *Gills:* yellow-ochre. *Stipe:* slender, swollen at the base, longitudinally striate.

Ecology Coniferous woods, in glades, along woodland paths, on brushwood heaps. Rare to occasional in Europe. August to November.
Edibility unknown.

Melanoleuca grammopodia
Fruiting body *Cap:* soon becoming depressed, with prominent dark, central umbo, remainder of cap greyish-brown, margin thin. *Gills:* decurrent, arcuate, whitish to cream. *Stipe:* base slightly bulbous and

minutely hairy, above striate with dark lines on fuliginous background. *Flesh:* whitish to fuscous brown from base upwards. *Smell:* nauseating.

Ecology In rows or troops in moist places in woods and fields, especially in mountain areas. Widespread but uncommon in Europe. Edible but smell makes it unattractive.

Melanoleuca melaleuca
This, and several other closely related species, may be mistaken for species of *Tricholoma*, and they can only be distinguished with certainty by microscopic examination which reveals their warty spores.

Fruiting body
Cap: sooty-brown, darker in the centre when moist, paler when dry. 4–8 or sometimes 10cm in dia-

Top: Marasmius ramealis
Top, right: Melanoleuca grammopodia
Centre: Melanoleuca cognata
Bottom, right: Melanoleuca melaleuca
Below: Marasmius rotula

meter. Convex, then flat, with a central hump. Cuticle smooth. Flesh white, becoming dark, translucent when wet. *Gills:* white, sharply cut away next to the stipe, broad, crowded. *Stipe:* tall, slightly swollen at the base, 5–7cm long, up to 1cm thick. White, longitudinally streaked with brown. Flesh flushing brown from the base upwards, elastic, solid. *Spores:* white to ochre in mass, ellipsoid, rough, in iodine warts turn blue-black, average size 8.0 × 4.6 microns.

Habitat and distribution
Grows in association with carnation grass (*Carex flacca*) in woods and pastures. Frequent to common in Europe, uncommon in North America. It is found in South Africa.

Occurrence
August to November.

Culinary properties
It is eaten in Europe.

Mycena alcalina
Fruiting body *Cap:* dull grey-brown, striate when moist. Bell-shaped, then convex with a central hump. *Stipe:* tall, slender, whitish-grey, with a hairy, rooting base. Smells distinctly acidic when broken.
Ecology In tufts, troops on or around conifer stumps. Frequent to common in Europe. August to October.
Edibility unknown.

Mycena epipterygia
YELLOW-STEMMED MYCENA
When grown in the laboratory, the mycelium of this species emits a glow, known as bioluminescence. The gills also show luminous patches when they are examined in the dark.

Fruiting body
Cap: olive-brown to yellow when wet, paler when dry. 1–2cm in diameter. Bell-shaped, striate, margin toothed in young specimens. Flesh white, thin. *Gills:* white, adnate with a decurrent tooth, relatively broad, rather distant. *Stipe:* slender, parallel-sided, sometimes wavy, rooting, up to 7cm long, 2mm thick. Yellow, white at the base. Flesh tough, hollow. *Spores:* white in mass, ellipsoid, smooth, in iodine they turn blue-black, average size 10.0 × 5.0 microns.

Habitat and distribution
Grows in troops, among moss and ferns, in coniferous and deciduous woods, on heaths. Common in Europe and North America. It is found in South Africa.

Occurrence
August to November.

Culinary properties
This species is too small to be worth gathering for worthwhile use on the table.

Mycena flavo-alba
Fruiting body Wholly ivory white. *Cap:* pale yellow in old specimens, margin finely striate. Convex then flat. *Stipe:* short, curved.
Ecology In grassland, especially on lawns, heaths, open woodland. Common in Europe, reported from South Africa. August to November. Edibility unknown.

Above: Mycena epipterygia
Left: Mycena alcalina
Bottom: Mycena flavo-alba

Mycena galericulata
BONNET MYCENA
The colour of this species varies with changing weather conditions. It often grows in dense tufts with several stipes 'glued together' by the soft hairy down at their bases.

Fruiting body
Cap: grey to brown. 2–5cm in diameter. At first conical or bell-shaped, becoming flat with a cen-

tral umbo. Margin striate to the centre, cuticle smooth, silvery shining when dry. Flesh white, thin. *Gills:* at first white, finally pink. Adnate with a decurrent tooth, broad, rather distant, cross-connected by veins near the stipe. *Stipe:* long, slender, with a spindle-shaped root, 5–10cm long, up to 5mm thick, greyish-brown, smooth, with long, coarse hairs at the base. Flesh tough, hollow. *Spores:* white in mass, ellipsoid, smooth, with iodine they turn blue-black, average size 10.5 × 7.0 microns.

Habitat and distribution
Grows in dense clusters, on stumps of deciduous trees, especially alder and birch, on coniferous stumps in mountainous areas. Common in Europe, North America, Australia and South Africa.

Above: Mycena galericulata
Top: Mycena galopus
Bottom: Mycena haematopus

Occurrence
January to December in Europe, September to November in North America.

Culinary properties
Young specimens have a delicate flavour and good texture when stewed gently in their own juice and then seasoned with salt, pepper and butter.

Mycena galopus
MILK-DROP MYCENA
This species which is also called the Milk Stalk, plays an important part in breaking down litter in woods, and thus in the recycling of nutrients back to the soil. It is very variable in colour, but can be recognized by its slender fruit bodies and by the white milk exuded from wounds in its stipe. A pure white variety, var. *alba*, is frequently found in deci-

duous beech woods. *Mycena leucogala*, a dark grey fungus common on burnt ground and bonfire sites in woods, is described by some as a variant, var. *nigra*, of *Mycena galopus*.

Fruiting body
Cap: varies from pale greyish-brown to dark grey, darker in the centre. 1–1.7cm in diameter. Bell-shaped to conical, expanding slightly and retaining a central hump. Striate from the margin to the centre. Flesh greyish-white, very thin. *Gills:* white to greyish-white, narrowed next to the stipe, fairly crowded. *Stipe:* very slender, slightly thickened at the base, 5–8cm long, 2–4mm thick. Pale greyish-brown to dark grey, paler at the apex. Smooth, woolly at the base. Flesh brown, very fragile, exudes a white juice when broken.

Spores: white in mass, ellipsoid, smooth, in iodine they turn blue-black, average size 13.5 × 6.5 microns.

Habitat and distribution
Grows singly or in small groups, among fallen leaves, needles and twigs, in woods, copses and hedgerows. Common in Europe and North America.

Occurrence
August to December.

Culinary properties
This species is too small to be worth gathering for food.

Mycena haematopus
BLEEDING MYCENA
When broken this species exudes a blood-red juice which accounts for the other common name, Big Blood Stalk. The amount of juice produced depends on the prevailing weather conditions. It can also be recognized by the teeth around the edge of its cap.

Fruiting body
Cap: deep brownish-red, often with a white bloom. 1–3cm in diameter. Bell-shaped to convex. Margin striate, toothed. Flesh turns blood-red when cut, thick in the centre. *Gills:* white to flesh-colour, with reddish-brown edges. Adnate, crowded, alternate gills shorter. *Stipe:* slender, parallel-sided, 5–10 cm long, 5–7mm thick. Deep brownish-red, with a white bloom at first. Flesh when broken yields blood-red to brownish latex. *Spores:* white in mass, broadly-ellipsoid, smooth, in iodine they turn blue-black, average size 10.3 × 6.3 microns.

Habitat and distribution
Grows in tufts, sometimes in troops, on stumps and fallen branches of deciduous trees, on coniferous wood

in mountainous areas. Occasional in Europe, frequent on birch in northern North America, in mountainous areas of Venezuela.

Occurrence
August to November.

Culinary properties
It is worth cooking, when available in large quantities.

Mycena inclinata

Fruiting body *Cap:* at first black becoming greyish-brown. Margin toothed, overlaps gills. *Stipe:* long, slender. Whitish-yellow, flushing red-brown upwards from the coarsely hairy base.

Ecology In tufts on trunks of oak, often growing from knot holes. Occasionally on beeches, rarely on conifers. Variable in Europe, becoming more common towards the south.

Edibility unknown.

Mycena polygramma

Fruiting body *Cap:* steel-grey, occasionally with a whitish bloom. Bell-shaped then convex with a central hump. Margin striate. *Stipe:*

tall, siff, rooting. Grey with paler, raised, longitudinal ribs.

Ecology Singly or in small groups, on or near stumps of deciduous trees, especially alder, hazel. Frequent to common in Europe. Reported from South Africa. July to November.

Edibility unknown.

tinged pink. Adnate with a decurrent tooth, broad, connected by veins. *Stipe:* slender, parallel-sided or tapering upwards, wavy or twisted, sometimes rooting, 4–7cm long, 2–4mm thick. Pale pink, smooth, shining, woolly at the base. Flesh tough, hollow. *Spores:* white in mass, ellipsoid, smooth, in iodine they turn blue-black, average size 6.9 × 3.9 microns.

Habitat and distribution
Grows singly or in tufts, among humus, leaves and decayed wood in deciduous and coniferous woods. Common in Europe and North America. It is found in Venezuela.

Occurrence
May to December in Europe, June to October in North America.

Culinary properties
Smells strongly of radish when bruised. Not recommended.

Mycena vulgaris

Fruiting body Small. *Cap:* greyish-brown, slimy, margin striate. Cuticle peels. Convex to flat. *Gills:* white, almost decurrent, edges swollen gelatinous. *Stipe:* slender, greyish, base with long, coarse hairs.

Mycena pura
LILAC MYCENA

When collections of this toadstool are examined in the dark, luminous patches show on its gills and stipe. The beautiful, clear, rose to lilac coloration of its fruit body distinguishes it from the other largish *Mycena* species.

Fruiting body
Cap: pale rose to lilac. 2–5cm in diameter. Convex, soon becoming flat. Cuticle smooth. Flesh pink, thick in the centre. *Gills:* white,

Top: Mycena polygramma
Top, far left: Mycena inclinata
Left: Mycena pura
Bottom: Mycena vulgaris

Ecology In troops, on needle cover of coniferous woods. Frequent in Europe and northern North America. August to November. Edibility unknown.

Right: Nolanea cetrata
Far right: Nyctalis asterophora
Bottom, right: Nolanea staurospora
Bottom, left: Nolanea sericea

Nolanea cetrata

Fruiting body *Cap:* yellowish-tan, margin striate halfway to centre when moist, drying paler, non-striate. Broadly conical, finally convex. *Stipe:* tall, slender, pale brownish-ochre, silky-striate.

Ecology Coniferous woods, among moss, on rotten wood. Europe. August to November. Edibility unknown.

Nolanea sericea

Gardeners regard this insignificant species as a menace as it is often found growing in troops on lawns.
Fruiting body
Cap: dark reddish-brown when moist, margin fading to greyish-brown when dry. 2–6cm in diameter. At first convex, expanding and slightly umbonate. Margin in-curved and striate at first and when moist, finally becoming split. Cuticle silky shining, fibrillose. Flesh very thin and fragile, pale grey when dry, darker and translucent when wet. *Gills:* at first greyish-white, finally pink. Cut away next to the stipe, broad, crowded. *Stipe:* slender, sometimes tapering upwards, it can be compressed or twisted, 2–5cm long, varies with the length of the grass, 3–5mm thick. Shining greyish-brown, with a white base. *Spores:* deep flesh-colour in mass, broadly ellipsoid, angular, average size 9.0 × 7.8 microns.

Habitat and distribution
Grows gregariously or in troops. Common among grass, especially on lawns, in meadows and along grass verges. Rare on the ground in open woodland. Common in Europe, infrequent in North America where it appears to be found only in woods.

Occurrence
May to October in Europe, June to July in North America.

Culinary properties
Tastes and smells of meal. Not recommended.

Nolanea staurospora

Fruiting body *Cap:* date-brown, margin striate halfway to centre when moist, yellowish-brown, not striate when dry. Broadly conical. *Stipe:* slender, straight, yellowish-brown, distinctly striate. White, downy at the base. *Spores:* cruciform stellate.

Ecology Grassland, glades in woods, under conifers in mountainous areas. Frequent to common in Europe. June to October. Edibility unknown.

Nyctalis asterophora

This parasitic fungus attacks the rotting fruiting bodies of certain species of *Lactarius*, especially *Lactarius piperatus* and *L. vellereus*, and *Russula*, usually *Russula delica* and *R. nigricans*. It has been grown successfully on a culture medium containing *Russula nigricans*. This is the only *Nyctalis* species found in North America.

Fruiting body
Cap: at first white, soon becoming powdered with brownish chlamydospores. 1–2cm in diameter. Almost globular. Flesh pale-grey, thick, moist. *Gills:* frequently not developed, whitish-grey, adnate, rather narrow, thick, distant. *Stipe:* short, stout, 2–3cm long, 3–8mm thick. White becoming brown, powdery or silky. Flesh becoming hollow. *Spores:* often absent, white in mass, ellipsoid, smooth, average

size 5.5 × 3.5 microns. *Chlamydospores:* abundant, brown in mass, bluntly star-shaped, average size 19.0 microns in diameter.

Habitat and distribution
Grows singly or in clusters, on rotting fruiting bodies of *Lactarius* and *Russula* species, less frequently on *Cantharellus* and *Clitocybe* species. Common in Europe, infrequent or locally common in North America.

Occurrence
July to November in Europe, August to September in North America.

Culinary properties
Inedible due to strong, rancid taste and smell.

Nyctalis parasitica
Fruiting body Small. *Cap:* whitish-grey, tinged lilac, smooth, silky. Convex to flattened. *Gills:* soon become obscured by brownish, powdery covering of chlamydospores. *Stipe:* long, slender, wavy, greyish-white.
Ecology Often in clusters, parasitically on rotting fungi, especially species of *Lactarius* and *Russula*. Occasional to frequent in Europe. July to December.
Edibility unknown.

Omphalina ericetorum
This small, funnel-shaped fungus varies in colour according to the weather.

Fruiting body
Cap: colour variable, usually pale brownish-olive, darker in the centre. 1—2cm in diameter. At first convex, finally umbilicate. Margin at first incurved, finally scalloped and grooved. Coarsely striate. Flesh pale, thick in the centre, translucent when moist. *Gills:* short, narrowing from apex to base, up to 2cm long. Usually pale brownish-olive, smooth, with white hairs at the base. Flesh firm, hollow. *Spores:* white in mass, broadly-ellipsoid to pip-shaped, smooth, average size 8.0 × 3.9 microns.

Habitat and distribution
Grows gregariously, sometimes in large numbers, on peaty ground, occasionally among wet moss, on heaths, bogs, pastures and along roadsides, variable in Europe, becoming more common towards the north and in mountainous areas. Widespread and common in North America from sea level to 1,200m. Found in the mountains of the Dominican Republic.

Culinary properties
This species is only worth gathering for food if one is otherwise faced with starvation!

Omphalina fibula
Fruiting body Small. *Cap:* colour varies from orange to almost white, somewhat translucent. Convex, finally depressed. *Gills:* white to yellowish-white, deeply decurrent, arched. *Stipe:* very slender, pale orange.
Ecology In grass, in moist shady places, in woods, bogs, heaths,

moors, pastures. Common in Europe and northern North America. May to November.
Edibility unknown.

Omphalina pyxidata
Fruiting body Small. *Cap:* orange-brown with coarse, radial, red-brown striations. Finally funnel-shaped. *Gills:* yellowish-brown.

Top: Omphalina ericetorum
Left: Omphalina fibula
Far left: Nyctalis parasitica
Bottom: Omphalina pyxidata

Stipe: slender, wavy, pale orange brown.
Ecology Grasslands, moist sandy soil, along roadsides. Frequent to common in Europe, reported from South Africa. August to November. Edibility unknown.

Right: Omphalotus olearius
Centre: Oudemansiella mucida
Far right: Oudemansiella radicata
Bottom: Panellus mitis

Omphalotus olearius
Fruiting body *Cap:* becoming funnel-shaped with a central umbo, margin inrolled, streaked with flat hairs, bright orange to orange-yellow. *Gills:* decurrent. yellow-orange, luminescent in dark (and hence common names—Jack O' Lantern in America and Lantern Funnel Fungus in Europe), thin. *Stipe:* tapering to a narrow base, minutely downy or scaly, light orange.
Ecology Forms clusters on stumps, buried roots and other debris of olive trees, oaks and chestnuts. Common in southern Europe and the eastern and southern states of America. Late summer and autumn.
Poisonous.

Oudemansiella mucida
SLIMY BEECH CAPS
This beautiful, glistening, white fungus sometimes called the Porcelain Fungus is often found growing several metres up on the trunks of beech trees.
Fruiting body
Cap: at first grey, then shining white, translucent. 3–8cm in diameter. At first hemispherical, becoming flattened and radially wrinkled. Margin striate. Cuticle very slimy. Flesh white, soft, slimy. *Gills:* white, shining, rounded and with a decurrent tooth next to the stipe, broad, distant. *Stipe:* short, tapering upwards from the base, curved, 1–7cm long, 5–10mm thick. White, striate above the wide membranous ring, greyish and scaly below. Flesh tough. *Spores:* white in mass, globose, smooth, with a very thick wall, average size 15.5 × 14.0 microns.
Habitat and distribution
Grows singly, in troops or small clusters, on dead trunks or weakened deciduous trees, especially beech. Variable in Europe, becoming more common towards the south. Frequent in eastern North America.
Occurrence
August to November.
Culinary properties
When chopped finely and cooked with care this species can be made into a good dish.

Oudemansiella radicata
Although this toadstool often grows on soil, its long tap-root always originates from decaying timber or roots. The mycelium causes a white rot in infected wood.
Fruiting body
Cap: colour varies from pale brownish-grey to dark olive-brown. 3–9cm in diameter. At first bell-shaped, finally flat with a slight, central hump. Cuticle slimy, radially wrinkled. Flesh white, thin, soft. *Gills:* clear white, sometimes edged with brown. Rounded or notched next to the stipe, broad, distant. *Stipe:* tapers towards the top, with a long tap-root, 10–20cm long. Whitish-brown, becoming vertically striate or grooved, often twisted. Flesh white, cartilaginous. *Spores:* white to yellow in mass, ovoid, smooth, average size 14.0 × 11.0 microns.
Habitat and distribution
Grows singly or in groups, on or around decayed stumps in deci-

duous woods, especially beech. Common in Europe and North America.
Occurrence
June to November.
Culinary properties
The caps have a delicious flavour and pleasing texture when cooked with care. They are best broiled or fried.

Panellus mitis
Fruiting body Small. *Cap:* whitish-brown, kidney- to shell-shaped, cuticle peels. *Stipe:* lateral, flattened and expanded at junction with cap.
Ecology On felled coniferous woods, especially spruce, balsam fir. Frequent to common in Europe and North America. October to December.
Edibility unknown.

Panellus serotinus

Fruiting body *Cap:* colour varies from olive-green to dingy yellow, at first cushion-shaped, hairy, finally fan-shaped, slimy. *Gills:* yellow. *Stipe:* lateral, yellow with brownish scales.

Ecology Singly, in tufts, or overlapping tiers, on trunks and stumps of deciduous trees, especially birch. Occasional in Europe and northeastern North America. August to December.

Edible.

Panellus stipticus
STIPTIC FUNGUS

The gills, caps and mycelium of the North American form of this species are luminous in the dark. The European form is not luminescent, but if mycelia from these two forms are mated, then luminescent mycelium is produced. The small, ear-shaped, fruit bodies are frequently attacked by slugs, which may be important agents in the dispersal of its spores.

Fruiting body

Cap: cinnamon when moist, pale clay when dry. 1–3cm in diameter. Kidney or ear-shaped, convex then flat. Margin incurved. Cuticle

minutely mealy. Flesh white to pale yellow, thin, tough. *Gills:* sometimes pale cinnamon, narrow, crowded, connected by veins. *Stipe:* lateral, flattened, widening into the cap, up to 3cm long. Almost white, powdery to downy. Flesh tough, solid. *Spores:* white in mass, ellipsoid to cylindrical, in iodine they turn blue-black, average size 4.5 × 2.5 microns.

Habitat and distribution

Grows in crowded, overlapping tiers, on the stumps and dead trunks of deciduous trees especially beech, oak and birch. Common in Europe and eastern North America.

Occurrence

January to December in Europe, August to February in North America.

Culinary properties

Inedible due to the unpleasant, bitter taste. It has been used in the past as a violent purgative.

Panaeolus foenisecii
HAYMAKERS' TOADSTOOL

This species of meadows and pastures in summer and autumn is well known to farm workers who come across it as they cut hay, hence the common English names. It is also called the Brown Hay Cap.

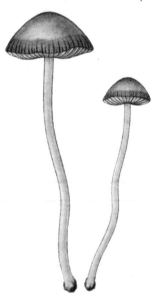

Fruiting body

Cap: when moist, dull darkish-brown with slight rufous tinge, slowly drying from the apex to pale clay colour, often leaving a dark marginal belt, smooth. 1–2cm in diameter. Bell-shaped to convex, never flat. Flesh thin, a dingy pale colour. *Gills:* pale brown at first, becoming mottled as spores ripen, finally dull dark-brown. Edge fringed with white. Adnate, often notched near the stipe, broad, inflated, almost subdistant. *Stipe:* slender, equal, fragile and hollow,

4–8cm long, 1.2–2cm thick. Paler than cap, smooth, powdered at the top. *Spores:* dark brown to blackish in mass, narrowly lemon-shaped, slightly warty, average size 14.5 × 8.0 microns, very variable.

Habitat and distribution

A common species growing singly or in groups in grassy places throughout the temperate regions of Europe, North America, and South Africa.

Occurrence

July to October, also occasionally in spring.

Culinary properties

Tastes and smells very slight, edible but unremarkable and too small to be worth collecting for food.

Left: Panaeolus semiovatus
Centre: Panaeolus foenisecii
Far left: Panellus serotinus
Bottom: Panellus stipticus

Panaeolus semiovatus

This is one of the most frequent toadstools to grow on dung. It is very hardy and can even be found growing in the snow on mountains. Enthusiasts describe it as being edible, with an excellent flavour. A closely related species *Panaeolus sphinctrinus*, has an overall grey-coloured cap with a distinct white fringe around its margin. It grows on herbivore dung. An alpine form occurs with a larger cap and shorter stipe than those growing in lower areas. These can be found fruiting through the melting snow for the few weeks of the year that the grass is exposed.

Fruiting body

Cap: greyish to very pale tan. 1–6cm in diameter approximately the same in height. Bell-shaped, not expanding, margin fringed with remnants of veil. Slimy when moist, shining when dry, becoming wrinkled with age. Flesh rather thick, whitish, yellow under cuticle. *Gills:* greyish, mottled, finally black with paler edge. Adnate ascending, broad, crowded. *Stipe:* straight, slender or stout, usually narrowing upwards from thickened base, with an expanded membranous ring just above the middle, 8–12cm long. Whitish shining, striate above ring. Flesh white, yellow in the base. *Spores:* black in mass, lemon-shaped, smooth, average size 19.0 × 12.0 microns, size very variable.

Habitat and distribution
Found always on dung or manured ground, usually in pastures. In the Alps on cow dung deposited the previous summer. Common in temperate areas of Europe, North America, South Africa and mountains of West Indies.

Occurrence
July to November in Europe, May to October in North America.

Culinary properties
Tastes and smells pleasant, must be cooked straight away and for not more than 15 minutes.

Panus torulosus
Fruiting body *Cap:* colour varies from pinkish-yellow to reddish-brown to violet, smooth. Margin lobed. Deeply, irregularly depressed in the centre. *Stipe:* eccentric to lateral, stout. At first covered with violet down. Completely wrinkled and grooved.

Ecology Often in small clusters on stumps of deciduous trees, especially oak, birch. Variable in Europe, becoming more common towards the south. Common in deciduous forest areas of North America. May to October.
Edible.

Paxillus atrotomentosus
This species is found at the base of living and dead coniferous trees. It is easily recognized by its stout stature and its velvety stipe. Cottony, thread-like mycelium can often be seen around its fruit bodies. The variety *bambusinus* grows on bamboo in Trinidad.

Fruiting body
Cap: dark sometimes reddish brown, tinged olive. 12–27cm in diameter. Convex then flattened and deeply depressed in centre. Margin thin, incurved, frequently minutely grooved. Cuticle persistently minutely downy especially at centre, moist and dark-spotted in wet weather. Flesh whitish, compact, turns buff with ammonia and dirty leaf-green with ferrous sulphate. *Gills:* at first olive-buff, soon pale-ochre then cinnamon, sometimes slightly spotted with rust or with rusty edges, dries olivaceous. Decurrent, branched, frequently forming a network at the junction with the stipe. *Stipe:* more or less eccentric, short, stout, narrowed at base, 3–9cm long, 2–5cm thick. Dark-brownish black with dense velvety down. Flesh cream to pale ochre, turns very slightly lavender when cut. *Spores:* sienna in mass, smooth, ellipsoid, turn pale straw in ammonia, average size 5.8 × 3.8 microns.

Habitat and distribution
Grows singly or in tufts, on stumps and at the base of living conifers, especially Scots Pine. Widespread and frequent in Europe, infrequent in North America, reported from Trinidad.

Occurrence
August to November in Europe, July to September in North America.

Culinary properties
No distinct smell. When cooked it has the consistency of marshmallow and a marked, but pleasant, flavour. Enthusiasts do not agree about the value of this species.

Paxillus involutus
This is a woodland fungus and can often be found abundantly even during comparatively dry seasons. It can easily be recognized by its strongly in-rolled, cottony, cap margin, by the brown bruising of its gills and by its overall ochreous-brown colour. As an edible species it is not highly regarded by enthusiasts.

Fruiting body
Cap: ochreous to tawny-yellow, at first with olive tinge on margin, finally snuff-brown with hazel blotches. 5–12cm in diameter. Convex at first, then flattened and sometimes depressed. Margin persistently inrolled and densely downy when young, becoming smoother and grooved with age. Cuticle downy at first, becoming slimy in the centre when wet, smooth and shining when dry. Flesh thick, soft, yellowish-brown, becoming firm and pliant with age. Turns reddish-buff then tawny-yellow with ammonia, turns leaf-green then olive

Right: Paxillus atrotomentosus
Below: Panus torulosus

with ferrous sulphate. *Gills:* at first yellow, finally olive-yellow to dark clay-brown, bruising brown and tinged olive when dry. Deeply decurrent, narrow, crowded, branching and forming a network at the top of the stipe. *Stipe:* sometimes eccentric, thickening upwards from narrow base, up to 7.5cm long, 8–12mm thick. Cap colour or paler, smooth, becoming spotted and streaked dark brown, particularly when handled. Flesh tawny yellow towards base, brown when bruised or cut. *Spores:* sienna in mass, smooth, ellipsoid, turn deep ochre in ammonia, turn sienna in Meltzers reagent. Average size 9.0 × 5.5 microns.

in damp coal-mines, but is not a serious problem in houses as wood must have a high moisture content for its development. The fibrous yellow mycelium is often seen on the surface of infected wood, which first becomes bright yellow, soft and cheesy before finally turning dark, reddish-brown with longitudinal cracks. This species has two varieties, var. *ionipes* which has a strongly developed violet or amythyst zone at its base, and var. *rubrosquammulosus* which has prominent reddish scales on its cap.

Fruiting body
Cap: dark buff to tawny-yellow, sometimes with a lavender or lilac zone at junction with substrate.

Occurrence
August to November in Europe, July to August in North America.

Culinary properties
No distinct taste or smell. Not recommended.

Phaeolepiota aurea
There are few more handsome mushrooms than *Phaeolepiota aurea*. It is one of the most distinctive of all the gill fungi with a golden cap and flared ring. Caution should, however, be exercised when eating this toadstool for the first time, as some people are allergic to it.

Above: Paxillus panuoides
Left: Paxillus involutus
Below: Phaeolepiota aurea

Habitat and distribution
Grows singly or in groups, sometimes in rings, in mixed and broad-leaved woods, particularly under birch and oak, on rocky mossy embankments by roadsides, along borders of marshes. Common in Europe and in the northern coniferous regions of North America, reported from South Africa.

Occurrence
August to November in Europe, July to October in North America.

Culinary properties
Tastes and smells slightly acidic. It is slightly poisonous to some people when raw, harmless when cooked. Flesh dry, coarse and tasteless, is not improved by cooking. It is, however, reported as being highly prized in Russia.

Paxillus panuoides
This fungus is easily recognized by its lateral habit, by its buff or ochre colour, and by its reduced or absent stipe. It grows on damp coniferous timber. It commonly causes decay

1–4cm infrequently 7cm in diameter. Bracket-like or shell-shaped. Margin thin, wavy or crisped. Cuticle at first minutely downy, then coarsely downy with even, reddish-brown scales. Flesh thin, ochraceous, paler towards the margin, turns tawny-yellow with ammonia and leaf-green with ferrous sulphate. *Gills:* buff to pale tawny-yellow, darkening slightly when handled, decurrent, crowded, branched. *Stipe:* lateral, rudimentary or absent. *Spores:* ochraceous-rust in mass, smooth, ellipsoid, dextrinoid, turn dark blue in cotton blue, average size 4.8 × 3.8 microns.

Habitat and distribution
Grows gregariously or in overlapping tiers, on decaying coniferous wood, or on sawdust heaps, in cellars, on pit-props down mines, on old pine stumps. Widespread and occasional in Europe, rather rare in North America, has been recorded in South Africa and Australia, and found on imported timber in Venezuela.

Fruiting body
Cap: golden-brown. 8–20cm in diameter. At first convex, becoming flattened. Cuticle and margin at first covered by a flaky, powdery veil which soon rubs off. Flesh whitish-yellow. *Gills:* at first clay-colour, soon becoming rusty-brown, adnexed. *Stipe:* tall, stout, 8–15cm high, 2–3cm thick. Sheathed upwards from base by the ochre-brown flaky veil, which expands near the apex into a conspicuous

membranous ring. *Spores:* yellowish-brown in mass, ellipsoid to spindle-shaped, smooth or finely roughened, average size 12.0 × 5.0 microns.

Habitat and distribution
Found on rich loamy soil, in pastures under hedges, in parks and woods, especially among stinging nettles and under beech and alder. Frequent in central Europe, becoming rare towards the west, rare in North America generally, but locally abundant on the Pacific Coast from Alaska southwards.

Occurrence
September to November.

Culinary properties
Tastes slight, smells aromatic and pleasant. The stipes should be discarded before cooking. When trying this species for the first time only a small quantity should be taken, as it causes an allergic reaction in some people.

Right: Phaeomarasmius
erinaceus
Far right: Pholiota
alnicola
Bottom, right:
Pholiota adiposa

Phaeomarasmius erinaceus
This very small fungus has a distinctive prickly cap. It grows on damp, dead branches of broad-leaved trees and is remarkable for its ability to quickly revive from a completely dried up state.

Fruiting body
Cap: yellowish, rusty-brown. 0.5–1 cm in diameter. Convex, then flattened. Margin at first incurved and connected to stipe by a fibrillose veil. Cuticle dry, with erect pointed scales. Flesh pale tan, tough. *Gills:* pale brown, then cinnamon, adnate and rounded behind, broad, rather distant. *Stipe:* short, equal curved upwards from base, up to 1cm long. Brown, scaly, like the cap, up to indistinct ring, smooth at apex. *Spores:* rusty-brown in mass, smooth, broadly ellipsoid, average size 12.3 × 8.0 microns.

Habitat and distribution
In small groups on dead branches or twigs of deciduous trees, in damp places in woods. Found occasionally in Europe.

Occurrence
August to November.

Culinary properties
Small and tough, inedible.

Pholiota adiposa
This striking woodland species is not regarded as edible by Europeans but it is eaten and enjoyed in North America.

Fruiting body
Cap: golden brown, 5–10cm in diameter. At first hemispherical then expanded and nearly flat. Margin even, hanging down, incurved when young. Cuticle sticky, beset with glutinous, brownish triangular scales. Flesh pale-yellow, thick and firm. *Gills:* at first straw-yellow, finally rusty-ochre. Adnate becoming cut away against the stipe, broad, crowded. *Stipe:* stout, slightly thickened at base, curved, 5–10cm long, 6–12cm thick. Cap colour, smooth above the very slight cottony ring, scaly below. Yellow flesh, tough, turning to rusty brown in the base. *Spores:* rusty-brown in mass, ellipsoid, smooth, average size 6.0 × 3.5 microns.

Habitat and distribution
Occurs occasionally at the base of trees or stumps, or on fallen logs especially beech. Also from wounds in living trees. Reported on maple and white ash in North America, found in S.E. Australia and Europe.

Occurrence
August to October.

Culinary properties
Tastes mild, no smell. Caps must be peeled before cooking, makes a substantial and agreeable dish.

Pholiota alnicola
Fruiting body *Cap:* bright yellow becoming olive tinged towards the edge, reddish in the centre. Convex then flat. *Stipe:* more or less horizontal. Pale yellow, becoming rusty towards the base, dry. Tastes bitter.
Ecology Solitary or in tufts on stumps and trunks of deciduous trees, especially alder, willow. Occasional to frequent in Europe. August to November.
Inedible.

Pholiota destruens

Fruiting body Large. *Cap:* pale brownish-yellow, covered with white cottony scales. Convex, sometimes with a broad central hump. *Stipe:* short, stout, covered with scales up to ring. Smells strong, nauseous, aromatic.
Ecology Singly or in tufts on trunks of deciduous trees, especially poplar, also birch, willow. Rare to occasional to Europe, and northern North America. August to November.
Edibility unknown.

Pholiota aurivella

Fruiting body Fairly large. *Cap:* deep rusty-yellow, with rusty-brown concentrally arranged scales, very slimy. Convex to flat. *Stipe:* usually short, curved. Rusty-yellow, dry, fibrillose below ring-like zone.
Ecology Singly or in small tufts, usually high up on deciduous trees. Occasional to frequent in Europe. September to November.
Edibility unknown.

Pholiota carbonaria

Fruiting body Small. *Cap:* yellowish-foxy-brown, paler towards the margin, slimy. *Stipe:* pale yellow becoming more brown towards the base.
Ecology In clusters, in burnt areas in coniferous forests, on burnt roots. Frequent to common in Europe, reported from South Africa. September to November.
Edibility unknown.

Pholiota flammans

This very striking fungus of coniferous woods is distinguished by its bright yellow colour and by the prominent scales on its cap and stipe. It is well worth cooking and eating, but is not particularly easy to find.

Above: Pholiota destruens
Top: Pholiota aurivella
Far left: Pholiota astragalina
Bottom: Pholiota carbonaria

Pholiota astragalina

Fruiting body *Cap:* orange-flame with a yellow margin, slimy, smooth. Convex to flat. *Stipe:* pale yellow, with minute rusty scales, especially towards the base. Tastes bitter.
Ecology In small tufts on conifer stumps, especially scots pine. Rare in Europe. August to November.
Inedible.

Fruiting body

Cap: bright tawny-yellow with sulphur-yellow scales. 2–6cm in diameter. Convex then flat, sometimes slightly umbonate. Margin at first in-curved then spreading. Cuticle with concentrically arranged, curved, triangular scales. Flesh yellow, becoming reddish-brown. *Gills:* at first bright yellow, finally rust. Adnate, narrow, crowded. *Stipe:* slightly thickened at base, often curved, 5–7cm long, 5–10cm thick. Yellow, scaly up to torn ring. *Spores:* rusty-brown in mass, smooth, ellipsoid, minute, average size 4.3 × 2.5 microns.

Habitat and distribution

Grows singly on decaying trunks and stumps of conifers. Occasional in Europe, and Australia, frequent in North America.

Occurrence

August to October in Europe, September to after frosts in North America.

Culinary properties

Tastes and smells slight, caps are delicious when fried.

Centre: Pholiota lenta
Far right: Pholiota lucifera
Below: Pholiota flammans
Bottom: Pholiota gummosa

Pholiota gummosa

Fruiting body *Cap:* convex becoming flat, pale straw colour with white margin, becoming slightly greenish, numerous small white squammules, viscid. *Gills:* straw-whitish. *Stipe:* slender, with scales, same colour as cap except at base which is rusty both inside and out.

Ecology Small clusters in open spaces in woods, on and around stumps of deciduous and conifer woods. Fairly common in Europe and North America. Inedible.

Pholiota lenta

Fruiting body *Cap:* whitish-olive-yellow, with white cottony tufts which soon disappear, slimy. Convex to flat. *Stipe:* almost white, covered with brownish-white cottony scales from the base up. Smells faintly of radish.

Ecology Deciduous woods, especially under beech, under conifers in mountainous areas. Frequent in Europe. September to December. Edibility unknown.

Pholiota lucifera

Specimens of this fungus have a striking tawny-yellow cap. They sometimes appear to be growing in soil, but on investigation are always found to be attached to buried stumps or logs.

Fruiting body

Cap: bright yellow with rusty scales. 4–6cm in diameter. At first convex, then expanded, finally bluntly umbonate. Margin even, incurved at first, then hanging down. Cuticle slimy, with inconspicuous scales. Flesh whitish, yellow under cuticle. *Gills:* at first bright yellow with paler edges, finally rusty. Adnate becoming wavy, edges scalloped with flask-shaped sterile cells. *Stipe:* cylindrical, often curved upwards from base, 2–5cm long, 5–7mm thick. Yellow, dry, scaly up to narrow woolly, short-lived ring, pale above. Flesh rusty in the base. *Spores:* rusty-brown, smooth, ovoid, average size 8.5–5.5 microns.

Habitat and distribution

Grows gregariously, often in tufts,

usually on deciduous wood, but on coniferous wood in mountainous areas. Found in damp places in woods. Rare, becoming more frequent southwards in Europe, rare in North America.

Occurrence

August to November in Europe, August to September in North America.

Culinary properties

Not recommended.

Pholiota squarrosa
SCALY CLUSTER FUNGUS

This species forms magnificent tufts on dead or living trees. It can be recognized by the shaggy red-brown scales on its yellow cap and stipe. The American form of this species is smaller and, unlike Euro-

yellow, becoming blue where bruised, connected by cross veins. *Stipe:* tapering towards base, buff with reddish stain, smooth above but pubescent below.

Ecology Single or in groups under conifers and mixed hardwoods including chestnut and oak. Frequent in Europe and North America. Spring through to autumn.
Edible (good).

Pleurotus dryinus

This fungus differs from the other large species of *Pleurotus* by having a strong smell of bitter almonds when mature.

Fruiting body

Cap: whitish-grey, often becoming yellowish with age. 5–12cm in diameter. At first convex, then flattened, margin incurved and hung with remnants of veil. Cuticle with dense grey down which breaks up into soft, woolly scales. Flesh white, thick, finally corky. *Gills:* white, discolouring yellowish, deeply decurrent, forming a network on the

pean specimens, it is usually restricted to the trunks of living trees. It is a weak parasite, entering through wounds in the bark.

Fruiting body

Cap: straw-yellow with hazel-brown scales. 3–8cm in diameter. Convex then flattened, commonly bluntly umbonate or lop-sided. Cuticle dry, with shaggy, curved scales. Flesh tough, yellowish. *Gills:* at first straw-yellow, finally olive-brownish, adnate with a decurrent tooth, narrow, crowded. *Stipe:* long, narrowing downwards, curved or wavy, length variable 7 to 15 even up to 20cm. Straw-yellow with brown scales up to a small, frayed, dark brown ring, smooth above. Flesh dark yellow in the base. *Spores:* rusty-brown in mass, smooth, ellipsoid, average size 7.3 × 4.5 microns.

Habitat and distribution

Grows in large tufts on living or decaying deciduous or coniferous trees. Frequent in Europe, uncommon in North America, where it used to be common until the virgin forests were felled, it is now most frequent in the forests of the Rocky Mountains.

Occurrence

September to November in Europe, August to November in North America.

Culinary properties

Sweet mealy taste at first, then of stale grease when old, with a heavy, stinking, but disappearing, smell. Can only be eaten when young, when cooked the caps are of good substance and flavour.

Phylloporus rhodoxanthus

Fruiting body *Cap:* convex, dry and felty, sometimes cracked, brown to red or orange-brown, yellow flesh exposed by cracking, 2–10cm diameter. *Gills:* decurrent,

stipe, narrowing at each end, rather distant. *Stipe:* eccentric or lateral, stout with a short blunt root, 2.5cm long and thick. White and downy, especially towards the base, with a membranous ring, which disappears as the cap expands. *Spores:* white in mass, cylindrical to ellipsoid, smooth, average size 11.8 × 3.9 microns.

Habitat and distribution

Grows on trunks of living deciduous trees or on felled wood, especially oak, ash and willow. Occasional to frequent in Europe, eastern North America and South Africa.

Occurrence

September to February.

Culinary properties

Tastes pleasant, smells strongly of bitter almonds when old. When

Top: Pholiota squarrosa
Left: Pleurotus dryinus
Bottom: Phylloporus rhodoxanthus

cooked the caps of young specimens are tender with a similar flavour to that of *Agaricus campestris*.

Pleurotus eryngii
Fruiting body *Cap:* brownish-grey fading with age, convex then expanded with depressed centre, slightly velvety but soon glabrous. *Gills:* decurrent, whitish becoming dirty ochre, widely separated. *Stipe:* usually eccentric, thick and tapering to base, smooth, whitish.
Ecology On decaying umbellifer stems. In southern Europe and Asia. Spring through to autumn. Edible and good. It is dried and sold as human and donkey food in India and Pakistan.

Above: Pleurotus eryngii
Top: Pleurotus ostreatus
Right: Pleurotus ulmarius

Pleurotus ostreatus
OYSTER MUSHROOM
Known as the 'shellfish of the woods' young specimens are cooked in the same way as oysters. Some experts believe that this mushroom is not excelled by any other vegetable. The base of its cap can be tough and should be removed. Care must also be taken to clean collections thoroughly as the gills are often infested by beetles. It is eaten everywhere and fruits throughout the year. In Japan it is called *hira-take*. Successive crops can be produced if a trunk or stump where it is known to grow is kept watered. This species attacks living or dead trees, forming sheets of vegetative hyphae under the bark of its host. A beautiful, peacock-blue variant of this species is frequently found on poplars.

Fruiting body
Cap: at first deep greyish-blue to almost black, finally paler bluish or brownish. 3–15cm in diameter. Shell or fan-shaped. Margin inrolled. Cuticle waxy lustrous, sometimes becoming cracked. Flesh whitish, grey under cuticle. *Gills:* whitish, sometimes light yellow. Deeply decurrent, often fused or forming a network at the top of the stipe, broad. *Stipe:* short, eccentric or lateral, thickening gradually into the side of the cap, sometimes absent, up to 2cm long, 1–2cm thick. Whitish, coarsely hairy towards the base. Flesh firm, tough and elastic. *Spores:* lilac in mass, ellipsoid, smooth, average size 9.5 × 3.5 microns.
Habitat and distribution
Often growing in large shelving clusters, on deciduous trees and stumps, especially beech, occasionally found on conifers. It also occurs on posts and old telegraph poles. Common in Europe, North America, Australia, Venezuela and Japan.
Occurrence
January to December, but most plentiful in autumn.
Culinary properties
Tastes and smells agreeable. When young and blue the flesh is tender and delicious. It can be fried, stewed and served in a sauce, or baked in a slow oven. It dries easily over a stove or in a warm room.

Pleurotus ulmarius
ELM TREE MUSHROOM
This parasitic species is frequently found on shade-trees, usually elms, in cities but it appears to be rare in rural areas. It enters its host by way of natural cracks in the bark or through pruning wounds. This fungus can be found fruiting in the same place for several years, and dried specimens persist on the tree

long after the growing season has finished. Young specimens of this toadstool are regarded by Italians as providing a special gastronomic treat.
Fruiting body
Cap: white with orange or brownish centre, finally dull brown. 5–15cm in diameter. Moderately regular or slightly eccentric, convex or nearly flat. Cuticle smooth or slightly downy, becoming cracked with age.

Flesh white, thick and tough. *Gills:* whitish to pale ochre, rounded next to the stipe, broad and somewhat crowded. *Stipe:* stout, narrowing upwards, somewhat eccentric, usually curved, up to 11cm long and 4cm thick. Whitish, downy, sometimes only at the base. Flesh solid, firm and elastic. *Spores:* white in mass, globose, smooth, average size 5–7 microns in diameter.
Habitat and distribution
Grows singly or in tufts on dead or living deciduous trees, in semi-urban areas. Locally common in Europe and North America.

Occurrence

Summer and autumn in Europe, September to November in North America.

Culinary properties

Tastes and smells pleasant. When young it is tender and well-flavoured only the tender cap margins should be used from older specimens. It is delicious when stewed or cooked with cheese. Dries and stores well.

Pluteus cervinus
DEER MUSHROOM

This fungus is valuable as a source of food because it can often be found throughout the year. There are many related species which are smaller and are not streaked. A very

large form of this toadstool can be found growing on sawdust heaps. It is also known as the Common Fawn Agaric.

Fruiting body

Cap: dark brown, often with darker radiating streaks. 4–10cm in diameter. At first bell-shaped or conical, soon becoming flat, with a slight, persistent, central hump. Cuticle sticky when wet, occasionally cracking. Flesh white, soft. *Gills:* at first white, finally salmon-pink. Free, rounded next to the stipe, broad, very crowded. *Stipe:* tall, parallel-sided, or slightly swollen at the base, 7–12cm long, 10–15mm thick. Grey, streaked with dark brown lines. Flesh white, solid. *Spores:* salmon-pink in mass, ovoid, smooth, average size 7.3 × 5.3 microns.

Habitat and distribution

Grows singly, in groups, occasion-ally in rings, on stumps, fallen trunks, decaying roots and sawdust of deciduous trees, on coniferous wood in mountainous areas. Common in Europe and North America, it is found in Australia.

Occurrence

January to December, most common from May to October.

Culinary properties

Tastes and smells pleasant but becomes tasteless when cooked. Caps and stipes are of different textures and should be cooked separately. Caps are best fried in butter, stipes should be stewed.

Pluteus pellitus

Fruiting body *Cap:* convex or somewhat hump-shape, white to

pale ivory, 5–7cm diameter. *Gills:* flesh colour. *Stipe:* white, glabrous. In most respects this is a pale form of *Pluteus cervinus*.

Ecology On beech stumps. Rare in Europe and the north-west of North America.
Edible.

Pluteus petasatus

Only a few of these large, fleshy mushrooms are needed to make quite a substantial meal.

Fruiting body

Cap: whitish-grey, becoming brown towards the centre. 5–15cm in diameter. Convex then almost flat. Cuticle with fine pointed, overlapping scales. Flesh white, thick. *Gills:* white, finally tinted red. Free, 1cm or more broad, very crowded. *Stipe:* stout, narrowed and grooved at the base, 10–12cm long, 1–2cm thick. Whitish-grey. Flesh solid. *Spores:* dark pink in mass, ovoid, smooth, average size 8.5 × 4.5 microns.

Habitat and distribution

Grows in tufts on sawdust heaps, on heaps of straw and dung. Uncommon in Europe and North America.

Occurrence

Autumn.

Culinary properties

The caps are good when fried in butter.

Left: Pluteus pellitus
Far left: Pluteus cervinus
Bottom: Pluteus petasatus

Pluteus salicinus

Fruiting body *Cap:* grey, tinged blue-green, brown in the centre, scaly. Bell-shaped, then flat with a central hump. *Stipe:* slender, white becoming grey towards the base.

Ecology On stumps of deciduous trees, especially willow, alder, beech. Occasional in Europe. April to October.

Edibility unknown.

Top: Pluteus salicinus
Above, right:
Porphyrellus
porphyrosporus
Right: Pluteus
thomsonii
Bottom: Psathyrella
candolleana

Pluteus thomsonii

Fruiting body *Cap:* campanulate or slightly umbonate when expanded, hygrophanous, wrinkled or veined especially in central area, striate at margin, blackish-brown when young, becoming umber or sepia at maturity. *Gills:* free, pink at maturity. *Stipe:* 2–5cm tall, grey or olive tints to sepia, covered with a fine down and later striate.

Ecology On fallen deciduous twigs and logs, especially of beech. or on ground. Rare to uncommon in Europe. July to November.

Inedible.

Porphyrellus porphyrosporus

Fruiting body *Cap:* hazel to snuff-brown, darkening when bruised, velvety. *Pores:* pale vinaceous-buff and then olivaceous or ochraceous, bluish-green when bruised. *Stipe:* attenuated towards top, same colour as cap, smooth, covered with dark granules. *Spores:* brown vinaceous in mass.

Ecology In deciduous, mixed and conifer woods, especially in mountainous areas. Uncommon in Europe. Autumn.

Edible but not recommended.

Psathyrella candolleana

Fruiting body *Cap:* honey-colour when moist, dingy white when dry. Bell-shaped to convex. Margin with tooth-like remains of veil. *Gills:* at first greyish-lilac. *Stipe:* slender, fragile, sometimes with thread-like ring.

Ecology In tufts on or near stumps of deciduous trees, at the base of wooden fences. Common in Europe and North America, reported from South Africa. May to November.

Edible.

Psathyrella gracilis

This graceful fungus is distinguished from a number of similar species by the pink edges of its gills.

Fruiting body

Cap: dark-brown when moist, drying to pale tan. 1–3cm in diameter. More or less convex with a slight umbo. Margin striate. Flesh thin, white, translucent when wet. *Gills:* white at first, finally cindery-black with pink edges (seen through a lens). Adnate, becoming broader towards the stipe, rather distant. *Stipe:* slender, tense and straight, thickening slightly at the base, which has a short hairy tap-root, up

to 10cm long. White and smooth. *Spores:* black in mass, ellipsoid, smooth, with a germ pore, average size 12.0 × 6.0 microns.

Habitat and distribution
Grows singly on rich soil and among debris, deciduous woods, along woodland paths, among grass in hedgerows, in gardens and on ploughed soil. Common in Europe and North America, it is also found in South Africa.

Occurrence
August to November in Europe, June to October in North America.

Psathyrella spadiceo-grisea
Fruiting body *Cap:* dark brown when moist, pale greyish-brown when dry. Conical becoming flat with a central hump. *Stipe:* tubular.
Ecology Grows singly or in twos or threes, on or around stumps in deciduous woods. Occasional in Europe. April to November.
Inedible.

Psilocybe coprophila
Fruiting body Small. *Cap:* shining hazel, transparent, slimy when moist, leather-yellow when dry. Cuticle peels. Hemispherical. *Stipe:* slender often curved, rigid.
Ecology Gregarious in pastures on dung, especially horse droppings, cow pats. Occasional to frequent in Europe. August to November.
Edibility unknown.

Top Psathyrella hydrophila
Left: Psilocybe coprophila
Far left: Psathyrella gracilis
Bottom: Psathyrella spadiceo-grisea

Psilocybe ericaea
In Europe and Australia this is an open grassland species, but in North America it is found in deciduous woods.
Fruiting body
Cap: bright tawny-brown. 2–3cm in diameter. Convex, becoming

Culinary properties
No distinctive taste or smell, but it is said by some to be useful when cooked as a flavouring to other species.

Psathyrella hydrophila
Fruiting body *Cap:* chestnut-brown when moist, pale ochre when dry. Margin striate, often wavy. *Stipe:* shining white, sometimes with a brown, ring-like zone near the apex.
Ecology In dense tufts on or near stumps of deciduous trees. Common in Europe and North America. August to November.
Inedible.

flattened with a slight blunt umbo. Margin with white fibrillose remains of the cortina in young specimens. Cuticle slimy when wet, smooth and shining when dry. Flesh yellowish, firm, rather thin, faintly translucent in wet weather. *Gills:* white at first, then blackish-brown with white edges. Adnate, becoming notched next to the stipe, broad, rather crowded. *Stipe:* slender, wavy, parallel-sided, 5–10cm long, 3–4mm thick. Pale yellowish, turning red. Smooth, powdery at the apex. Flesh tough, cartilaginous, finally hollow. *Spores:* dark purple in mass, ovoid to ellipsoid, smooth, with a germ pore, average size 11.5 × 7.8 microns.

Habitat and distribution

Grows among grass and moss in damp pastures and on heaths. Frequent to common in Europe and Australia, in North America, it has been recorded growing from fallen leaves in deciduous woods in the north.

Occurrence

July to October.

Culinary properties

Not recommended.

Top: Psilocybe semilanceata
Right: Psilocybe ericaea
Bottom, right: Rozites caperata

Psilocybe semilanceata
LIBERTY CAPS

This small fungus was given the name Liberty Caps because the shape of its cap is like that adopted as the symbol of the first French Republic. It contains the hallucinatory drug psilocybin, and may have been tried by those seeking new drug experiences. In a recent English court case it was judged not to be an offence to possess the fruiting bodies of this species.

Fruiting body

Cap: pale-clay colour, becoming yellowish-olive or dingy brown. 0.5–1cm in diameter, up to 2cm high. Acutely conical, often with a sharp point, never expanding. Margin inrolled at first, slightly striate. Cuticle slimy, peeling in wet weather. Flesh membranous, white. *Gills:* finally purplish-brown with white edges, adnate, narrow, crowded. *Stipe:* slender, usually wavy, up to 7.5cm long. Whitish at the top, pale clay lower down. Smooth, with remnants of veil in young specimens. Flesh pliant, tough. *Spores:* purple-brown in mass, ellipsoid, smooth, with a germ pore, average size 13.0 × 7.8 microns.

Habitat and distribution

Grows gregariously, often in troops, among grass, in fields, pastures, heaths and along roadsides where animals have grazed. Frequent to common in Europe and North America, it also grows in Australia.

Occurrence

August to November.

Culinary properties

It is said to be poisonous when raw, even fatal if eaten by children. Harmless when cooked.

Rozites caperata
THE GYPSY

This rather rare species grows singly or in groups always on acid soil under conifers. It is identified by the silky white traces of universal veil remaining on the cap and a hint of a volva at the base of the stipe. An edible fungus, it is highly prized in North America and Europe, where it is sold in local markets.

Fruiting body

Cap: dull ochre colour with filmy white scales. 5–10cm in diameter. Ovate when young becoming bell-shaped or convex. Dry, smooth except for remains of universal veil, cottony on disc becoming scaly towards the radially wrinkled margin. Flesh white, thick in centre, thin towards the margin. *Gills:* at first whitish becoming brownish rusty with age, adnate, sides vertically wrinkled, edges eroded, crowded. *Stipe:* stout, cylindrical, sometimes bulbous. 5–12.5cm long, 7–12mm thick. White with an upward turning membranous thick-

edged ring. There are slight remnants of volva in the form of fine, upward-turned scales around the base of the stipe. Flesh white and solid. *Spores:* rusty-brown in mass, ellipsoid, rough, average size 11.5 × 8.5 microns.

Habitat and distribution
Found on the ground in coniferous woods, in mossy swamps or light sandy soils, also among bilberries, especially in mountainous areas. Locally common in Europe and North America.

Occurrence
August to December in Europe, July and September in N. America.

Culinary properties
Tastes acrid, smells mild, highly prized for its succulent flesh. The acrid taste disappears in cooking.

Russula adusta
Fruiting body *Cap:* white then grey and finally blackish-grey, convex and then strongly depressed, 7–12cm diameter, smooth, margin inrolled. *Gills:* adnate to slightly decurrent, crowded, white then blackish-grey, unequal. *Stipe:* colours as the cap, stout. *Flesh:* white becoming rose coloured and then slowly brown.
Ecology On ground in beech and other deciduous woods. Rare in Europe. Autumn.
Edible but not recommended.

Russula aeruginea
Fruiting body Becomes covered with brownish spots. *Cap:* grass-green, margin grooved, slimy when moist, powdery when dry. Convex then depressed. Flesh: white and firm. *Gills:* whitish at first becoming straw coloured and finally brownish in old specimens. *Spores:* cream in mass.
Ecology Singly or in groups in mixed woods, usually under birch occasionally in open coniferous woods. Frequent to common in Europe, infrequent in northern North America. July to November. Edible mild flavour, but of poor quality.

Russula alutacea
Similar to *Russula olivacea* but with muter colouring and definitely more greenish.
Fruiting body
Cap: fleshy, convex becoming flatter and slightly hollow. Purplish-red, prone to discoloration in the centre, sometimes fading to light green or olive brown, margin incurved. 8–14cm in diameter, cuticle inseparable from cap. *Gills:* from creamy yellow to ochraceous, broad and thick with almost free adnates. *Stipe:* cylindrical and stout, rosy or reddish on a white background, seldom without any trace of red, tends to be slightly wrinkled.
Spores: light yellow in mass.
Habitat and distribution.
Found in deciduous woods, especially under beech on calcareous soil. Common in Europe in summer. Edible, mild and sweet-tasting. One of the few Russulas with a sweet flesh, faint smell and having a pinkish-red stalk.

Left: Russula alutacea
Below: Russula adusta

Fruiting body
Cap: varies from scarlet, to orange, sometimes wholly or partly yellow. 4–9cm in diameter. At first hemispherical, becoming flattened and depressed in the centre. Margin sometimes wrinkled, slightly striate in old specimens. Cuticle thin, slimy in wet weather, peels up to half-way to the centre. Flesh white, yellow below the cuticle, firm. *Gills:* white at first, becoming pale ochre with bright yellow edges. Rounded next to the stipe, free, broad, connected by veins, shiny. *Stipe:* stout, parallel-sided or sometimes narrowed at the base, 3–8cm long, 1–2.5cm thick. White, flushing yellow, especially towards the base. Flesh firm, spongy in the middle. *Spores:* egg-yellow in mass, ovate, with prominent warts, average size 8.8 × 7.0 microns.

Habitat and distribution
Grows in troops, in deciduous woods, especially under beech, and under conifers in mountainous areas. Uncommon in Europe, becoming slightly more common towards the south, frequent in mountainous

Top: Russula azurea
Right: Russula aurata
Below: Russula atropurpurea

Russula atropurpurea
This common species fruits during the summer and early autumn, and is rarely found later in the year. It is edible, but the flesh is dry and the taste can be bitter. The variety *depallens*, which grows in damp places, has a cap with irregular yellow or brownish to creamy areas. Sometimes an entirely green variant can be found.

Fruiting body
Cap: deep purplish-red, with a darker centre. 4–10cm in diameter. Convex becoming flattened or depressed in the middle. Margin at first incurved, then spreading, smooth except in old specimens when it is striate. Cuticle smooth, slimy when wet, often wrinkled when dry, peels up to half-way to the centre. Flesh white, greyish or greyish-purple under the cuticle, thick and firm. *Gills:* white to pale cream, often with rusty spots. Slightly decurrent, rather broad, becoming narrower and forked towards the stipe. *Stipe:* parallel sided, 3–5cm long, 1–2cm thick. White-rusty at the base, if moist becoming grey, somewhat wrinkled. Flesh firm at first, becoming spongy and fragile. *Spores:* creamy-white in mass, almost spherical, warted, with a rounded projection at one end, average size 8.0 × 6.5 microns.

Habitat and distribution
Grows singly, in deciduous and coniferous woods, especially under oak. Common in Europe, locally frequent in North America.

Occurrence
July to October.

Culinary properties
Tastes mild to moderately hot, produces an unpleasant smell as it dries. Only specimens in good condition should be eaten, and these must be cooked as soon as they are gathered, otherwise they should not be eaten at all.

Russula aurata
GOLDEN RUSSULA
The cap colour of this toadstool varies through beautiful shades of red, orange and yellow and, with its bright-yellow gill edges and yellow stipe, it is one of the most striking of woodland fungi. It is very abundant in open woodland in the mountains of southern Europe.

areas of north-east North America.
Occurrence
August to November in Europe, July to October in North America.
Culinary properties
Is said to taste slightly of cherry bark, when cooked it is one of the most delicious *Russula* species.

Russula azurea
Fruiting body *Cap:* becoming depressed, with a whitish bloom, dry, blue-lilac-green or olive coloured with darker spots. *Gills:* white to cream, adnate. *Stipe:* cylindrical, white.
Ecology On ground in woods such as fir and pine. Rare in

Europe. Early autumn.
Edible.

Russula badia
Fruiting body *Cap:* depressed and umbonate, cherry-red to brownish and almost black in centre, viscid becoming dry. margin becoming grooved. *Gills:* yellowish becoming ochraceous, *Stipe:* white with pinkish tinge, rugose. *Taste:* mild and then very hot. *Smell:* when bruised of cedarwood.
Ecology Coniferous woods, especially in mountains. Rare in Europe.
Edible but of poor quality.

Russula caerulea
Fruiting body *Cap:* conical at first becoming flatter and hollow in the centre with a characteristic umbo. Deep violet or purple, blackish at the centre, viscous when wet, shiny in dry weather, cuticle separable. Subtle, slightly inturned margin, becomes streaked in older specimens.
Gills: Close, narrow towards stipe broad towards the margin, pale ivory

in colour, thin. Stipe: clavate and slender, 4–10cm long with a diameter of 1–2.5cm. White, becoming darker (muddy coloured) and streaked.
Spores: yellowish in mass.
Habitat and distribution
Found in grassy places in pine woods on non-calcareous soil. Common in Europe. July to October.
Culinary properties
Flesh is firm and white, has a mild smell and taste after the bitter-tasting cuticle is removed, not recommended.

Russula cyanoxantha
This is a very common and beautiful

toadstool whose cap is usually variegated with shades of purple and green. It is an excellent source of food, and is one of the species permitted to be sold in Munich markets.
Fruiting body
Cap: usually a mixture of colours, bluish-green to violet. 5–15cm in

diameter. At first globose, finally flattened and depressed in the centre. Margin incurved at first, often becoming bright blue or purple, slightly striate and wavy. Cuticle greasy when moist, sometimes wrinkled, with a faint radial network of veins. Flesh firm, white, red under cuticle, with ferrous sulphate flesh is unchanged or sometimes turns very faintly olive. *Gills:* white or very pale cream, rounded next to the stipe, rather narrow, flexible, oily to touch, forked and with intermediates, gills present. *Stipe:* parallel-sided, 5–10cm long, 1.5–3cm thick, white, sometimes flushed purplish, smooth and shiny. Flesh firm, spongy in middle. *Spores:*

white in mass, broadly ellipsoid, densely and bluntly warted with a rounded projection at one end, in iodine spores turn faintly blue-black, size 8.0 × 6.5 microns.
Habitat and distribution
Grows singly or gregariously in deciduous woods, especially under beech, on calcareous soil, and under conifers in mountainous areas. Common in Europe and North America.
Occurrence
July to November in Europe, August to October in North America.
Culinary properties
Tastes mild and agreeable.

Russula decolorans
Fruiting body *Cap:* brick to orange-red, fading to yellowish-red. At first slimy. Hemispherical then flat, depressed. Flesh almost black in old specimens. *Stipe:* tall, stout. white, becoming grey, striate, rough. *Spores:* pale ochre in mass. Tastes mild.
Ecology Singly or scattered on boggy ground, in coniferous woods, heaths, especially in mountainous areas. Variable in Europe and north

Top: Russula cyanoxantha
Centre: Russula caerulea
Below: Russula decolorans

Right: Russula delica
Far right: Russula
emetica
Bottom: Russula
foetens

America, becoming more common towards the north. August to November.
Edible (good).

Russula delica

This species superficially resembles *Lactarius vellereus* and *L. piperatus* but its gills do not exude milk or juice when broken. It is a large, coarse, cup-shaped fungus, which is not highly rated as a source of food.

Fruiting body

Cap: dirty white, often with rusty spots when old. 5–18cm in diameter. At first convex, finally becoming funnel-shaped, with a strongly incurved margin. Cuticle delicately downy, becoming smooth, sometimes cracked. Flesh white, hard, brittle, not very thick. *Gills:* white often tinged bluish near the stipe. Decurrent, thin, distant with intermediate shorter gills. *Stipe:* short and stout, 2–6cm long, 2–5cm thick. White, bluish at the apex, becoming tinged with brown, smooth. *Spores:* white to very pale cream in mass, broadly ellipsoid, warty, with a short rounded projection at one end, average size 10.0 × 8.0 microns.

Habitat and distribution

Grows gregariously, on sandy soils, in mixed woods. Common in Western Europe, locally common in North America.

Occurrence

September to November in Europe, July to October in North America.

Culinary properties

Tastes rather hot and bitter, with a distinctive fruity smell. It is rather dry and tasteless when cooked and is much inferior to other *Russula* species.

Russula emetica
THE SICKENER

This species is quite unmistakable due to its startling red cap. It forms a mycorrhizal association with conifers, especially pine. The closely related species *Russula mairei* is distinguished by the grey-green flush to the gills and by the cream spots on the red cap. It is also smaller.

Fruiting body

Cap: pure scarlet to cherry-red, fades in sunlight and rain to almost white. 5–10cm in diameter. At first convex, then flattened and often depressed in the centre, often with coarse striations at the margin. Cuticle is slimy and glistens in wet weather, peels off easily to reveal reddish flesh which is thin and very fragile. With guaiacum flesh turns pale blue, with sulphovanillin cuticle turns violet-purple to greyish. *Gills:* white to very pale cream, equal in length, adnate, broad, rather distant and fairly elastic. *Stipe:* rather short 5–8cm long, 1–2cm thick club-shaped, white and spongy. *Spores:* white in mass, ovoid, with distinct network of warts, and a round projecture at one end, average size 10.0 × 8.0 microns.

Habitat and distribution

grows gregariously or scattered in coniferous woods especially under pines or on wet heaths and moors where it can usually be found on moss. Common in Europe and North America.

Occurrence

August to November in Europe, July to October in North America.

Culinary properties

Tastes very hot and acidic, smells like coconut. It contains a mild toxin which causes gasteroenteritis if eaten raw. In Northern Europe it is eaten after careful washing and simmering for a long time. It would seem prudent not to gather this species for food.

Russula fellea

Fruiting body *Cap:* dull ochre-yellow 3–7cm in diameter. Convex to flat, margin grooved when mature, thin-fleshed. Cuticle is vis-

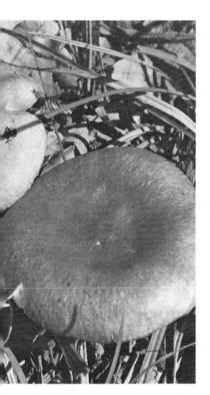

fragility, pale colour, sweet smell and extremely acrid taste.

Russula flava

This species in common with *Russula decolorans*, *Russula obscura* and *Russula paludosa*, is characterised by the fact that the flesh turns grey with age.

Fruiting body *Cap:* hemispherical becoming wide and hollow at the centre and even cyatiform in old specimens. Colour varies from chrome yellow to lemon yellow or gold, 4–10cm in diameter. Margin often paler than rest of cap, streaked when mature. *Gills:* whitish then pale ochre, free or slightly partitioned and wavy. *Stipe:* tall up to 9cm, cylindrical often slightly stouter at the base, white. *Spores:* ochre in mass.

Habitat and distribution
found on boggy ground in damp woods on rather acidic soil. Common in Europe especially in Northern Europe, July to October. Edible.

Russula foetens

The strong unpleasant smell, together with the warty, ribbed, cap margin, makes this fungus easy to identify. It is frequently eaten by slugs, but humans find it inedible or even poisonous.

Fruiting body
Cap: dull brownish-yellow to honey-coloured. 5–15cm in diameter. At first almost globular with a smooth margin, finally flat, margin with radial ribs decorated with raised knobs. Cuticle thin, slimy, radially veined, peels slightly. Flesh whitish, fragile. *Gills:* dirty-white to cream at first, becoming spotted with brown. Cut-away next to the stipe, thickish, distant, intermixed with many intermediates. With sulphovanillin gills turn slowly deep blue. *Stipe:* stout, thickening towards or below the middle, 5–12cm long, 1.5–4cm thick. Whitish at first, becoming dark and furrowed or wrinkled. Flesh hard, rigid but fragile, turns red-brown when exposed to the air. *Spores:* cream in mass, subglobose, warted, with a distinct projection at one end, average size 9.0 × 8.0 microns.

Habitat and distribution
Grows gregariously, sometimes in clusters, on humus in deciduous or coniferous woods and under hedges. Common in Europe and in the deciduous forests of eastern North America, rare in the coniferous forests of the Rocky Mountains.

Occurrence
August to November in Europe, July to October in North America.

cous and can only be separated from the cap at the margins. *Gills:* pale honey colour, thin, pointed toward the stipe, rounded toward the margin. *Gills* exude drops of moisture. *Stipe:* short, 2–6cm, thick similar colour to the cap. *Spores:* pale cream in mass. Flesh is pale yellow, brittle and fragile, smell reminiscent of *Geranium*, tastes bitter and very hot.

Ecology occurs frequently even abundantly in deciduous woods especially under beeches and oak, more rarely among conifers. Not edible.

This species may be confused with *Russula ochroleuca* (Page 249) from which it can be distinguished by its small size firmness and

Culinary properties
Inedible due to bitter, oily taste and rancid, nauseous smell. It is said by some to be poisonous.

Russula fragilis

Fruiting body *Cap:* red, centre purplish-red, finally tinged olive, slimy when wet. Convex then flat, depressed. *Gills:* white, edge minutely toothed. *Stipe:* white, very fragile. *Spores:* white in mass. Tastes very acrid.

Ecology Deciduous and coniferous woods, on boggy ground. Frequent to common in Europe, infrequent in North America. July to November.
Edibility unknown.

Russula grisea

Fruiting body *Cap:* greyish-lilac mixed with pink-yellow and olive, smooth, margin striate when old. *Gills:* cream to pale yellow, brittle, adnexed. *Stipe:* white or flushed purple, cylindrical or clavate. *Taste* slightly acrid when young.

Ecology Deciduous woods such as birch. Common in Europe. Edible.

Top: Russula flava
Above: Russula fragilis

Russula lepida
Fruiting body *Cap:* deep rose-red to pink with white bloom, 4–8cm in diameter. Colour can fade becoming pale yellow or white but retaining some red spots usually near margin. Convex to flat. Flesh white and hard. *Gills:* white to cream, often with faint blue-green hues, fragile. *Stipe:* white, often tinged with pink or red, hard and brittle. *Spores:* cream in mass. Smell is reminiscent of cedar wood. Tastes mild at first then resinous.
Ecology Singly or in groups, in deciduous woods, especially beech and oak, also in coniferous woods in mountainous areas. Common in Europe, frequent in North America becoming less frequent in the north. July to November.
Edible.

Russula lutea
Fruiting body *Cap:* mid-yellow to ochraceous yellow, colour often deeper at the centre. 2–6cm in diameter, convex then flattened. Cuticle sticky in wet weather, can be easily separated from the cap. *Gills:* at first creamy-yellow turning a deeper golden-yellow, connected by small veins, fragile. *Stipe:* white and slender. *Spores:* yellow-ochre in mass.
Ecology Singly or scattered in damp deciduous woodland. Europe and North America. Autumn fruiting. Edible.

Top: Russula nauseosa
Right: Russula nigricans
Bottom: Russula lepida

Russula mairei
Fruiting body *Cap:* bright scarlet becoming discoloured with spots when old, minutely powdery, velvet texture, convex at first then flat or slightly depressed. 4–7cm in diameter. Margin often lobed. Cuticle peels to one third cap diameter. Flesh white and brittle. *Gills:* white, adnate, fairly narrow. *Stipe:* white, rarely pink, 5cm high, slightly attenuated towards cap. Becomes tinged with brown at base with age. *Spores:* white in mass. According to some experts it smells faintly of honey.
Ecology typically under beech, in beech woods or mixed woods containing some beech. Rarely in coniferous woods on calcareous soil.
Occurrence
Infrequent both in Europe and North America. July to September. Inedible.

Russula nauseosa
This small and delicate fungus is common in coniferous forests on mountains, but rare in the lowlands. It is distinguished from several similar species by its nauseous smell.
Fruiting body
Cap: varies from dark wine-red to pink, fading to yellowish-brown with age. 2–7cm in diameter. Convex at first, soon becoming flattened or slightly depressed in the centre. Margin thin, can be furrowed and warted. Cuticle peels easily, revealing white flesh which is thin and very fragile. *Gills:* light yellow, becoming saffron, rounded next to the stipe, thin, brittle, distant, with a few short intermediate gills. *Stipe:* slender, 2–7.5cm long, 0.5–1.5cm

thick. White, becoming faintly yellow or brown when old, slightly veined. Flesh soft and fragile. With sulphovanillin surface turns blue-black. *Spores:* egg-yellow in mass, ovoid to ellipsoid, with isolated warts and a distinct projection at one end, average size 9.0×7.5 microns.

Habitat and distribution
Found in coniferous forests, especially in mountainous areas. Locally common in Europe and north-east North America.

Occurrence
August to November in Europe, August to October in North America.

Culinary properties
Tastes unpleasant, smell is often nauseous, but this disappears when cooked.

Russula nigricans
The colour of this toadstool varies greatly. As it matures and dries out its whole fruiting body turns black. These dry, black specimens persist on the ground long after the growing season has finished. When old, it is frequently attacked by two parasitic toadstools, *Nyctalis asterophora* and *Collybia tuberosa.*

Fruiting body
Cap: white, turning brown and finally black. 10–20cm in diameter. Convex at first, becoming deeply depressed when mature. Margin at first incurved. Cuticle dry, smooth, partially peeling. Flesh firm, white, turning red then black when exposed to the air. With ferrous sulphate flesh turns salmon-pink then olive-green. *Gills:* straw-colour to olive, bruising greyish-pink. Decurrent, very thick and distant, with smaller intermediates. *Stipe:* stout, of a rather unequal shape, 3–8cm long,

1–4cm thick. White, turning brown, becoming black where bruised. Flesh firm. *Spores:* white in mass, broadly ellipsoid, warted and netted, with a distinct projection at one end, average size 7.5 × 6.5 microns.

Habitat and distribution
Grows singly or gregariously among fallen leaves or on the bare earth of deciduous or coniferous woods. Common in Europe and northern North America.

Occurrence
August to November in Europe, June to November in North America.

Culinary properties
Tastes mild, turning slowly hot on the tongue, with a fruity smell. Makes a good dish when cooked, but is inferior to most other edible *Russula* species.

Russula ochroleuca
Fruiting body *Cap:* yellow-ochre, smooth and slippery, 4–10cm in diameter, convex then almost flat. *Gills:* white and broad. *Stipe:* white becoming watery-grey, with faint network of veins. *Spores:* pale cream in mass. Tastes almost mild. The variety *citrina* has a definate yellow cap and the flesh under the cuticle is also yellow.
Ecology Singly, in deciduous and coniferous woods. Frequent to common in Europe and North America. Edible.

Russula olivacea
This handsome mushroom is recognized by its concentrically zoned cap and bright yellow gills. It is closely related to *Russula alutacea.* Highly recommended by enthusiasts, it is one of the fungi to be found on sale in Munich markets.
Fruiting body *Cap:* colour vari-

able, purplish-red brown, olive-brown or even ochraceous, often concentrically zoned, paler at the margin. 6–16cm in diameter. At first subglobose, soon becoming flattened and depressed in the centre. Margin inrolled at first, thin, with concentric cracks when old. Cuticle slimy when wet, powdery when dry, peels up to one third of the way to the centre. Flesh white at first becoming yellowish and often very wormy. *Gills:* at first lemon yellow becoming wholly egg yellow. Near the margin the edges may be tinged with cap colour. Adnate, broad and distant, flexible at first becoming brittle. *Stipe:* stout, sometimes thicker at the base, 5–10cm long 1.5–4cm thick. Basically white, flushed purplish-pink beneath cap. Flesh spongy. With phenol water flesh turns purplish-

Top: Russula mairei
Above: Russula paludosa
Left: Russula ochroleuca

red in 10–15 minutes. *Spores:* egg-yellow in mass, broadly ovoid, warted, average size 9.5 × 8 microns.

Habitat and distribution

Grows singly or in troops, on calcareous soils. Frequent in beech woods or under spruce, in mountainous areas in Europe, in oak and maple woods in North America. Edible tastes of hazlenuts.

Russula paludosa

Fruiting body *Cap:* brick-red with brown tints, shiny. Margin grooved in mature specimens. Convex to flat. *Gills:* finally cream, edges often tinged red. *Stipe:* stout, with reddish tinge. *Spores:* creamy-yellow in mass. Tastes mild. Old specimens smell slightly of honey.

Ecology On boggy ground in coniferous woods, especially with *Sphagnum* or *Vaccinium*. Variable in Europe, becoming more common towards the north. August to November.

Edible.

Russula pectinata

Fruiting body *Cap:* dark brown in centre, paler at margin, margin undulate and with pronounced radial grooves, viscid. *Gills:* crowded, white then pale cream, adnexed. *Stipe:* white or rusty stained.

Ecology Under oaks and conifers and on lawns near conifers. Common in Europe and North America. Autumn.

Edible but needs prolonged cooking to remove peppery taste.

Russula puellaris

This species is easily recognized but it is too small and fragile to be worth collecting for food. Older specimens can easily be recognised by their uniform dull yellow coloration which suffuses over the whole of the fruiting body.

Fruiting body

Cap: purple to brick-red, sometimes faded with a darker, often brownish, centre. 2.5–4cm in diameter. Sharply convex at first, soon becoming flat and depressed in the middle. Margin grooved and toothed. Cuticle almost dry, spotted, peels up to half way to the centre. Flesh wax yellow, very thin except in the centre. *Gills:* white at first, finally pale ochre, adnate but narrowing next to the stipe, thin, crowded. *Stipe:* slender, thickening towards the base, 2–6.5cm long, 0.5–1.5cm thick. At first white, becoming pale ochre, especially along the fine longitudinal veins. Flesh soft and fragile, becoming hollow with age. *Spores:* cream to pale ochre in mass, subglobose with conical warts, average size 7.8 × 6.3 microns.

Habitat and distribution

Grows in troops, mostly in coniferous woods. Frequent to common in Europe, common in North America.

Occurrence

August to November in Europe, July to September in North America.

Culinary properties

Tastes mild, but not generally considered to be worth gathering for food unless it can be found in very large numbers.

Russula queletii

Fruiting body *Cap:* wine-red to purplish-violet, finally flushed dirty olive, at first slimy. Finally flat with a slight central hump. *Gills:* at first white, finally cream, often flecked with grey. *Stipe:* pale wine-red, minutely powdery. *Spores:* pale creamy-ochre in mass. Tastes acrid.

Ecology On sandy soil in open coniferous woods, especially spruce. Frequent to common in Europe. August to November.

Inedible.

Russula romellii

Fruiting body *Cap:* reddish-purple or violet with greenish centre, margin striate, 8–15cm diameter. *Gills:* white and finally pale yellow and ochraceous with spores. *Stipe:* white, pruinose, striate. *Flesh:* white; does not become red with ammonia solution.

Ecology In deciduous woods. Common in Europe. June to November.

Edible.

Top: Russula puellaris
Above right: Russula queletii
Bottom right: Russula pectinata
Bottom: Russula rubra

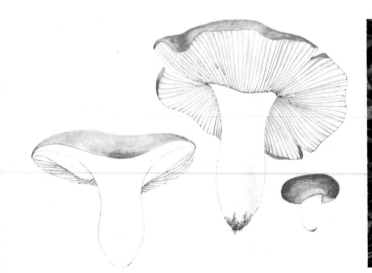

Left: Russula turci
Below left: Russula sanguinea
Bottom: Russula sardonia

Russula rubra

Fruiting body *Cap:* carmine-red, similar in form to that of *Russula lepida* but does not become discoloured, convex then flat or even hollow in the centre. 5–11cm in diameter. Flesh white. *Gills:* ivory colour. *Stipe:* slightly rounded, blunt, white. *Spores:* cream in mass. **Ecology** Mainly deciduous woods. *Odour:* fruity, of old honey. Tastes bitter. Inedible.

Russula sanguinea

Fruiting body *Cap:* blood-red, fading with age. Margin smooth, convex to flat, slightly depressed. *Gills:* finally yellow, slightly decurrent. *Stipe:* tapers towards the base, pinkish-red, slightly striate. *Spores:* cream in mass. Tastes bitter.
Ecology Coniferous woods. Rare to occasional in Europe and North America. July to November.

Russula sardonia

Fruiting body *Cap:* hemispherical then flat and depressed. From violet to purplish-red, becoming tinged with olive. Margin, inturned and slightly striated when mature. 4–10cm in diameter. Flesh white or yellowish, firm, yellowish under cuticle. *Gills:* Creamy yellow, quite thick, annexed or adnate. *Stipe:* cylindrical, stouter towards the base, similar in colour to cap or paler, soft, up to 8cm high. *Spores:* pale ochre in mass.
Ecology in pinewoods on sandy soil. Common in Europe from September to November.
Inedible the flesh is bitter with a sour or acrid smell.

Russula solaris

Fruiting body *Cap:* lemon-yellow to bright yellow, occasionally tinged orange, smooth, slimy. Margin striate, warty in mature specimens. *Gills:* at first white, finally straw colour. *Stipe:* narrowed towards the apex, sometimes curved. White, rarely spotted yellow. *Spores:* deep cream in mass. Tastes extremely acrid. Smells sometimes of mustard.
Ecology Beech woods. Occasional in Europe. September to November.
Inedible.

Russula turci

Fruiting body *Cap:* flat with a depressed centre, viscid becoming dry, purple-violet and nearly black in centre, margin not striate, cuticle peeling off when dry. *Gills:* cream becoming ochre, free, often forked.

Right: Russula velenovskyi
Below right: Russula virescens
Bottom right: Russula vesca

Stipe: white with perhaps tinge of red, 5–7cm tall, wider at base, which smells of walnut husks.
Ecology Under pines and firs. Europe. Autumn.
Edible.

Russula velenovskyi

Fruiting body *Cap:* reddish-orange to bright red with a central disc of a stronger orange becoming ochraceous. Hemispherical becoming umbonate and depressed in the centre, margin grooved in mature specimens. *Gills:* whitish to light ochre, unequal and widely spaced. *Stipe:* cylindrical sometimes curved, white occasionally spotted pink, 6cm high.
Habitat and distribution
Deciduous woods, especially beech. Common in Europe from June to October.
Edible.

Russula vesca

It can be recognized by its receding cuticle which leaves the gills protruding like teeth around the edge. This is one of the first fungi to fruit after the late summer rains and is highly regarded by enthusiasts.
Fruiting body
Cap: brownish-red to pinkish, often darker in the centre. 6–10cm in diameter. Hemispherical at first, becoming flat and depressed in the centre. Cuticle rather slimy and shiny when wet, dull when dry, smooth in the centre and radially wrinkled towards the margin, which in mature specimens falls short of the edge, exposing a band of white flesh. Flesh firm, white, reddish under cuticle, often with rusty spots. With ferrous sulphate flesh rapidly turns deep salmon-pink. *Gills:* white or very pale cream, often brown-spotted. Narrowed near the stipe, broader towards the margin, often protruding beyond the cap cuticle,

crowded, forked, especially near the stipe. *Stipe:* can be very short, narrows downwards to a more pointed base, 3–10cm long, 1.5–2.5cm thick. White, rarely tinged pinkish, sometimes with rusty spots and delicate wrinkles. Flesh cheesy and firm. *Spores:* white in mass, broadly ellipsoid, very finely warted, with a distinct projection at one end, average size 6.5 × 5.5 microns.
Habitat and distribution
Grows singly, not very abundantly. Found in and along the margins of deciduous woods, especially under birch and oak or solitary horse chestnut trees, under conifers in mountainous areas. Becoming rarer towards the north in Europe and North America.
Occurrence August to November.
Culinary properties
Tastes mild and nutty, smells fishy

in old specimens. It blends well with all types of egg dishes and can be good raw.

Russula virescens

Found mainly in beech woods, this striking fungus is regarded as a delicacy throughout Europe. In Northern Italy peasants toast it on a

griddle over a glowing wood fire. It is also sold in Munich markets.
Fruiting body
Cap: verdigris to dull green, but often completely or partially ochre-buff to cream. 5–12cm in diameter. At first globose becoming flattened and finally depressed, often unequally and broadly lobed. Margin incurved at first, smooth to slightly grooved. Cuticle dry, coarsely mealy, soon becoming cracked. Flesh white and compact. *Gills:* white or cream, free, narrow and connected by veins, somewhat brittle. *Stipe:* stout, slightly tapering downwards, 4–9 cm long, 2–4cm thick. White to pale cream, becoming brown where damaged. Smooth, mealy at first. Flesh white, spongy and brittle.

Spores: pale cream in mass.
Habitat and distribution
Grows singly or in small groups, in glades in deciduous woods, especially under beech, but also under oak and maple, and under conifers in mountainous areas. Variable in Europe and North America, becoming common towards the south.

Occurrence
August to November in Europe, July to September in North America.

Culinary properties
Tastes of hazelnut, young specimens smell fruity when cut, older specimens smell of fish. It should only be eaten when fresh. Good when sliced raw with a salad of watercress, tomato and French dressing, or when roasted or crisply fried in butter. It needs to be well seasoned. Develops a strong smell while being dried for storage.

Russula xerampelina
Experts have described several varieties of this species, each one being associated with a different kind of tree. The variety *pascua* is small, has a pale cherry-red to brownish cap, and grows under *Salix repens* on

pale-ochre, rounded behind, moderately broad and thick, often forked and connected by veins. *Stipe:* parallel-sided or swollen in the middle, 3–11cm long, 1–3cm thick. White, becoming red, bruising yellowish-brown, with a fine network of veins. Flesh firm. *Spores:* ochre in mass, broadly ovate, with sharply conical warts, average size 9.5 × 7.8 microns.

Habitat and distribution
Grows in large scattered troops, in all types of woodland. Common in Europe and northern North America, especially in the Rocky Mountains, it is also found in South Africa and Australia. Often found growing with the inedible *R. sardonia*.

Occurrence
August to November in Europe, July to August in North America.

mountains. The variety *rubra* has a dark wine-red cap and grows under conifers, but the varieties *barlae*, which is straw to pale yellow-ochre, sometimes with red tints, and *elaeodes*, which is greenish, are found under beech. All these varieties are identified by the immediate olive-green colour which develops when ferrous sulphate is put on their flesh. This edible toadstool is as sweet as a fresh hazelnut when young.

Fruiting body
Cap: varying from purplish-red to brown to yellow. 5–14cm in diameter. Convex, becoming flattened and depressed in the centre. Margin smooth, finally becoming grooved. Cuticle slimy at first, soon becoming dry and dull. Flesh white, compact, staining brown when cut. With ferrous sulphate flesh instantly turns deep olive-green. *Gills:* cream to

Culinary properties
It has a characteristic smell of shellfish when mature. Young specimens are sweet and nutty, and are good when cut into small pieces, marinated in French dressing and used in green salad. They are also excellent when sautéed in butter.

Strobilomyces floccopus
OLD MAN OF THE WOODS
In spite of its rather off-putting appearance, this fungus can be delicious if prepared with care, and it is a great favourite with many people. It is very highly regarded in Bohemia.

Fruiting body
Cap: at first smoke-grey with white areas, finally black 5–10cm in diameter. Convex, margin hung with scales and white cottony veil fragments. Cuticle ornamented with large, thick, overlapping scales.

Flesh thick, whitish, becoming reddish and finally blackish when cut. With ammonia it turns rusty-tawny, with ferrous sulphate it turns leaden grey and with Meltzer's reagent it turns dark wine-red. *Tubes:* whitish, flushing red where bruised, adnate, rather long, shorter next to stipe. *Pores:* white, then greyish-olive, bruising reddish, larger and angular. *Stipe:* rather unequal in width, 8–12cm long, 1–2cm thick. Covered with a greyish black cottony sheath from base up to thick, cottony ring near the white to grey, grooved apex. *Spores:* blackish-brown in mass, broadly ellipsoid, rough, average size 11.0 × 9.8 microns.

Habitat and distribution
Grows singly, in troops or occasionally in tufts, in coniferous, deciduous or mixed woods, often in deep shade. Becoming common in Europe towards the south, rare but

Above: Strobilomyces floccopus
Left: Russula xerampelina

sometimes locally abundant in the United Kingdom, common in North America.

Occurrence
September to November in Europe, July to November in North America.

Culinary properties
Taste and smell at first indistinct, increasing with age. Stipe, tubes and scales must be removed before cooking. It cooks well by any method. Highly recommended.

Stropharia aeruginosa
VERDIGRIS AGARIC
This is a common and spectacular woodland and grassland toadstool. The green colour, which is contained in the thick slime which covers the cap and stipe, is soluble in water and is washed out by rain.

Fruiting body
Cap: deep blue-green, fading to yellowish-green. 2–8cm in diameter. Bell-shaped to convex, becoming flattened, with a slight umbo. Margin hung with small white scales in young specimens. Cuticle very slimy. Flesh white, tinged blue, rather soft, thin except in the centre. *Gills:* whitish, becoming dusky and finally dark

Right: Stropharia coronilla
Below: Stropharia aeruginosa
Bottom: Stropharia ferrii

chocolate-brown with white edges. Adnate, broad, rather distant. *Stipe:* parallel-sided, usually curved at the base, 4–7cm long. Tinged pale blue-green, slimy, at first covered with white cottony scales below the narrow ring. Flesh soft, hollow. *Spores:* dark-brown in mass, ellipsoid, smooth, average size 8.0 × 4.5 microns.

Habitat and distribution
Sometimes grows in tufts, in grass, in deciduous or coniferous woods, meadows and gardens. Common in Europe and eastern North America and it is found in New Zealand.

Occurrence
May to November in Europe, July to November in North America.

Culinary properties
It is regarded with suspicion because of its disagreeable taste and unusual appearance, and although it is eaten in parts of Europe, it is not highly regarded.

Stropharia coronilla
Superficially this species resembles *Agrocybe praecox*, from which it is distinguished by its blackish spore print, and *Agaricus comtulus*, which differs in having free gills. In Europe and Australia it is found in open grassy places, but in North America it grows in pine or beech woods. Experts disagree as to the edibility of this fungus, and it would seem prudent not to gather it for food.

Fruiting body
Cap: yellow-ochre, sometimes bright yellow. 2–6cm in diameter. Convex becoming flattened. Margin at first white and sometimes wavy. Cuticle slimy when wet, smooth and minutely powdery when dry. Flesh white, thick, firm. *Gills:* pale brownish, then dark brown with white edges. Adnate but wavy next to the stipe, broad, rather crowded. *Stipe:* stout, narrowed at the base, 5–7cm long, 5–10mm thick. White, becoming yellow with age, minutely woolly above the narrow, radially-grooved ring, fibrillose, finally shiny below. Flesh faintly yellow, solid. *Spores:* dark brown to blackish in mass, ellipsoid, smooth, with a faint germ pore, average size 9.3 × 5.0 microns.

Habitat and distribution
Found among grass in pastures, parks, on lawns, heaths, sand dunes, cultivated ground and along grass verges. Frequent in Europe and Australia. Infrequent in northern

North America where it is found on the ground in white pine or beech woods. It is found in New Zealand.

Occurrence
May to November.

Culinary properties
Smells faintly unpleasant. It is said by some to be poisonous, but it is eaten in parts of Europe.

Stropharia ferrii
Fruiting body *Cap:* conical subglobose to flat, purple or maroon-red fading to straw colour, 5–12cm diameter, fibrillose, margin undulate. *Gills:* adnate, smoky-grey to violet, with white edges, arcuate or linear. *Stipe:* thick, up to 3cm wide, white or pale yellow, smooth, with a conspicuous ring whose lower part divides into several large triangular segments.

Ecology On cultivated ground and especially mulched areas and on rotting debris. Common in North America but rare in Europe. Autumn but sometimes earlier.
Edible and good.

Stropharia semiglobata
DUNG ROUNDHEAD

This common and widespread toad-stool can be found growing on dung from spring to late autumn. It is well worth gathering for food.

Fruiting body

Cap: straw-yellow to tan, colour fades with age. 1—4cm in diameter. Persistently hemispherical. Cuticle at first slimy, shiny when dry. Flesh pale, soft, thick in the centre, thin at the margin. *Gills:* olive-grey becoming purplish-brown. Adnate, very broad with white cottony edges, crowded. *Stipe:* slender, parallel-sided, firm and straight, 5—12cm long, 2—5mm thick. White to yellow, slimy below the viscous ring or ring-like zone. Apex powdered with spores in mature specimens. *Spores:* purple-brown in mass, ellipsoid, smooth, average size 18.5 × 10.0 microns.

Habitat and distribution

Grow singly or gregariously on dung, on richly manured lawns and pastures. Very common in Europe, North America, Australia, Venezuela.

Occurrence

April to November.

Culinary properties

Tender and good when cooked. Stipes require long, slow cooking.

Suillus aeruginascens

Fruiting body *Cap:* convex, very sticky, pale straw coloured to smoke-grey, flesh turning blue where cut. *Pores:* adnate or slightly decurrent, dirty-white to grey-olivaceous. *Stipe:* white to pale straw colour with yellow or green tint at top, grey network above ring.

Ecology Common under larch. Europe, especially in south, and North America. Spring to autumn. Edible except for sticky cuticle, which should be peeled off before cooking.

Suillus badius
CHESTNUT BOLETUS

This species looks rather like a well-baked, sticky bun. It is much prized not only for its flavour, but also because it is rarely attacked by maggots.

Fruiting body

Cap: bay, chestnut or dark brick-colour, flushing ochraceous-brown. 7—13cm in diameter. Convex then expanded and nearly flat. Cuticle at first minutely to distinctly downy, soon becoming smooth and polished when dry, sticky when wet. With Meltzer's reagent or ammonia, cuticle instantly turns deep blue-black. Flesh white to pale yellowish, turns faintly bluish especially above tubes, soft, up to 1.5cm thick. Flesh with ammonia or KOH turns buff or tawny-yellow, and with ferrous sulphate, olive green. *Tubes:* cream or lemon-yellow, blue to bluish-green when cut, adnate or depressed around the stem, up to 1.5cm long. *Pores:* are the same colour as the tubes, blueing when bruised, large and angular. *Stipe:* fairly slender, can taper upwards or downwards 4.5—12.5cm long, 0.8—4.0cm thick. Pale brown, streaked with darker lines and minutely dotted. Flesh turns bluish especially at apex. *Spores:* olivaceous snuff-brown in mass, smooth, ellipsoid, spindle-shaped, average size 14 × 5.0 microns. In ammonia spores turn pale straw colour.

Habitat and distribution

Common in conifer plantations in Australia, Cape Province (South Africa), Britain, Europe and North America, also under isolated coniferous trees and especially common under Scots Pine. May continue to fruit long after conifers disappear from an area.

Occurrence

August to November.

Culinary properties

Mild taste, earthy or fragrant smell. Rated highly as an edible species wherever it is found.

Top: Suillus aeruginascens
Left: Stropharia semiglobata
Below: Suillus badius

Right: Suillus bovinus
Bottom: Suillus granulatus

Suillus bovinus
COW BOLETUS

This distinctive species can be recognized by its pale-edged, reddish-buff cap. It is found under pine trees almost everywhere.

Fruiting body

Cap: buff to reddish with a distinct persistently paler margin. 3–10cm in diameter. At first rounded then flattened, sometimes slightly depressed. Cuticle smooth, very slimy when wet. Flesh whitish-yellow, turning slowly pinkish and slightly blue above the tubes when cut. With ammonia or potassium hydroxide flesh turns rose or dark red, and with ferrous sulphate it turns bluish-green. *Tubes:* dirty-yellow, decurrent. *Pores:* at first dirty yellow, finally olive-brown, darkening slightly when bruised. Compound, angular, wide and unequal in size. *Stipe:* quite short, tapering downwards, 4–6cm long, 5–8mm thick. Buff to reddish, very minutely dotted especially at apex, smooth elsewhere. *Spores:* pale brownish-olive in mass, smooth, ellipsoid to spindle-shaped, average size 9.0 × 3.5 microns.

Habitat and distribution

Grows singly or sometimes in small clumps. In coniferous woods, plantations and under isolated pine trees. Especially associated with pines, it grows under Scots Pine and Atlantic Pines in Europe, *Pinus radiata* in South Africa and *Pinus densiflora* in Japan. Widespread and common in Europe, North America, South Africa and Japan.

Occurrence

July to November.

Culinary properties

Tastes strong but unpleasant, the smell is indistinct. It has a soggy consistency and is not highly regarded, although it can be of good quality when cooked well.

Suillus granulatus

This cosmopolitan species occurs wherever pines are growing. It is recognized by the granules on its stipe and the droplets on the pores of young specimens. In Mediterranean regions a gross form is often found in winter. It is firm with a white cap and large, fluffy, yellow or brown granules at the top of the stipe.

Fruiting body

Cap: reddish-yellow when moist, yellow when dry. 2–8cm in diameter. Convex then expanded. Margin at first felted with white fibres and incurved, finally expanding beyond the tubes. Cuticle very slimy, translucent, is easily peeled. Flesh thick, pale yellow, turning coral with ammonia and dirty bluish-green with ferrous sulphate. *Tubes:* buff to pale yellow, unchanging, adnate to subdecurrent. *Pores:* yellow then olive, at first oozing milky drops, which harden and darken on drying. Small, up to 1mm across. *Stipe:* equal or very slightly swollen downwards, often crooked, 3–7cm long, 7–10mm thick. Yellow, covered at apex or all over with small yellow or whitish granules, which exude pale droplets, these becoming dark reddish-brown or blackish when dry. Flesh lemon-chrome. *Spores:* an ochraceous-sienna colour in mass, smooth, ellipsoid to spindle-shaped, average size 9.0 × 3.0 microns.

Habitat and distribution

A gregarious species which forms a mycorrhizal association with pines. It sometimes grows in rings, occasionally in clusters. Common in Europe, eastern North America, Mexico, Australia, Madagascar and the Philippines.

Occurrence

August to November in Northern Europe, spring, rarely autumn, in Southern Europe, July to October in North America.

Culinary properties

Tastes and smells pleasant, but the slimy cuticle must be removed before cooking. In France it is regarded as one of the best on the gastronomic scale.

Suillus grevillei
LARCH BOLETUS

This very attractive, shining-yellow, species is edible and can only be found growing under larch trees.

yellowish-olive, small, simple. *Stipe:* stout, rather short, 2.5–5cm long, with a large purplish-brown membranous ring. Yellow, granular above ring, white or brownish below. Flesh tough, elastic sometimes faintly greenish at apex. *Spores:* clay to ochre in mass, smooth, spindle-shaped, average size 8.5 × 3.3 microns.

Habitat and distribution

Widespread and common in coniferous woods. Australia, Britain, Europe and North-east America. Introduced into Columbia with two-needle pines.

Occurrence

August to November.

Culinary properties

It is good when fried, but will not keep and is not suitable for drying.

Top, left: Suillus grevillei
Left: Suillus luteus

Fruiting body

Cap: light yellow, sometimes tinged rust to apricot especially at centre. 3–12cm in diameter. Unevenly convex, later flattish, margin thin. Cuticle glutinous when wet, smooth, often wrinkled, polished and shining when dry. Flesh thick and soft, remaining pale yellow or straw colour. Turns dark wine-red with ammonia, and bluish-olive with Meltzer's reagent. *Tubes:* pale lemon-yellow, finally ochre, adnate to decurrent. *Pores:* lemon-chrome to lemon-yellow, later tinged or bruised rust; angular, small. *Stipe:* tallish, slender to medium, 5–7cm long, 1.5–2cm thick. Yellow above, yellowish-white membranous ring, more cinnamon below, bruising rust. Apex cottony, granular sometimes with faint network. Flesh darkish-chrome-yellow; when cut frequently temporarily turns blue. *Spores:* ochre-sienna in mass, ellipsoid or spindle-shaped, smooth, average size 9.5 × 3.5 microns.

Habitat and distribution

Forms a mycorrhizal association with larch, grows singly but more often in rings or groups. Common and widespread in temperate zones of Australia, Europe, New Zealand and North America.

Occurrence

March to November.

Culinary properties

Tastes and smells pleasant, although not delicate, the caps have a good flavour and consistency, are best fried or braised. Debris and larch needles adhere to the very sticky cap, which must be carefully cleaned before cooking.

Suillus luteus
SLIPPERY JACK

This edible species grows in conifer woods. It has a very sticky cap which is always covered in debris

and, as it is also eaten by larvae, careful cleaning is necessary before cooking.

Fruiting body

Cap: brown to brownish-yellow, sometimes purplish, radially streaked with darker lines or of mottled colour, fading with age. Lopsided, convex, sometimes nearly flat. 5–10cm diameter. Remnants of veil sometimes on margin. Cuticle slimy with brown gluten when moist, shiny when dry. Flesh pale yellow or white, unchanging. *Tubes:* adnate, soft, short, 5–8mm. *Pores:* at first covered by a white membranous veil, pale yellow, finally

Not rated as one of the best Boleti, but is described as having a choice consistency and good flavour, and seems to be universally enjoyed.

Suillus placidus

Fruiting body *Cap:* off-white becoming yellow, dingy olive when water-soaked, glabrous and viscid, broadly convex becoming flat with a wavy margin. *Pores:* pale yellow, not altering when damaged. *Stipe:* 4–12cm tall and 0.5–1.2cm wide, usually narrowed towards base, white becoming yellow when old.

Ecology Under eastern white pine in North America and intro-

Tricholoma aurantium
Fruiting body *Cap:* dark rusty-orange, slimy, mealy in the centre. Margin incurved. Convex. *Stipe:* stout, pale yellow, densely covered with dark rusty-orange scaly belts.
Ecology Coniferous woods, especially spruce, also under willows. Rare to occasional in Europe, becoming more frequent towards the south. September to November. Edibility unknown.

Tricholoma caligatum
Fruiting body *Cap:* broadly convex to flattened, slightly depressed, dry, centre with hairy flattened reddish-brown scales, surface pallid to pinkish cinnamon, margin silky. *Gills:* white, crowded, sometimes conspicuously veined. *Stipe:* dry, smooth, light tan above ring, covered with reddish-brown fibrils below, ring dull white and flared upwards.
Ecology There is much confusion between this species and the closely related *Armillaria matsutake* and *Armillaria ponderosa*. Indeed

Tricholoma argyraceum
Fruiting body *Cap:* mouse-grey, densely scaly. Margin downy. Convex then flat. *Stipe:* whitish-grey, ring absent.
Ecology Tufted on leaf litter of deciduous woods especially under beech, on chalk. Under conifers in mountainous areas. Frequent in Europe and North America. August to November.
Edible.

duced into Europe on pine. July to September.
Edible.

Suillus variegatus
Fruiting body *Cap:* tawny, yellowish-brown, with small, soft darker scales. Slightly greasy when wet. *Pores:* olive, becoming ochre-yellow. *Stipe:* stout, may be club-shaped, tawny-yellow.
Ecology In coniferous woods and plantations. Common in Europe and North America. August to November.
Edible.

Top, left: Suillus placidus
Top, right: Tricholoma acerbum
Right: Tricholoma argyraceum
Bottom, right: Tricholoma aurantium
Below: Suillus variegatus

Tricholoma acerbum
Fruiting body *Cap:* flattened, coarsely grooved at the margin, yellowish to red-brown, viscid, margin inrolled. *Gills:* whitish or cream becoming dingy reddish from edge upwards. *Stipe:* stout, same colour as cap, apex mealy.
Ecology Grows in open spaces in deciduous woods, especially beech and oak. Rare in Europe. Inedible.

the present species is frequently called *Armillaria caligata*. These may all be the same species or simply very close relatives. Under mixed hardwoods and conifers. Widespread in North America and Europe. Autumn.
Edible.

Tricholoma colossus
Fruiting body An especially large fleshy species with a thick stipe. *Cap:* pink to hazel, convex with an involute margin, cuticle sometimes cracked, viscid in wet weather. *Gills:* thick, white with reddish spots. *Stipe:* short, squat, with a short-lived ring in the middle.
Ecology Solitary in conifer woods. Europe.
Edible but indigestible.

Tricholoma columbetta
Fruiting body Wholly white. *Cap:* with a silky sheen, often stained blue on the wavy margin. *Stipe:* stout, rooting.
Ecology Deciduous woods, on acid soils, often under beech, birch.

In coniferous woods in mountainous areas. Occasional to frequent in Europe, widespread in North America. August to November.
Edible (good).

Tricholoma flavovirens
MAN ON HORSEBACK
Mushroom lovers, knowing where to look, often dig through layers of pine needles in search of this tasty mushroom. Buried specimens usually have a yellow cap and this mushroom is often commonly known as the Yellow Knight Fungus.
Fruiting body
Cap: greenish-yellow, tinged brown in the centre. 5–10cm in diameter. Convex, soon becoming flattened and undulating. Margin smooth, incurved, irregularly wavy. Cuticle slimy, slightly scaly in the centre. Flesh white or tinged yellow, compact. *Gills:* at first off-white, finally sulphur-yellow. Rounded next to the stipe, almost free, crowded. *Stipe:* stout, slightly swollen at the base, 2–5cm long, 1–2cm thick. Pale yellow, fibrillose. Flesh white, solid. *Spores:* white in mass, ellipsoid, smooth, with a central oil drop, average size 6.5 × 4.5 microns.
Habitat and distribution
Grows gregariously, in loose clusters or in rings, on sandy soil, in pine woods, sometimes under birch. Frequent in Europe, infrequent in North America but appears to be increasing.

Occurrence
August to November.
Culinary properties
Tastes and smells mild, mealy when young, old specimens have an unpleasant taste. Flesh tender when cooked, they are good when baked, fried or stewed.

Tricholoma fulvum
Fruiting body *Cap:* reddish-chestnut, radially streaked, slimy. At first conical, then convex with a slight central hump. *Gills:* pale yellow, becoming brown-spotted. *Stipe:* reddish-chestnut, streaked, flesh-yellow.
Ecology On peaty ground in deciduous woods, on heaths, es-

Top, left: Tricholoma caligatum
Top, centre: Tricholoma columbetta
Left: Tricholoma colossus
Above: Tricholoma flavovirens

Right: Tricholoma
fulvum
Right, centre:
Tricholoma ionides
Far right: Tricholoma
lascivum
Bottom, left: Tricholoma
imbricatum

red, fibrillose. Flesh white, some-what hollow. *Spores:* white in mass, ellipsoid, smooth, with a central oil drop, average size 6.9 × 4.8 microns.

Habitat and distribution
Grows gregariously or in dense groups in coniferous woods. Occasional to frequent in Europe, locally abundant in north-east North America.

Occurrence
September to November.

Culinary properties
Tastes faintly mealy. They are good when cooked.

Stipe: paler than cap, fibrous, with white, stiff hairs at base.

Ecology In both deciduous and conifer woods. Rare in Europe. Autumn.
Edible.

Tricholoma lascivum
Fruiting body *Cap:* pale cha-mois-leather colour, margin almost white. Flat with slight central hump. *Stipe:* white, tinged pale brown. Tastes and smells sweet and aro-matic.

Ecology Forms groups on the ground in deciduous woods, in coniferous woods, in mountainous areas. Frequent in Europe. September to November.
Edible and particularly good when cooked.

pecially under birch. Under conifers in mountainous areas. Common in Europe and North America. September to November.
Edibility unknown.

Tricholoma imbricatum
This scaly-capped fungus is closely related to *Tricholoma vaccinium* which also grows in coniferous woods.

Fruiting body
Cap: reddish-brown, 5–9cm in dia-meter. Conical. Margin persistently incurved. Cuticle dry, smooth, break-ing up into coarse, overlapping scales. Flesh white, thick, firm. *Gills:* white, red-spotted in old specimens. Slightly notched next to the stipe, rather crowded. *Stipe:* tapers towards the top, slightly rooting, 5–7cm long, 1–1.5cm thick. At first white, becoming brownish-

Tricholoma ionides
Fruiting body *Cap:* convex then flattened, smooth, violet becoming purplish-brown, up to 3cm diam-eter. *Gills:* white with a tinge of yellow, sinuate, narrow, crowded.

Tricholoma pardinum

Fruiting body *Cap:* covered with numerous small hairy grey-brown scales, convex with a slight umbo, margin inrolled. *Gills:* whitish with blue-green hues, then yellowish, adnexed, edges serrated. *Stipe:* striate, with long soft hairs at top, light ochre at base, slightly enlarged at base.
Ecology Single or in groups in conifer woods in mountain areas. Frequent in Europe and North America. Autumn.
Poisonous.

Ecology Solitary under deciduous trees and conifers, especially spruce and pine. Rare in Europe and North America. Autumn.
Inedible, and can be confused with the poisonous *Tricholoma montanum*.

Tricholoma populinum

Fruiting body Large. *Cap:* pale flesh-brown becoming darker, smooth, slimy. Margin wavy. Convex then flat. *Gills:* finally tinged red. *Stipe:* stout, white, tinged pale red. Tastes and smells mealy.

radially streaked from darker centre. Convex to flat, uneven. *Stipe:* stout, slightly rooting. White tinged yellow.
Ecology In coniferous woods, especially under old pine trees, also under beech. Occasional to frequent in Europe and north-eastern North America. May to November.
Edible (good).

Above: Tricholoma portentosum
Far left: Tricholoma pessundatum
Bottom, left: Tricholoma pardinum
Below: Tricholoma populinum

Tricholoma pessundatum

Fruiting body *Cap:* 6–12cm diameter, red or chestnut-brown with paler margin, viscid when wet, shiny when dry, flesh with strong smell of meal or linseed oil. *Gills:* white with tinges of red-brown, sinuate. *Stipe:* slender, tall, whitish, speckled with reddish tufts.

Ecology Tufted on the ground, under poplars. Widespread and frequent in Europe. September to October.
Edibility unknown.

Tricholoma portentosum

Fruiting body *Cap:* sooty-brown, sometimes tinged violet,

Tricholoma saponaceum
SOAP-SCENTED TOADSTOOL

The size and colour of this species are very variable, but it can always be recognized by its strong soapy smell.
Fruiting body
Cap: colour variable, blackish-grey to olive or brown, margin pale.

Top: Tricholoma saponaceum
Right: Tricholoma sulphureum

America, becoming more common towards the south.

Occurrence
August to October.

Culinary properties
Inedible, because of its strong, unpleasant taste and its smell, which resembles coal gas.

Tricholoma terreum

This very pleasant edible toadstool grows in coniferous woods. It is recognized by its dark grey cap and paler grey gills. The variety *atrosquamosum* has black scales on its cap and black dots on the top of its stipe.

Fruiting body
Cap: very dark grey, often almost black in the centre. 5–7cm in diameter. Convex, then flattened with a central hump. Margin incurved. Cuticle felty to scaly with darker fibrils. Flesh whitish-grey, thin, soft, fragile. *Gills:* grey, cut away next to the stipe, up to 5mm broad, with uneven edges. *Stipe:*

3–8cm in diameter. Convex, then flattened, with a central hump. Margin incurved at first. Cuticle fibrillose to scaly, moist in wet weather, sometimes becoming cracked. Flesh white, bruising red, firm. *Gills:* white to pale yellow, becoming tinged or spotted with red, sometimes minutely hairy. Notched next to the stipe, thin, distant. *Stipe:* sometimes swollen in the middle, narrowing at the base, rooting, 5–10cm long, approximately 1cm thick. Pale, with a network of black fibrils or scales. *Spores:* white in mass, broadly ellipsoid, smooth with a central oil drop, average size 5.5 × 3.8 microns.

Habitat and distribution
Grows singly or in small groups, on the ground, in pine and birch woods. Common in Europe, relatively infrequent in north-east North America. It has also been reported from South Africa.

Occurrence
August to November.

Culinary properties
Inedible due to the unpleasant soapy taste and smell, which resembles that of kitchen soap.

Tricholoma sulphureum
NARCISSUS BLEWIT

This toadstool is unmistakable due to its sulphur-yellow fruit body and strong foetid smell. It is also known to taxonomists as the Sulphurous Tricholoma.

Fruiting body
Cap: sulphur-yellow, centre sometimes tinged with brown. 4–8cm in diameter. At first subglobose, then

becoming irregularly flattened. Margin at first incurved. Cuticle smooth, silky. Flesh yellow, thick, fragile. *Gills:* sulphur-yellow, notched next to the stipe, sometimes somewhat arched, thick, rather distant. *Stipe:* long, bulbous toward middle, narrowed at the base, wavy, invariably growing in a distinct curve. Sometimes rooting, 5–10cm long, up to 1cm thick. Sulphur-yellow, smooth. Flesh yellow, fibrous, finally hollow. *Spores:* white in mass, ellipsoid, smooth, with a conspicuous central oil drop, average size 9.5 × 5.5 microns.

Habitat and distribution
Grows gregariously, on the ground, in deciduous woods, especially oak, in coniferous woods in mountainous areas. Variable in Europe and North

parallel-sided or slightly swollen at the base, 5–7cm long, approximately 1cm thick. Whitish-grey, mealy at the apex. Flesh spongy. *Spores:* white in mass, ellipsoid, smooth, with a central oil drop, average size 6.5 × 4.1 microns.

Habitat and distribution
Grows gregariously, sometimes in rings, on the ground, in coniferous woods and newly established pine plantations, beside woodland paths. In mixed pine and beech woods in North America. Frequent to common in Europe, frequent in North America.

Occurrence
August to November.

Culinary properties
Tastes and smells pleasant, of fair quality, can be eaten raw or cooked.

Tricholomopsis platyphylla
BROAD-GILLED AGARIC

The fruiting bodies of this species, originate from a network of cord-like mycelium, which extends out to 1m from the base of each stipe. It is attached to buried twigs, dead roots or leaves. These cords used to be called *Rhizomorpha xylostroma*

Above: Tricholoma virgatum
Above, left: Tricholoma terreum
Below, far left: Tricholoma ustale
Below, left: Tricholoma vaccinum

Tricholoma ustale

Fruiting body *Cap:* reddish-brown, becoming darker, slimy, smooth. Convex then flat. *Gills:* white at first, becoming flecked with red. *Stipe:* slender, club-shaped. Brownish-red, paler at the apex.

Ecology Deciduous woods, especially under beech, under conifers in mountainous areas. Widespread and frequent in Europe and North America. August to November. Edible.

Tricholoma vaccinum

Fruiting body *Cap:* reddish-brown with coarse, soft scales. Margin downy, shaggy, incurved. Convex to almost flat. *Stipe:* tall, slender, hollow. Pale reddish-brown. Tastes slightly bitter.

Ecology In groups in coniferous woods, especially in mountainous areas. Occasional to frequent in Europe and eastern North America. August to November. Edible.

Tricholoma virgatum

Fruiting body *Cap:* grey with darker radiating streaks, shining. Unevenly conical. *Gills:* with white edges. *Stipe:* tall, slender, whitish-grey, powdery at the apex. Tastes peppery and sharp. Confused with *T. sciodes*, which, however, is not umbonate.

Ecology Coniferous woods, beech woods, on heaths. Occasional in Europe. September to November. Edibility unknown.

before their relationship with *Tricholomopsis platyphylla* was discovered.

Fruiting body

Cap: dusky-brown or grey, streaked with darker radiating fibrils. 4—9cm sometimes, 12cm in diameter. At first convex, finally flat. Margin at first incurved. Cuticle dry, often cracking or tearing. Flesh white, thin, fragile. *Gills:* white, cut away obliquely next to the stipe, up to 1.2cm broad, soft, distant. *Stipe:*

parallel-sided, with prominent basal mycelial cords, 7—10cm long, approximately 1cm thick. Whitish-grey, fibrillose, striate. Flesh white, soft. *Spores:* white in mass, globose, smooth, with a central oil drop, average size 6.0 × 6.5 microns.

Habitat and distribution
Grows singly, or gregariously, rarely in clusters, on the ground in deciduous woods, around stumps, on decayed wood or rotten leaves, in coniferous woods in mountainous areas. Frequent to common in Europe, frequent in north-east North America.
Occurrence
May to November, sometimes December.
Culinary properties
Old or decayed specimens have a disagreeable smell. Fresh caps are good when broiled or fried but not really satisfactory if prepared by any other method.

Top, left:
Tricholomopsis
platyphylla
Top, right: Tylopilus
felleus
Bottom, right:
Volvariella bombycina
Below: Tricholomopsis
rutilans

Tricholomopsis rutilans
This beautiful variegated toadstool grows on rotten conifer stumps. It has an unusual, marshmallow-like, texture when cooked, and is well worth experimenting with.
Fruiting body
Cap: densely flecked rich purplish-red on a yellow background. 5—9cm in diameter. Convex, then flattened. Margin thin, incurved at first. Cuticle scaly, especially in the centre. Flesh yellow, thick, soft. *Gills:* chrome-yellow, rounded behind, broad, with thick and sometimes woolly edges, crowded. *Stipe:* parallel-sided or slightly swollen at the base, 5—10cm long, 1—2cm thick. Yellow, variegated with purplish-red cottony scales. Flesh yellow, soft. *Spores:* white in mass, ellipsoid, smooth, with a central oil drop, average size 7.3 × 4.5 microns.
Habitat and distribution
Grows on and around old conifer stumps. Frequent in Europe and eastern North America and found in New Zealand.
Occurrence
August to November in Europe, May to November in North America.
Culinary properties
When cooked the flesh becomes gummy, rather like the consistency of a marshmallow. It is highly recommended.

Tylopilus felleus
Specimens of this species are usually large and heavy with very broad caps and relatively short stipes. They can be recognized by the dark network of veins on their stipes and by their clay-pink spore prints.
Fruiting body
Cap: ochre to honey colour. 6—12cm in diameter. Convex, later flattened. Cuticle at first slightly downy, soon becoming smooth. Flesh thick, soft, white tinged flesh-colour where wounded. With ammonia, potassium hydroxide or ferrous sulphate flesh, turns grey-olivaceous. *Tubes:* at first white then pink, 1—2cm long, adnate, depressed around stipe. *Pores:* same colour as tubes, bruising dirty brown, angular. *Stipe:* slightly club-shaped, 7—10cm long, 2—3cm thick. More creamy-ochre than cap at the top. Covered with a dark-brown network. Flesh white, solid. *Spores:* clay-pink in mass, smooth, ellipsoid to spindle-shaped, average size 12.0 × 4.5 microns.
Habitat and distribution
Grows singly on rotting conifer stumps and on humus under oak and other deciduous trees. Common and widespread in Europe and North America.

Occurrence
August to November.
Culinary properties
Inedible due to its bitter taste.

Volvariella bombycina
This is an uncommon, but widespread species, and as it fruits in the same place for several years, it can be quite a valuable source of food. It sometimes grows high up on living trees, but it is not a proven parasite. If a young, egg-like fruiting body, is placed in a bell-jar, it will continue to expand and develop to full size.
Fruiting body
Cap: at first yellowish-white, becoming fawn. 5—10cm in diameter. At first ovoid, then bell-shaped, finally convex with a central hump. Cuticle with silky hairs. Flesh white, thin, soft. *Gills:* flesh colour, free, very crowded in unexpanded cap. *Stipe:* narrows upwards from bul-

bous base, curved when growing on tree trunks, 7—15cm long, at least 1cm thick. White, smooth, with a long, yellowish, membranous volva surrounding the base. Flesh white, solid. *Spores:* salmon-pink in mass, broadly ovoid, smooth, average size 9.3 × 5.5 microns.

Habitat and distribution
Grows singly, occasionally in tufts, on trunks, decayed stumps and sawdust of deciduous trees. Uncommon in Europe, North America and Australia.

Occurrence
June to October.

Culinary properties
It is worth eating if found in large enough quantities.

brown, smooth, with a free, torn, bulbous volva enclosing the base. *Spores:* salmon-pink in mass, ellipsoid, smooth, average size 13.0 × 8.0 microns.

Habitat and distribution
Grows singly or gregariously, on rich manured ground, dung hills, rotting grass, straw, compost heaps, in gardens, greenhouses, on cultivated land. Occasional to frequent in Europe, common in North America, especially California. It is found in Australia and South Africa.

Occurrence
July to October in Europe, May to July in North America.

Culinary properties
Best avoided altogether.

cybe clavipes and *Amanita vaginata*. Rare in Europe and North America.

Occurrence
October.

Culinary properties
Not recommended.

Xeromphalina campanella
This small fungus can be gathered in great quantities in mountainous coniferous woods, and is highly recommended when stewed.

Fruiting body
Cap: rusty yellowish-brown, paler when dry, 1—2cm in diameter. Bell-shaped or hemispherical. Striate when moist. Flesh yellow, thin, membranous, translucent when moist. *Gills:* yellow, powdery when

Top: Volvariella surrecta
Far left: Volvariella speciosa
Left: Xeromphalina campanella

Volvariella speciosa
ROSE-GILLED GRISSETTE
This fungus is eaten in Europe, but not in North America, where it is regarded by some experts as being poisonous. It can be mistaken for some of the poisonous *Amanita* species, from which it is distinguished by the lack of a ring on its stipe. It is also commonly called the Dung-hill Agaric.

Fruiting body
Cap: whitish at first, becoming greyish-brown especially in the centre. 5—10cm in diameter. At first conical, becoming flattened with a central hump. Cuticle smooth, shiny. Flesh white, soft, fragile. *Gills:* white, finally deep salmon-pink. Free, broad, soft, very crowded. *Stipe:* tall, gradually tapering upwards from a slightly bulbous base, 10—20 cm long, up to 2cm thick. Greyish-

Volvariella surrecta
A parasite on *Clitocybe nebularis*, this species appears as a small greyish-white button, and develops as the host decays.

Fruiting body
Cap: whitish-grey, faintly tinted yellow, 2—5cm in diameter. At first convex, then becoming flat. Cuticle covered with short, white hairs. *Gills:* white at first, finally salmon-pink. Free, irregular, broad, rather crowded. *Stipe:* short, curved, tapering upwards from base, thickening immediately below the cap. White, often downy with a white torn volva surrounding the base. *Spores:* salmon-pink in mass, broadly ovoid, smooth, average size 6.3 × 3.9 microns.

Habitat and distribution
Grows in dense clusters on *Clitocybe nebularis* and more rarely on *Clito-*

mature. Decurrent, arched, narrow, distant, connected by veins. *Stipe:* very thin, rigid, curved, approximately 2.5cm long, 1mm or less thick. Date-brown, polished, apex paler. Tawny, coarsely hairy at the base. Flesh horny, cartilaginous. *Spores:* white in mass, ellipsoid, smooth, in iodine they turn blue-black, average size 7.0 × 3.0 microns.

Habitat and distribution
Grows in tufts, on rotten stumps in coniferous woods, especially pine, particularly in mountainous areas. Frequent in the mountainous areas of Europe and North America.

Occurrence
August to October in Europe, May to November in North America.

Culinary properties
The caps are tender and of fair flavour when stewed.

INDEX